LocoScript 3

USER GUIDE

**LOCOMOTIVE
SOFTWARE**

Written by Jean Gilmour, Locomotive Software
Produced and typeset electronically by Locomotive Software
Printed by Unwin Brothers, Old Woking, Surrey

Published by Locomotive Software
Dorking
Surrey RH4 1YL

First edition, published August 1993 (Reprinted with corrections June 1994)
ISBN 1 85195 118 0

Introduction

LocoScript 3 is the latest version of the word-processing software for your Amstrad PCW. It's easier to use than the version supplied with your PCW. It also has a number of extra features, such as the ability to print text in different fonts and sizes from small print to large headline-size which will let you to produce really impressive documents on your PCW.

It can be used on any model of PCW, while the documents it produces can be printed on a wide range of printers from simple dot-matrix printers to sophisticated laser printers. It can even be used on a PCW on which the original 3" Drive A has been replaced by a 3½" drive, provided you have a suitable .FIB file for this drive (available from the supplier of the disc drive).

About this User Guide

This User Guide starts with an Introductory section which introduces the main features of LocoScript 3 and explains the steps you need to take to install LocoScript 3 on your system. It also includes a short Tutorial in how to use LocoScript to prepare and style documents.

This is followed by the four main sections of the book which cover:

I: **The basics of using LocoScript 3** – *loading the program; using the menus; creating and editing documents; and printing*

II: **Text Layout** – *using different fonts, text styles and sizes; setting margins and tabs; centring, indenting and justifying text*

III: **Advanced features** – *such as setting up a document for different printers and different types of paper; adding headers and footers; using glossaries of 'Phrases'; setting up Templates; and exchanging text with other programs*

IV: **Troubleshooting** – *covering the more common types of problem that you might experience*

Finally, there are a number of appendices covering such things as converting your existing documents and datafiles to LocoScript 3 and the extra products that are available to enhance your use of LocoScript 3.

Conventions

The conventions used in this User Guide are as follows:

- Messages on the screen and options in the menus are written in a special style of text. For example, the 'Copy disc' option is shown as Copy disc.

- Keys that you need to press are shown symbolically. As far as possible, the keys shown match the keys on the keyboard. For example, the key marked ENTER is shown as [ENTER].

- An italic (slanting) *n* is used to represent one or more digits of a number: the actual number will depend on the document etc. you are working on

---

LocoScript 3 User Guide

Customer Support

If you are having difficulty with LocoScript 3 or other Locomotive Software products and cannot find the answer in this User Guide, we can help in two ways.

Written Support

This is available free of charge by writing with full details of the problem to:

LocoScript Support, Locomotive Software, Dorking, Surrey RH4 1YL

Telephone Support

This is available 10am – 12 noon and 2pm – 4pm any working weekday by calling 0891 515717. This service is funded by the call charges. Please note that, at the time of printing, calls are charged at 49 pence per minute at the above times – and that we can rarely help with LocoMail applications or BASIC programs over the 'phone.

Help us to help you

Whichever method of support you choose to use, before contacting us write down:

- **The version number of LocoScript you are using.** This is shown as LocoScript is loaded into your PCW and is also shown on the first line of the menu that appears if you press ⌑ from the Disc Manager.
- **Details of your PCW and any add-ons you have fitted** (eg. PcW9256 with 512K memory and Amstrad PCW matrix printer, with Locomotive Power Pack.)
- **If the problem concerns an alternative printer, details of the interface you are using and of the printer manufacturer and model number** (eg. Locomotive Power Pack with Canon BJ-10ex used in LQ mode).
- **A brief summary of the problem**, including sufficient details for us to repeat your actions and, if appropriate, the exact messages that have been shown on screen. If you don't tell us how to repeat the problem, it's unlikely that we will be able to help you.

If you're writing to us, include all the above, plus your name, address and a daytime phone number. Also, if possible, include a copy of your Start-of-day disc(s) onto which you have also copied any document or datafile which illustrates the problem. If the problem concerns printing, please include a printout of the document as well as a copy on disc. We will of course treat documents as confidential and return any discs with our reply.

If you're calling us, if possible call from a phone where you can also operate your PCW. Have your PCW turned on and LocoScript running.

Note: The Screen Displays you see when using LocoScript won't necessarily match the Screen Displays shown in this book. In particular, pictures of the Disc Manager Screen may not show the same range of files as you have on your discs. There is no need to worry unless what is described in this book bears no relation to what is happening on your screen.

CONTENTS _____

_____

Part II: Text Layout

Part III: Advanced facilities

Part IV: Troubleshooting

Appendices

Index

Introducing LocoScript 3 ——————

LocoScript 3 is a very powerful word processor, providing a very wide range of word-processing 'tools' so that you can:

- *Prepare all sorts of documents – letters, contracts, invoices – very easily*

- *Use different printers for your documents*

- *Use different character sizes and styles*

- *Type text in a variety of languages – including Ancient Greek*

- *Centre headings; put addresses over to the right-hand side of the page; prepare tables*

- *Take pieces of text from one document and put them in another*

- *Put special text at the top and the bottom of each page*

- *Have letter-head documents with your address etc. ready set up in them*

- *Put in page numbers and make these consecutive across a series of documents*

etc. etc.

And to work alongside LocoScript 3, there are a range of 'add-on' programs – LocoSpell to check your documents for spelling mistakes; LocoMail to help you prepare everything from a mailshot to invoices and VAT returns; while LocoFile provides a 'pop-up' database which allows you to pull information from a datafile and slot it straight into the document you are preparing.

If you have used either LocoScript '1' (the version of LocoScript supplied with the PCW8256/8512, the PcW9256 and the PcW10) or LocoScript 2 (the version supplied with the PCW9512 and the PcW9512+), the menus, keystrokes and the layout of the screen will all seem very familiar to you. LocoScript 3 is a more sophisticated version of LocoScript, which offers a number of extra features. But there are also a number of important differences, especially from LocoScript '1'. Some of the more complex aspects of LocoScript – such as Layout and using different types of stationery – were made very much easier to use in LocoScript 2 and these changes have been carried on in LocoScript 3.

The following pages take a brief look at the main features of LocoScript 3.

9402

Multiple fonts in a document *(see Chapter 6)*

LocoScript 3 lets you use up to four different typefaces – or 'fonts' – in a document and to switch between these at will. The fonts you mix in this way can be LocoScript 3's LX fonts (see opposite), the printer's own built-in fonts, 'Download' fonts (if your printer supports these), or a mixture of the LX fonts with one of these other types.

In order to use this feature, you need a printer that either has a range of built-in fonts (and can switch between these fonts) or works with LocoScript 3's LX fonts. The chances are that you have such a printer already. If you have a PCW8256, PCW8512, PcW9256 or a PcW10, you will be able to use a mixture of fonts (including the LX fonts) on your PCW's own matrix printer. The same is true if you have a PcW9512+ with a built-in bubblejet printer. You can also use a mixture of fonts on most other dot-matrix, inkjet and laser printers.

The main exceptions are daisy-wheel printers. The problem here is that you can only change font on a daisy-wheel printer by changing the printwheel. This isn't practical to do in the middle of printing a document so you are restricted to just one font per document when you print on a daisy-wheel printer.

Text at different sizes *(see Section 7.1)*

If the fonts you are using can be printed at more than one size, LocoScript 3 lets you take advantage of this in your documents. Depending on the fonts available on your printer, this could let you include anything from really small print (half the size of normal text) to headlines ¾" tall.

The chief range of fonts that can be printed at different sizes are the LX fonts provided for use with LocoScript 3 (see opposite). 'Scalable' fonts such as the Times and Univers fonts on HP LaserJets and compatible printers and the Roman and Sans Serif fonts on 'ESC/P2' printers can also be printed at a range of different sizes.

LocoScript 3 also includes an 'Auto' Line Pitch setting which automatically makes the basic spacing between one line and the next approximately 20% larger than the largest size of characters used on the line. This is the spacing recommended by typesetting experts.

The improvement you can make in the appearance of a document simply by using different sizes of text for headings is quite spectacular – as you will see from the examples shown on the following pages.

LX fonts *(see Appendix II)*

Among the fonts that LocoScript 3 supports are some special 'LX' fonts, two of which – 'LX Roman' and 'LX Sanserif' – are supplied either in the LocoScript 3 pack or, for external printers, in the Printer Support Pack.

Possibly the most important feature of these fonts is that they can be printed at a variety of different character sizes. We provide each of these fonts in five basic sizes – 8, 10, 12, 14 and 18pt – but each of these basic sizes can be doubled, trebled or even quadrupled giving you in all a very extensive range of sizes to use in your documents. This lets you include everything from 'small print' (characters ½" high – using 8pt text) to headlines up to ¾" high (using 72pt text) in your documents.

The fonts have also been professionally designed to give high quality results especially where the fonts are printed at their natural size. (Characters produced by doubling etc. are not quite as well-formed.)

You can achieve impressive results using the LX fonts. With just the two fonts and five sizes that we supply as standard, you can readily produce documents like those shown on the following pages. (These example documents are provided on your LocoScript 3 Master disc as the files BUSINESS, CHAPTER, MINUTES and NEWSLTR and they use just five of the LX files we provide for use with LocoScript 3: LX Roman 8pt, 10pt and 12pt and LX Sanserif 14pt and 18pt.)

Note: These samples were produced on a Bubblejet printer to show you the quality of result that can be produced with the LX fonts. Using the fonts on, say, the PCW8256/8512/9256/PcW10 built-in matrix printer gives equivalent results but the quality is not quite as good because the PCW printer works at a very much lower resolution (ie. using coarser dots) than a Bubblejet printer.

IMPORTANT: *The LX fonts can only be used to print LocoScript 3 documents: they cannot be used to print text prepared in any other way.*

Built-in word count *(see Section 2.5)*

In LocoScript 2, you could only count the number of words in a document as part of the process of using LocoSpell to check its spelling. In LocoScript 3, counting words is available as a separate option within LocoScript itself.

To count the words in a document, simply edit it, press `f7` to display the Spell menu and take the Count words option. LocoScript then proceeds to count all the words in the document, and it shows the result in a message in the centre of the screen. Press `ENTER` to return to editing the document.

What you need to use the LX fonts

To use LocoScript 3's LX fonts you need:

Either: A PCW8256/8512/9256/10 with its built-in matrix printer

Or: A PcW9512+ with built-in Inkjet printer

Or: Any PCW, a copy of the Printer Support Pack (LocoScript 3 version) and almost any of the following types of printer:

- A 9-pin dot-matrix printer
- A 24-pin dot-matrix printer
- A Bubblejet
- A Hewlett-Packard LaserJet or DeskJet (or compatible printer)

Note: The few printers that **aren't** suitable are marked ⊗ in the 'Alternative Printers' booklet supplied with your copy of LocoScript 3.

We also recommend that your PCW has at least 512k of RAM. It is possible to use LocoScript 3 on a PCW with just 256k of memory but you will be restricted in the range of fonts and sizes you will be able to use and you almost certainly won't be able to use add-on programs such as LocoFile and LocoSpell. With 512k, you should be able to work with a reasonable variety of fonts and sizes, though we would definitely recommend giving yourself extra room by changing over to the new more compact LocoSpell dictionary (see below). If you have all the add-ons and you want to use further fonts and sizes, we'd recommend having 768k, particularly if the documents you work on are at all large.

We offer a number of additional products to help you make better use of the LX fonts. In particular, the Locomotive LPP512 Power Pack will both increase your PCW's memory by 512k (ie. from 256k to 768k or from 512k to 1M) and provide a suitable socket into which to plug any additional printer on which you want to use the LX fonts. Another way of making more memory available for fonts is by replacing the original 160k 'large' LocoSpell dictionary by one which offers the same range of words but takes up less than 100k of your Drive M: it is also three times quicker to look up. These products are described in Appendix VI.

Newbell & Company

Chartered Surveyors and Land Agents
25 High Street, Draperston
Tel: (0125) 776432 Fax: (0125) 774611

BUSINESS

Mr J T Williams
48 West Street
Tillsbury

10th May 1993

Dear Mr Williams

5 Threspan Close

Thank you for your enquiry regarding a full structural survey and valuation of the above property.

Newbell & Co will be happy to carry out this work for you. Moreover, should you instruct us within the next seven days, we will be able to give you the finished report before the end of the month.

Our charges are as follows:

  Valuation survey
  Home purchaser's report
  Full structural survey

In addition, we would recommend taking o
This will provide you will a second survey
purchase of the above property fall through

All charges are exclusive of VAT which wi

We thank you for giving us the opportunity
receiving your instruction to proceed.

Yours sincerely

Newbell & Co

E.J. Newbell.

-

The Write Way

_____ *For writers everywhere*

LocoScript 3 breaks new ground

When the Amstrad PCW came out in 1985, it quickly became established as essential equipment for writers everywhere. Locomotive Software's LocoScript word-processing program provided precisely the tools needed to prepare everything from simple letters to major novels.

However, while LocoScript 2 would let you print different documents in different fonts (or typefaces), you could only ever use one font in any document - though you could always vary the type*style* in any way you liked, putting text you wanted to emphasise into Bold or Italic or even Bold+Italic. Also, all the characters would be the same height, though changing the Character Pitch on a dot-matrix printer would vary their width.

LocoScript 3 changes all that. With LocoScript 3, you can use up to four different fonts within one document. And with LocoScript 3's special 'LX' fonts, you can print characters at almost any size between 6pt - that's $^1/_{12}$" - and 72pt (1") in height. True, the LX fonts cannot be used on every type of printer but as they can be used on the PCW8256/8512/9256's built-in matrix printer, the PcW9512+'s Bubblejet printer and a wide range of dot-matrix, Bubblejet, LaserJet and DeskJet printers beside, it's highly likely that you will have a suitable printer.

Writer's Tips: Science Fiction

Story line — Science fiction stories may cover galactic adventures, military conflict or the paranormal. But what they all need is conflict, action, tension and a strong current of suspense. In addition, they need to maintain interest and to finish on a positive note.

The story should also take the reader into the world of Science Fiction and convince them that it's real.

Characters — The characters can be male, female or alien but must be realistic. When facing impossible situations, they must have the strength of character to overcome the enemy.

The Write Way   *March issue*

NEWSLTR

Chapter 4

Backing up your data

This chapter is possibly the most important chapter in the whole book. It describes how to make 'Back-up' copies to use if either a disc or a file is damaged or lost.

Now, don't run away with the wrong idea: data stored on computer discs is pretty reliable. You can leave a disc on a high shelf for years on end and still be able to read the data on it. Discs that you use every day, however, can get lost, be eaten by the dog, have coffee poured over them or simply wear out. Discs can also be damaged if you have a problem with a disc drive. You can also lose files simply through carelessness - formatting the wrong disc, for example! It's in case of accidents such as these that you need Back-ups.

There are two possible approaches to backing up data: you can either make copies of individual files or you can make copies of the whole disc. We can't tell you which is best because it depends how much data you hav[e]
a club with 200 members, whose names yo[u]
the dozen or so LocoMail Master docum[ents]
subscription reminders etc. etc. The best
making a copy of the whole disc in order t[o]
copy the membership file because the Loco

Your next decision is how often to back up
matter of balancing the time and effort spe[nt]
to spend re-doing the changes you have ma[de]
one-finger typist, you might begrudge re-ty[ping]
typist, it may only be worth backing up a
beware: if you don't back up at the end of
hard work will have to be done again!

If your membership file contains 2000 names and addresses ra[ther than] the whole disc rather than simply this one file.

The Layman's Guide

DRAPERSTON CHORAL SOCIETY
Minutes of the Committee Meeting
held on Wednesday, 4th August 1993
at 5 Threspan Close, Draperston

Present:

William Wykeham-Smythe	(Chairman)
Anthea Williams	(Secretary)
Belinda Davison	(Treasurer)
Anthony Robinson	(Librarian)
George Pratt	(Conductor)

1 **Apologies for absence**
Apologies had been received from Mary Bell (Ladies' Rep.) and Colin Davison (Men's Rep.).

2 **Minutes of the last meeting**
The minutes of the last meeting were read and signed by the Chairman as an accurate record.

3 **Matters arising**
There were no matters arising.

4 **Financial position**
There had been no major expenses to meet over the summer but the Treasurer had been warned that the Festival fees had gone up to £5 per singer. Once again, the importance of the raffles to the choir's funds would need to be emphasised to the members.

5 **New members**   CD
The choir is still very short of male singers. It was agreed that the usual poster should be prepared but this year the poster coverage should be extended to cover Coopernaught in the hope of attracting new members. Mr Davison would organise its distribution.

6 **Music for the Festival**   AR
The Festival organisers had announced the set pieces but hadn't said how many hire copies we would have so it was not known how many extra copies we would have to buy.

7 **Any other business**   AW
Rex Johnston (Hon Life member): The Secretary reported that Mr Johnston had died in July. It was agreed that the choir would make a donation to charity in his memory.

8 The Secretary was thanked for her (and her husband's) kind hospitality in their new home and the meeting closed at 9pm.

_____
Chairman

_____
Date

MINUTES ⟶

LocoScript 3 User Guide

Improved support for external printers

Using a printer either alongside or instead of the one provided with your PCW is easy in LocoScript 3. Both installing this printer and using it to print is basically just a matter of picking out its name from the appropriate list.

LocoScript 3 also offers extensive support for the fonts offered by such a printer. Moreover, any 'scalable' or 'multi-size' fonts can be used at a wide range of sizes (see Section 7.1).

IMPORTANT: To use an alternative printer with LocoScript 3, you must have a copy of the LocoScript 3 Printer Support Pack. (If you have the LocoScript 2 version of this pack or one of the earlier Printers Drivers Discs, you can upgrade to the new version for a nominal sum. Contact our Sales Department for further information and prices.) You will find full details of the steps used in installing your printer in the 'LocoScript 3 External Printers Guide' supplied in that pack.

Other features

Copying and formatting of discs from within LocoScript (see Chapter 5)

– rather than having to load CP/M and then use DISCKIT. Indeed, you may never need to use CP/M again!

Wide range of characters to use (see Appendix III)

LocoScript 3 supports over 400 different characters and symbols, including Cyrillic characters, ancient Greek characters (and breathing marks) and a wide range of mathematical and technical symbols. Moreover these characters can be used in combination with any of LocoScript 3's many accents. (The range of characters and accents is in fact the same as that supported by LocoScript 2 but with the additions introduced at v2.28.)

The range of characters is so wide that a system of 'Supershifts' is used to allow you to type all the different characters. This system is explained in Section 2.3.

User-defined characters

If you have either a PCW with a built-in matrix printer, the PcW9512+ with the built-in bubblejet printer or a 24-pin matrix printer that accepts characters 'downloaded' from LocoScript, you have the option of replacing up to 16 of LocoScript's characters by characters of your own design.

The way this is done is by running a special CP/M program called LOCOCHAR, the appropriate version of which is supplied alongside the fonts in the LocoFont, LocoFont 24 and LocoFont BJ packs. Contact our Sales Department for further information.

)308

Types of paper selected by name (see Chapter 12)

LocoScript 3 records the details of the different types of paper you use as named 'Paper Types' in your 'Settings file'. Setting up a document or setting up the printer for a particular type of paper is then just a matter of picking out the type of paper you want by name.

Find and Exchange options (see Section 3.5)

Options within the Find and Exchange menus allow you to tell LocoScript to treat capitals and small letters as the same when searching for your Find text, to search only for whole words and to set the case of the inserted text to match that of the replaced text. You can also use 'wild cards' in the text that is searched for.

Copying between documents (see Section 3.4)

LocoScript 3 remembers blocks of text that you copy until changed or until the PCW is turned off or reset. This means you can copy a block of text from one document, open another document and simply paste the text in. You don't have to save the block of text onto your disc first.

Jump to page (see Section 3.2)

LocoScript 3 lets you move directly to a given page. All you have to do is select the 'Find page' option, type the number of the page you require and press [ENTER].

What is more, large moves like this are very much quicker than they were in LocoScript '1' because LocoScript 3 jumps straight to the new position. It doesn't scroll through the whole document on the screen.

Additional 'paragraph' spacing (see Section 7.3)

As well as defining the spacing from line to line, LocoScript also lets you define an additional space to be left after lines ending in a carriage return. This allows you to leave a half-line space between paragraphs, for example.

Consecutive page numbers across a series of documents (see Section 11.5)

One of the more laborious tasks when you are preparing a book is ensuring that the separate documents that go to make up this book have consecutive page numbers. LocoScript 3 can do this for you: all you have to do is pick out the documents in the correct order.

Printing multiple copies (see Section 4.1)

With LocoScript 3, you can print up to 99 copies of any document or part thereof.

Preparation

Before you can use LocoScript 3 to prepare any documents, you need to make a 'LocoScript 3 Start-of-day' disc – perhaps together with an additional 'Start-up disc'. These are the discs that you will in future use to load the LocoScript 3 program into your PCW.

We also recommend you to make a 'LocoScript 3 Examples disc', containing the files needed to work through the Tutorial and the other examples given in this book.

This chapter explains what you need to do in order to prepare each of these discs.

You will need two or possibly three blank discs. (If you don't have any blank discs, you can always re-use 'old' discs, provided you don't want any of the files they contain any more.)

Write-protecting your LocoScript 3 Master disc

Before you do anything else, it is a good idea to check that your LocoScript 3 Master disc (and any other Master discs you have) are 'write-protected' so that there is no way these can be accidentally changed while you are making your Start-of-day and Examples discs.

To do this, you need to look at the corners of these discs: you should notice either one or two holes with shutters that move over them. To protect your Master discs, these holes should all be open. (*Note:* The corresponding holes on your blank discs should be closed.)

PCW8256/8512/9512 disc

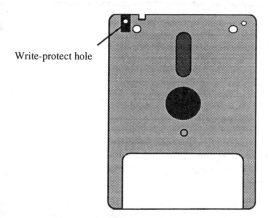

Write-protect hole

PcW9256/9512+/PcW10 disc

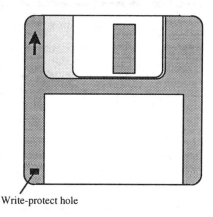

Write-protect hole

LocoScript 3 User Guide   9

Making your LocoScript 3 Start-of-day disc

You make your LocoScript 3 Start-of-day disc by running the special Installation program that we have provided on your LocoScript 3 Master disc.

This Installation program goes through a number of stages, because LocoScript 3 is only the core of the software that you can have on your Start-of-day disc. You can also add such things as the LocoSpell spelling checker, the LocoMail mailmerge program, the LocoFile database and a whole host of additional fonts and printer files – all of which the Installation program has to cater for.

However, the steps themselves are straightforward. You just have to switch on your PCW, load the Installation program from your LocoScript 3 Master disc, and then follow the instructions that appear on the screen. The process of creating this disc is then completed the first time you load LocoScript 3 from the discs the Installation program prepares for you.

Full instructions are given in the LocoScript 3 Installation booklet which you will find in your LocoScript 3 pack. This splits the process of creating a Start-of-day disc into a number of stages, starting with loading the Installation program (the steps for which depend on the type of PCW you have) and finishing with the final adjustments you make the first time you load LocoScript 3.

When you have finished creating your Start-of-day disc, return to this book in order to complete your preparation by making your LocoScript 3 Examples disc.

Be sure to follow the instructions given on the screen (and in the Installation booklet) carefully – particularly with regard to the option to select from the Installation program's 'System Installation' menu. Otherwise, you may find yourself at odds with the Installation program over the details of the system you are trying to set up.

Making your LocoScript 3 Examples disc

The Examples disc is made by copying your LocoScript 3 Master disc.

This copy is made from LocoScript's Disc Manager Screen. This is the screen that is shown immediately after loading, and it is probably the screen that your PCW is currently showing. It should look something like that shown opposite, though details such as the range of files could well be different from those shown here. (If your PCW is showing a different screen, it is probably easiest to insert your LocoScript 3 Start-of-day disc in Drive A and press [SHIFT], [EXTRA] and [EXIT] together to re-load LocoScript.)

The steps used to copy your LocoScript 3 Master disc are slightly different depending on whether your PCW has one disc drive that will accept this type of disc or two, so we give separate sets of instructions below.

Note: Side 2 of the PCW8256/8512 Master disc is not a standard disc and cannot be copied or used either with LocoScript 3 or CP/M.

```
                        Disc management.              Printer idle.  Using    M:
C=Create new document         E=Edit document      P=Print document      D=Direct printing
f1=Actions  f2=Disc  f3=File  f4=Group  f5=Document  f6=Settings  f7=Disc change  f8=Options
```

```
Drive A:                     Drive B:        empty        Drive M:
210k used 496k free  22 files   0k used   0k free  0 files  96k used 196k free  16 files

group 0 210k      group 4    0k                          group 0 96k      group 4    0k
group 1    0k     group 5    0k                          group 1  0k      group 5    0k
group 2    0k     group 6    0k                          group 2  0k      group 6    0k
group 3    0k     group 7    0k                          group 3  0k      group 7    0k

A: group 0   22 files  M: group 0   16 files
   1 limbo files          20 limbo files

DXR08__B.@XR    4k   DXR08__B.@XR    4k
DXR10__B.@XR    4k   DXR10__B.@XR    4k
DXR12__B.@XR    6k   DXR12__B.@XR    6k
DXR14__B.@XR    6k   DXR14__B.@XR    6k
DXR18__B.@XR    8k   DXR18__B.@XR    8k
DXS08__B.@XS    4k   DXS08__B.@XS    4k
DXS10__B.@XS    4k   DXS10__B.@XS    4k
DXS12__B.@XS    6k   DXS12__B.@XS    6k
DXS14__B.@XS    6k   DXS14__B.@XS    6k
DXS18__B.@XS    8k   DXS18__B.@XS    8k
MATRIX .#SS    12k   MATRIX .#SS    12k
MATRIX .#ST    12k   MATRIX .#ST    12k
MATRIX .#XR     2k   MATRIX .PRI     6k
MATRIX .#XS     2k      3 hidden    10k
PHRASES .STD    2k
SETTINGS.STD    2k
   6 hidden   122k
```

Note: In what follows, you will see messages referring to a 'Source' disc and a 'Destination' disc. For this copy, the 'Source disc' is your LocoScript 3 Master disc and the 'Destination disc' is the blank disc that is to be your LocoScript 3 Examples disc. We suggest you label this disc 'LocoScript 3 Examples disc'.

Single-drive system

Check that the disc drive is empty, then press `f2` (ie. `SHIFT` + `f1`) to display the Disc menu, check that the Copy disc option at the top of the menu is highlighted and then press `ENTER` to take this option.

Before copying starts, LocoScript asks you to confirm that you want to copy a disc in case you picked this option by mistake. Press the `↓` key once to move the highlighting to the 'Copy disc' option offered in this message and then press `ENTER`.

The process of copying the disc is carried out in a number of stages, each requiring you first to put in the Source disc and then to replace this disc by the Destination disc. Messages on the screen tell you how many stages your copy will take and record the progress of the copy through all the tracks on the disc.

The first message asks for the Source disc. Check that your LocoScript 3 Master disc is write-protected (as described on page 9), then insert this disc in the disc drive and press `ENTER`. (On an 8000 series machine, insert the disc with Side 1 to the left.) LocoScript then starts reading the data on the disc track by track into memory.

When a message appears asking for the Destination disc, remove the LocoScript 3 Master disc from the drive, insert the disc you labelled 'Examples disc' and press `ENTER`. (On an 8000 series machine, you again want to insert this disc with Side 1 to the left.) LocoScript now writes the section of the disc it had read into memory onto the new disc – then stops and asks for the Source disc again.

Preparation

Simply respond to this and other such messages by removing the disc currently in the drive, inserting the disc that's asked for and pressing [ENTER] until the entire side of the disc has been copied and you see the following message. When this message appears, simply press [ENTER] to return to the Disc Manager Screen.

```
Copying finished

   OK - return to Disc Manager
▶ OK - copy another disc
```

Two-drive system

Make sure that both disc drives are empty, then press [f2] (ie. [SHIFT] + [f1]) to display the Disc menu, check that the Copy disc option at the top of the menu is highlighted and then press [ENTER] to select this option.

Before copying starts, LocoScript checks that you want to go ahead and copy a disc. On an 8000 series machine (or a PCW with non-matching disc drives), this message will also ask you which type of disc you want to copy – 180k or 720k. Press the [↓] key once to highlight the first Copy disc option, and then press [ENTER].

If the disc can be copied directly from one drive to the other, a new message will ask you to put the Source disc in Drive B and the Destination disc in Drive A. (If this isn't possible, the message will ask for your Source disc and you will proceed as described for Single-drive systems.)

Check that your LocoScript 3 Master disc is write-protected (as described on page 9) then insert this disc into Drive B. Then insert the disc you labelled 'Examples disc' in Drive A. (On an 8000 series machine, you need to insert both these discs with Side 1 to the left). Press [ENTER] when you are ready. LocoScript then starts copying the data, track by track, from the disc in Drive B to the disc in Drive A. The message on the screen records its progress through all the tracks on the disc.

When the disc has been copied, you will see the message shown above. When this message appears, press [ENTER] to return to the Disc Manager Screen.

Final step

The disc you have made so far also includes a copy of the Installation program.

To free the space this program occupies for your own work, you need to erase the file with .EMS or .EMT as the second part of its name (full name something like INSTE300.EMT). To do this, use the Cursor keys [↑][↓][←][→] to move the highlighting to this file, press [f3] to display the Files menu, press [↓] twice to highlight the Erase file option in this menu, and then press [ENTER] twice.

> *You have now finished all the preparation you need to do and are ready to start using LocoScript 3. But first, put your LocoScript 3 Master disc (and any other Master discs) away somewhere safe. You won't need these discs in your general work but you will need them – undamaged and unaltered – when you want to update your system in any way, for example by adding other programs in the LocoScript family.*

Tutorial ━━━━━━━━━━━━━━━

The following Tutorial provides a quick introduction to preparing documents with LocoScript 3.

It is principally meant for people who either haven't used LocoScript before or have only used LocoScript '1' (the version of LocoScript supplied on the PCW8256/8512, PcW9256 and PcW10). If you have been using LocoScript 2 (the version supplied with the PCW9512 and PcW9512+), you probably don't need to follow the Tutorial in full but you may find it useful to read through Session 2 because this will show you how you use different fonts and different text sizes.

The main aim of the Tutorial is to give you the overall flavour of the different tasks involved in preparing documents. When you want to know how to carry out a particular task in detail, you should refer to the main part of this book.

To follow the Tutorial, you will need a LocoScript 3 Examples disc. If you have not yet prepared one of these, do this now: the instructions to follow are given in the Preparation section of this book (pages 10 – 12). You will also need a printer attached to your PCW – preferably either the PCW matrix printer, the PcW9512+ Inkjet printer or some other printer that supports LocoScript 3's LX fonts. If your printer doesn't support these fonts, you can still follow the Tutorial but you won't be able to apply the full range of styling that we show you.

Don't worry about hitting the wrong keys as you work through the Tutorial. In many cases, all that will happen is that your PCW will bleep to let you know that it couldn't do anything with the keystrokes you've just made. If instead you find yourself getting into a part of the program that isn't described in the instructions, first try pressing [CAN]; if that doesn't get you back to the right part of LocoScript, try pressing [EXIT], followed by [ENTER] if a menu appears.

If anything happens while you are following the Tutorial that isn't explained in the text, consult the 'Troubleshooting' section of this book (Part IV).

Note: The Tutorial assumes that you know how to switch your PCW on and off, how to insert discs into the disc drives and how to load paper into your printer. Consult either your PCW's own user guide or the manual supplied with the printer if you need any help with these actions.

9402

Creating a document

In this first session of the tutorial, we take you through the steps needed to create a document – starting from switching on your PCW.

The document we shall prepare is a letter to a publisher, to be sent with the manuscript of a book.

Stage 1: Load LocoScript

The first thing you need to do is to load the LocoScript program from the discs that the Installation program prepared for you – unless, of course, this is already loaded in which case you just need to return to the Disc Manager Screen. *(Turn to Section 1.3 in the main part of this book if you have any trouble displaying this screen.)*

To load LocoScript, first switch on your PCW – or if it already switched on, 'reset' it by holding down [SHIFT] and [EXTRA] and pressing [EXIT]. ('Resetting' your computer is equivalent to switching it off and then on again but is much better for it because the electronics don't suffer any sudden change of voltage.)

If your PCW has one disc drive, now put your LocoScript 3 Start-of-day disc in this drive. If your PCW has two disc drives, put any Drive B Start-up disc that the Installation program made for you in Drive B and your LocoScript 3 Start-of-day disc in Drive A. *Note: If you haven't got a LocoScript 3 Start-of-day disc, you need to run the Installation program as described in the Installation book.*

You should now see a pattern of horizontal lines as the LocoScript program is read from your Start-of-day disc. If the PCW doesn't automatically start reading your disc, press the Space bar to prompt it to do this. (If the PCW starts reading the disc but then bleeps, release the disc from the drive and check that you've inserted the correct disc the correct way round – because the bleep means that the PCW is failing to load from the disc. If you have a PCW8256/8512, remember that you insert discs with the side you want to use to the left.)

The pattern of lines is soon replaced by a copyright message which remains on the screen until LocoScript has finished loading. This screen also gives details of your PCW and of the version of LocoScript you are loading.

If the Installation program made any 'Drive A Start-up discs' for you, a message will appear asking you to insert the next disc. When this message appears, replace the disc currently in the drive by the first of these Start-up discs (this could well be Side 2 of your Start-of-day disc) and press [ENTER]. If the message appears again,

```
Insert next disc
▶ continue
```

replace this disc by the next in the sequence and press [ENTER] – and so on until the last of these Start-up discs has been inserted.

Loading has finished when a screen like that shown here is displayed. This is LocoScript's Disc Manager Screen, whose job is to show you the contents of the discs you are currently using. This screen is the central point of all operations within LocoScript. (*Note:* The files and figures shown on your screen will depend on the type of PCW you have and which additional programs you have installed.)

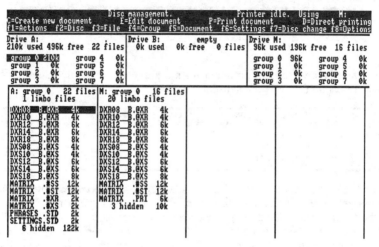

Finally, remove your Start-up disc(s) from the drive(s) and put them somewhere safe, ready for the next time you need to load LocoScript.

Stage 2: Pick where the new document is to be stored

Each document is ultimately stored as a 'file' on a disc. So the next task is to decide where you want to store your document and then pick this out on the Disc Manager Screen.

The first thing to sort out is which disc you want to store the document on and insert this in your PCW's disc drive. The place to store documents is on a 'Data disc' – that is, any disc other than either your Start-of-day disc or a Start-up disc (which should be used solely for the programs and other files that need to be loaded at Start-up). For this example case, we're going to store the document on your LocoScript 3 Examples disc, so insert this disc in your PCW's disc drive. (If you have a PCW8256/812, insert this disc in your (upper) disc drive with Side 1 to the left.)

Then after inserting the disc, you need to press ⎡f7⎤ to tell LocoScript that you have put a different disc in the drive. LocoScript promptly updates the display to show the contents of the disc you've inserted. *Note: You always need to press ⎡f7⎤ after you change the disc in the disc drive.*

You are now in a position to pick out where you want to store the new document, but to do this you need to understand both how files are organised on a disc and how the Disc Manager Screen is laid out.

The top three lines of the screen are Information lines – which tell you what you are currently doing and list the main actions you can carry out and the menus that are available for you to use from this screen.

Disc Manager functions

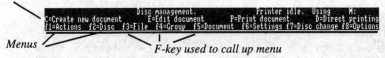

```
                        Disc management.                  Printer idle. Using   M:
C=Create new document        E=Edit document         P=Print document      D=Direct printing
f1=Actions f2=Disc f3=File  f4=Group  f5=Document  f6=Settings f7=Disc change f8=Options
```

Menus — *F-key used to call up menu*

Immediately below these Information lines are three boxes which summarise the contents of each of your PCW's disc drives.

Drive A:			Drive B:			Drive M:		
160k used 546k free 32 files			0k used 0k free 0 files			274k used 18k free 36 files		
group 0	18k	group 4	0k			group 0	274k	group 4	0k
group 1	86k	group 5	0k			group 1	0k	group 5	0k
group 2	0k	group 6	0k			group 2	0k	group 6	0k
group 3	0k	group 7	56k			group 3	0k	group 7	0k

The first box summarises your PCW's main disc drive (Drive A); the second summarises your PCW's second disc drive, if it has one of these (Drive B); while the third box summarises something called Drive M. This is an area of your PCW's memory which has been set up to store files in very much the same way as a disc – but with one important difference: the files on Drive M are lost if you switch off or reset your machine. The chief user of Drive M is LocoScript itself, which uses it to store the 'support files' it calls on (Printer files, Font files, dictionaries and the like) and for the temporary files it creates while you are working on your documents. You can use it for your own files as well if there's room – but do remember to copy these to a floppy disc before resetting your machine or switching off!

These summaries show how much space you have on the disc in the relevant drive and how much is used. They also show how the data that is stored on the disc is divided between the eight 'groups' into which the files on a disc can be placed. (The purpose of these groups is to help you to organise your files. You will soon find that files are easier to manage when you divide them into groups of similar files.)

The rest of the screen lists the files stored on these discs in their different groups.

There is only room to show the contents of at most four groups in this part of the screen, so for a start, LocoScript only shows groups that actually contain files. Then as you could still have more than four groups to display, this section of the screen is able to 'scroll' from left to right in order to display further groups.

The group in which you create a document depends on the type of document you want to create – partly because files are easier to manage when you group similar documents together, but also because LocoScript lets you set up a 'Template' in each group for documents created in that group. The point here is that you can save yourself a lot of work in setting up a document by creating it in a group that contains a Template for the type of document you want to create. (We'll be seeing more about this in Session 5.)

9402

For the purposes of this Tutorial, we want to create our example document in group 1 of the LocoScript 3 Examples disc, so that's the group you want to pick out here.

You pick out the group in which you want to create your new document by moving the Disc Manager Screen's 'cursor' to it. This cursor has two parts. The first is the band of highlighting in the upper part of the screen, which picks out the group you are currently in: this part of the cursor is also known as the Group cursor. The second is the band of highlighting in the bottom part of the screen, which is used to pick out the particular file you want to use: this is also known as the File cursor.

It is in fact possible to move the cursor directly from one group to another in the top part of the screen but when there are already files in the group you want, you can pick out the group you want simply by using the ⬅ and ➡ Cursor keys to move the File cursor across the bottom section of the screen until it is in the file list for the group you require. As the File cursor moves from group to group, the Group cursor automatically moves to select the same group as you will see if you try this out.

Finish with the cursor in group 1.

Stage 3: Create the document

Once the cursor is in place, type C.

LocoScript immediately puts up a short menu showing the details of the document you are about to create.

```
┌─────────────────────────┐
│ Create document         │
├─────────────────────────┤
│▐Name:     DOCUMENT.000▌ │
│ Group:      group 1     │
│ Drive:      A           │
└─────────────────────────┘
```

This menu gives the new document the name DOCUMENT.*number* but you don't have to use this name. Instead, you type the name you do want over this 'default' name, clearing any remaining characters by pressing the Space bar.

There are various rules about the form of the name you can give. In particular, it must have a main part of no more than 8 letters, to which can be added a dot and an 'extension' of up to three letters. Also, the letters used in the name are limited pretty much to the standard A...Z, 0...9. However, you can never give a document a name that breaks these rules as LocoScript won't let you set anything invalid.

We suggest calling our example document EXAMPLE.LET so simply type this over the DOCUMENT.000 that's currently shown, quickly check that the name been entered correctly and press ENTER. LocoScript then displays a new screen – its Editor Screen – all ready for you to type your document. (*Note: In time you'll think of this whole procedure as typing C, typing the name you want for the document (perhaps plus a couple of spaces) and then pressing* ENTER.)

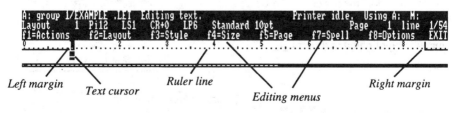

Left margin   Text cursor   Ruler line   Editing menus   Right margin

Tutorial

The document we are aiming to prepare is shown below, but before we can start on this, we need to ensure that the document is set up for the printer that you will be using to print it.

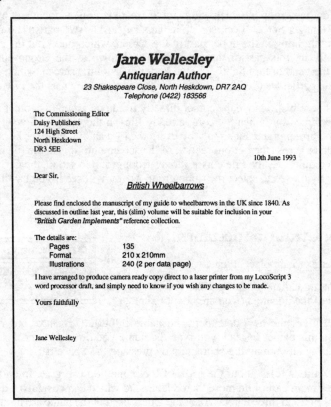

Jane Wellesley
Antiquarian Author
23 Shakespeare Close, North Heskdown, DR7 2AQ
Telephone (0422) 183566

The Commissioning Editor
Daisy Publishers
124 High Street
North Heskdown
DR3 5EE

10th June 1993

Dear Sir,

British Wheelbarrows

Please find enclosed the manuscript of my guide to wheelbarrows in the UK since 1840. As discussed in outline last year, this (slim) volume will be suitable for inclusion in your *"British Garden Implements"* reference collection.

The details are:
Pages   135
Format   210 x 210mm
Illustrations   240 (2 per data page)

I have arranged to produce camera ready copy direct to a laser printer from my LocoScript 3 word processor draft, and simply need to know if you wish any changes to be made.

Yours faithfully

Jane Wellesley

Stage 4: Set up the document for your printer

The printer you will be using to print a document is recorded in an area of the document known as its 'Document Set-up', along with other overall details about the document such as the type of paper that will be used.

So to set up this document for your printer, you have to go into its Document Set-up. To do this, press ▭ to display the Actions menu. When the menu appears, check that the Document setup option at the top of the menu is highlighted and press ▭.

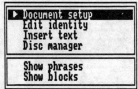

LocoScript then displays its Document Set-up screen.

```
A: group 1/EXAMPLE .LI1 Document setup.              Printer idle. Using A: M:
Layout    0  Pi12  LS1  CR+0  LP6  Standard 10pt              Page ---- line --/54
f1=Actions  f2=Layout  f3=Style  f4=Size  f5=Page  f6=Printing  f7=Spell  f8=Options  EXIT
0.........|.........2.........3.........4.........5.........6.........7.........8..|....
```

━━end of header 1 : used for all pages━━

━━end of footer 1 : used for all pages━━

━━end of header 2 : used for no pages at all━━━━━━━━━━━━━━━━━━━━━━━━━━━━━━━━━━━━

━━end of footer 2 : used for no pages at all━━━━━━━━━━━━━━━━━━━━━━━━━━━━━━━━━━━━

Most of the settings you can make on this screen are outside the scope of this Tutorial (you can read about them in Part III of this book). All you need to do is press ⬚f6⬚ to display the Printer Selection menu and see which printer the document is currently set up for. (This is shown under the Printer line of the menu.)

This menu has two different forms depending on whether the printer is 'multi-font' printer, allowing you to use a mixture of fonts in a document, or a 'single-font' one that restricts you to one font per document.

On a 'multi-font' printer   **On a 'single-font' printer**

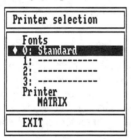

If the menu shows the printer you were intending to use, simply press ⬚CAN⬚ to close up the menu and then press ⬚EXIT⬚ followed by ⬚ENTER⬚ to leave Document Set-up and return to the main part of the document.

But if the menu shows a different printer, move the cursor (the band of highlighting) to the Printer line of the menu and press ⬚ENTER⬚. This displays a list of the printers installed on your system.

Simply move the cursor to the name of the printer you want to use, press the ⬚+⬚ key to tick this and then press ⬚ENTER⬚ to return to the Printer Selection menu which should now be set up for your printer. That done, press ⬚EXIT⬚ followed by ⬚ENTER⬚ to leave the Printer Selection menu and then press ⬚EXIT⬚ followed by ⬚ENTER⬚ again to leave Document Set-up and return to the main part of the document.

Note: If the printer you wanted to use isn't listed, you haven't installed it correctly. You should abandon what you are doing here, reset your PCW (by pressing either ⬚SHIFT⬚ ⬚EXTRA⬚ *and* ⬚EXIT⬚ *– or* ⬚SHIFT⬚ ⬚EXTRA⬚ *and* ⬚RELAY⬚ *on a 3½"-disc system) and run the Installation program again.*

9402

Stage 5: Type in the text

The next step is to type the text of the document. Later, when you're more experienced, you will probably style the text as you type it, but for now it's simpler to get the text right, then worry about the styling you want for it later.

Typing text on a word processor is just like typing at a typewriter – except that tasks like positioning headings centrally (where you want this), starting a new line or a new page, are done for you by LocoScript. You just need to type the actual text and then give instructions as to how you want it to be laid out.

In particular, you only have to press [RETURN] where you specifically need to start a new line – for example, at the end of a heading – or where you want to leave a blank line. You never have to press [RETURN] to start a new line in the middle of a paragraph because LocoScript automatically wraps the text onto a new line for you.

The text for our example document can be seen in the screen display opposite. To start with, just type as far as the short table of details part way down the letter. Moreover, simply type the words of this text, plus any carriage returns that are needed. Don't worry about centring the name and address at the top of the letter or styling it in any way: we'll show you how to do that in Session 2.

If you notice yourself making any mistakes as you type, use the [← DEL] key to rub out back to the place you made the mistake and then correct it.

Inserting the table

The first thing you need where you want to set up a table of details is some 'tabs' on your Ruler line specifying how the columns of the table are to be aligned. LocoScript offers four different types of tab (as you will see in Chapter 8), but for this table you just need a couple of 'Simple' tabs, marking where you want the left-hand edges of these columns to be. You want one 5 characters from the left margin and another 20 characters to the right of that.

To set these tabs, press [f2] ([SHIFT] + [f1]) to display the 'Layout' menu, move the cursor to Change layout and press [ENTER]. This puts you into an area of LocoScript known as the Layout Editor in which you can set a number of aspects about how your text is laid out. (**Note:** You can still see the text of your document while you are in the Layout Editor but you can't work on this again until you have left the Layout Editor.)

To set the first tab you need here, use the [→] key to move the cursor on the Ruler line five places to the right of the left margin (Character position 15), then press [f2] to display the Tabs menu, check that the cursor is on Set Simple tab and press [ENTER]. LocoScript then places a Simple tab at the position of the cursor.

```
0........1...◨..2..........3.........4.........5.........6.........7.........8...L....
```

Simple tab (overlaid by cursor)

To set the other tab, just move the cursor along to Character position 35 and call up the Tabs menu as before.

That done, press [EXIT] to leave the Layout Editor and type the table as follows:

[TAB]Pages[TAB]135[RETURN]
[TAB]Format[TAB]210 x 210 mm[RETURN]
[TAB]Illustrations[TAB]240 (2 per data page)[RETURN]
[RETURN]

Then type the remainder of the letter.

When you've finished typing the text, your document should look like this:

```
A: group 1/EXAMPLE .LE1  Editing text.              Printer idle.  Using A:  M:
Layout    1  Pi12   LS1    CR+0   LP6    Standard 10pt            Page    1  line  1/54
f1=Actions    f2=Layout    f3=Style    f4=Size    f5=Page    f7=Spell    f8=Options    EXIT
0........1.....↑..2.........3....↑...4.........5.........6.........7.........8...L....
          Jane Wellesley↵
          Antiquarian Author↵
          23 Shakespeare Close, North Heskdown, DR7 2AQ↵
          Telephone (0422) 183566↵
          ↵
          The Commissioning Editor↵
          Daisy Publishers↵
          124 High Street↵
          North Heskdown↵
          DR3 5EE↵
          10th June 1993↵
          ↵
          Dear Sir,↵
          British Wheelbarrows↵
          ↵
          Please find enclosed the manuscript of my guide to wheelbarrows in the UK
          since 1840. As discussed in outline last year, this (slim) volume will be
          suitable for inclusion in your "British Garden Implements" reference
          collection.↵
          ↵
          The details are:↵
       →     Pages→           135↵
       →     Format→          210 x 210mm↵
       →     Illustrations→   240 (2 per data page)↵
       →  ↵
          I have arranged to produce camera ready copy direct to a laser printer from
          my LocoScript 3 word processor draft, amd simply need to know if you wish
          any changes to be made.↵
          ↵
          Yours faithfully↵
          ↵
          ↵
          ↵
          Jane Wellesley↵
```

NOTE: The steps we took here in fact set up tabs for the whole document. It was all right to do this because none of the rest of the letter uses any tabs. In other cases, you will need to think more carefully about how and where you change the layout that's being used. This is explained in Chapter 8.

9402

Stage 5: Save the document

So far, the text that you have typed is only held in your PCW's memory. To preserve it, you need to save it on disc.

LocoScript offers several options for saving the work you have done. Which to choose depends on whether you want to finish work on the document at this point; or continue working on the document after saving the work you have done so far; or both save the document to disc and print it.

All three options are offered from the same 'Exit' menu, so the first step is to call up this menu by pressing EXIT.

```
► Finish edit
  Save and Continue
  Save and Print
  Abandon edit
```

When this menu appears, you will see it offers a choice of four options – the three actions we've just described, plus the option to abandon the work you have done. For the purposes of this Tutorial, leave the cursor on the Finish edit option at the top of the menu and press ENTER. LocoScript then saves the document to disc and returns you to the Disc Manager Screen. If you look at this screen, you will see that this shows the EXAMPLE.LET file you've created in group 1. Moreover, LocoScript has automatically placed the File cursor on this file – all ready for you to continue work on this document in Session 2.

Note: The 'Save and Continue' option is particularly useful when you are working on a large document. Because the work you do is initially only held in memory, it will have to be re-done if there's a sudden power cut. But if you use the Save and Continue *option every half-hour or so, you will only have to re-do the work you've done since the you last saved the document. It's worth thinking about!*

Styling a document

In the first session of this Tutorial, we set up the text of our example document – but if you were to print it now, it wouldn't look anything like the document we showed on page 18 because we haven't told LocoScript how we want it to be styled. In this session, we're going to put that right.

Note: (i) We assume that you have already got your PCW switched on and that the screen is showing LocoScript's Disc Manager Screen. If not, switch on (or reset your PCW) and load LocoScript now. (Turn back to Stage 1 of Session 1 if you are not sure how to do this.)

(ii) To follow this session in full, you need to be using a printer that supports LocoScript 3's LX fonts – such as the matrix printer supplied with the PCW8256/ 8512, the PcW9256 and the PcW10 and the bubblejet printer supplied with some models of the PcW9512. If your printer doesn't support these fonts, we will tell you to skip certain sections of this session where these cover styling that isn't available on your printer.

Opening up the document again

To change a document that you have stored on disc, you first need to display its current text on the screen. This is known as 'opening the document for editing' or, more simply, as 'editing the document'.

If you have come here straight from the previous session, all you need to do to open up EXAMPLE.LET again is check that the cursor is on this document, then type E (for Edit), and then press [ENTER].

But if you have switched off your PCW or done something else in the meantime, you will first need to insert your LocoScript 3 Examples disc (if you have a PCW8256/8512, insert this disc in your upper disc drive with Side 1 to the left) and press [f7] to signal the change of disc.

Then use the Cursor keys [↑], [↓], [←] and [→] to move the cursor EXAMPLE.LET, type E, check that EXAMPLE.LET is named in the menu that is displayed and press [ENTER].

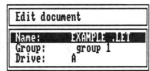

```
Edit document
Name:       EXAMPLE .LET
Group:      group 1
Drive:      A
```

The letter you prepared in the last session should now be displayed on the screen, ready for you to style it.

Positioning the headings and the date

The first styling to do is to centre Jane Wellesley's details at the top of the page and the title 'British Wheelbarrows', and to move the date over to the right.

To centre Jane Wellesley's details, you first need the cursor on the J of Jane. When the cursor is in place, press `f2` (`SHIFT`+`f1`) to call up the Layout menu, move the cursor to the Centre option and press `ENTER`. The text on this line then jumps to the middle of the screen.

That's centred the first line of these details. To centre the remaining lines (and the heading 'British Wheelbarrows'), you simply need to move to the beginning of each of these lines in turn (for example by pressing `LINE`), press `f2` and take the Centre option as before. That's all there is to centring any line of text.

Moving the date over to the right-hand side of the page uses much the same steps. Just move the cursor to the beginning of this date and press `f2` as before – but this time, take the Right align option. The date then jumps to the right of the screen.

Already, the document is showing much of the final shape we want for the letter.

```
0........1....?....2.........3...?....4.........5........6.........7█.......8...L....
                              Jane Wellesley↵
                            Antiquarian Author↵
                23 Shakespeare Close, North Heskdown, DR7 2AQ↵
                        Telephone (0422) 183566↵
↵
The Commissioning Editor↵
Daisy Publishers↵
124 High Street↵
North Heskdown↵
DR3 5EE↵
                                                        20th June 1993↵
↵
Dear Sir,↵
↵
                        British Wheelbarrows↵
↵
Please find enclosed the manuscript of my guide to wheelbarrows in the UK
since 1840. As discussed in outline last year, this (slim) volume will be
suitable for inclusion in your "British Garden Implements" reference
collection.↵
↵
The details are:↵
  →   Pages→              135↵
  →   Format→             210 x 210mm↵
  →   Illustrations→      240 (2 per data page)↵
↵
I have arranged to produce camera ready copy direct to a laser printer from
my LocoScript 3 word processor draft, amd simply need to know if you wish
any changes to be made.↵
```

Specifying the text styles

The next thing to do is to put in the different text styles (Bold, Italic etc.) that we want. The menu used to do this is the f3 Style menu and you need to use this menu first at the top of the document and then again at each point down the document where you want to change any aspect of the text style. *Note: If you have a daisy-wheel printer, selecting Italic has no effect because the characters on a printwheel can't be italicised – so we suggest you select Underline instead.*

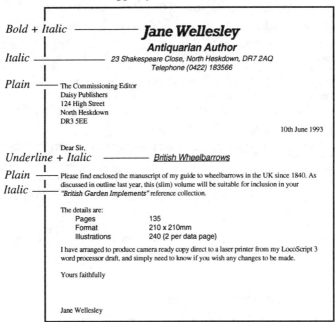

The standard way of moving the cursor is by using the Cursor keys but when you want to move somewhere like the beginning or end of a line or a page, it's usually easier to use LocoScript's 'Textual Movement' keystokes. The one that takes you to the start of a document is [ALT] + [SHIFT] + [PAGE], so press this now and then press [f3] to display the Style menu.

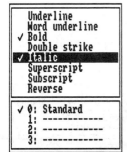

Note: Reverse is used to highlight text on the screen. It doesn't change the appearance of the text when it is printed.

Our scheme specifies Bold+Italic for the first line of the document and to get this, we need to tick the corresponding options in the Style menu ie. Bold and Italic. To do this, move the cursor to Bold and press the key marked [⊞] (which is known as the 'Set' key); then move down a couple of lines to the Italic and press [⊞] again. Then press [ENTER] to close up the menu. That's set the text style we want for Jane Wellesley.

Two lines down we've specified just Italic, so at the start of this line we need to clear the Bold styling. So place the cursor on the 2 of 23 Shakespeare Close and press ⌷f3. The menu appears with Bold and Italic ticked to show these are currently selected. To get the result we want, just move the cursor to Bold and press the key marked ⌷-⌷ key (the 'Clear' key) to clear the tick beside Bold, and press ⌷ENTER.

Carry on in this way down the document:

• Clearing Italic at the start of the Commissioning Editor's address

• Ticking Italic and Underline at the start of British Wheelbarrows

• Clearing Italic and Underline for the start of the first main paragraph

• Ticking Italic before "British Garden Implements" and clearing it again afterwards

As you do this, you will doubtless notice that, in the main, the text on the screen gives no hint of the styling you have set. Only Underline and Reverse can be shown directly on the PCW's screen – but it is still possible to see what styling you have set.

One way is to look at the Information lines at the top of the screen. The print style being used at the current position of the cursor is shown on the second of these lines.

The other way is to press ⌷f8 (⌷SHIFT+⌷f7) to display the Options menu, tick the Codes option at the top of this menu and press ⌷ENTER. The screen then changes to reveal all different codes you have been inserting into the text – (CEntre) where you've centred the line, (+Bold) where you've turned on Bold, (-Bold) where you've turned off Bold, etc. etc. (Codes that turn on effects generally start with a +, while those that turn effects off start with a -.)

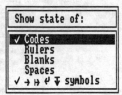

```
0........1....↑....2....↓....3....↑....4.........5.........6.........7.........8....↓....L....
           (+Bold)(*Italic)(CEntre)      Jane Wellesley↵
           (CEntre)               Antiquarian Author↵
           (CEntre)      (-Bold)23 Shakespeare Close, North Heskdown, DR7 2AQ↵
           (CEntre)               Telephone (0422) 183566↵

           (-Italic)The Commissioning Editor↵
           Daisy Publishers↵
           124 High Street↵
           North Heskdown↵
           DR3 5EE↵
           (RAlign)                                        10th June 1993↵
           ↵
           Dear Sir,↵
           (CEntre)               (*UL)(*Italic)British Wheelbarrows↵
           ↵
```

Showing codes can distort the text on the screen, possibly sending the right-hand end of each line off the display but it is worth doing because it shows you precisely what stylings that you have put into your document.

(Having done all this styling, it's probably worth saving the document before continuing. So before you carry on, press ⌷EXIT, move the cursor to Save and Continue and press ⌷ENTER.)

Specifying the fonts

* If your printer doesn't support the LX fonts, you should skip both this and the following section, and go on to 'What you have achieved so far' on page 30.

The next step is to carry out much the same procedure but this time to select the different fonts you want to use in the document. The menu used to do this is again the f3 Style menu, so press [ALT] + [SHIFT] + [PAGE] to return to the top of the document and then press [f3] to display the Style menu.

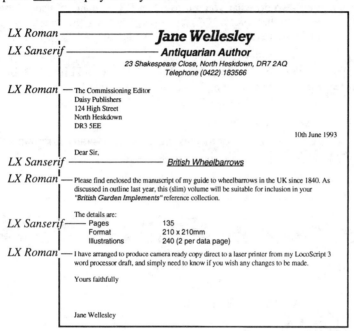

Our scheme specifies LX Roman for the first line of the document. LX Roman probably isn't listed in the Style menu at present but this is nothing to worry about. Just move the cursor to the first line of dashes in the Font section of this menu and use [⊞] to tick this. *(Notice how you don't have to clear the tick against the font that's currently selected: this is automatically cleared because you can only work with one font at a time.)*

Press [ENTER].

LocoScript now displays a message telling you that the Font number you've ticked is undefined. Press [ENTER] to this message and LocoScript then displays a list of the fonts that are available for you to choose from.

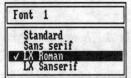

```
Font 1

  Standard
  Sans serif
✓ LX Roman
  LX Sanserif
```

If your printer supports the LX fonts, this list should include LX Roman. To select this, move the cursor to LX Roman, press ⊞ to tick it and then press ENTER. (You can confirm that you have selected LX Roman here by looking at the Information lines which should now be showing LX Roman on the second line.)

For the next line, we've specified LX Sanserif. So move the cursor to the A of Antiquarian and press f3 to call up the Style menu again. Again, LX Sanserif probably isn't listed – so do what you did to select LX Roman, ie. use ⊞ to tick another of the lines of dashes, press ENTER, press ENTER again to the message appears, tick LX Sanserif in the list of fonts you are shown and press ENTER once more.

For the Commissioning Editor's address, we've specified LX Roman again. So place the cursor on the T of The Commissioning Editor and press f3. Because you have already used this font, the Style menu does include LX Roman this time. So just move the cursor to LX Roman, press ⊞ to tick it and press ENTER.

Carry on in this way down the document:

• Ticking LX Sanserif at the start of the heading British Wheelbarrows
• Ticking LX Roman for the start of the first paragraph
• Ticking LX Sanserif at the start of the book details
• And finally ticking LX Roman again at the beginning of the last paragraph

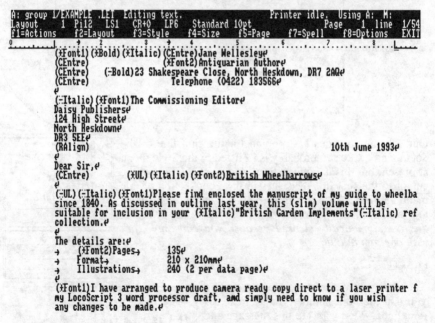

(At this point it's probably worth saving the document again. So before you carry on, press EXIT, move the cursor to Save and Continue and press ENTER.)

Setting different sizes

Different fonts and text styles do a lot for the appearance of a document but really impressive results come from using different sizes of text. To produce the effects we want in our example letter, we need to specify 'Point Sizes' from 28pt for Jane Wellesley's name to 12pt for the main part of the text. *(The Point Size of text is basically the height of the characters from the tops of capital letters to the lowest point on a letter like p or g, measured in 'Points' where 1 Point (or pt) = ½₂".)*

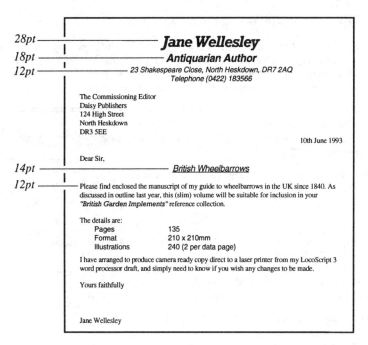

The procedure for setting these sizes is much like that used to set the font and the print style, only this time you use the f4 Size menu. So hold down [ALT] and [SHIFT] as you press [PAGE] to move the cursor back to the top of the document and then press [f4] ([SHIFT]+[f3]) to call up the Size menu.

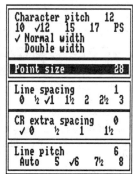

Our specification shows 28pt for Jane Wellesley, so move the cursor to the Point size line of the menu, type 28 followed by [ENTER] (to 'finish' this value). Then press [ENTER] again to close the menu. LocoScript then inserts a (+PoinT28) code at the start of the document, setting the Point Size of the text to 28pt.

For the next line, we've specified 18pt. So move the cursor to the A of Antiquarian, press [f4] to call up the Size menu and set the Point Size to 18. Then carry on down the document, positioning the cursor at each point the Point Size changes, pressing [f4] to call up the Size menu and setting the required size.

Note: The reason we can use different sizes of text here is because we are using LocoScript 3's LX fonts in our document. Most other fonts can only be printed at one size which limits the results you can achieve with these fonts.

What you have achieved so far

If you have a printer that supports LocoScript 3's LX fonts (eg. the PCW matrix printer or the bubblejet supplied with some models of the PcW9512+), it's worth printing the document out at this point to see what the document looks like now you have positioned headings and set fonts, text styles and point sizes.

The way to do this is via the Save and Print option offered in the Exit menu, so press [EXIT] to call up the Exit menu, move the cursor to the Save and Print option and press [ENTER].

```
Finish edit
Save and Continue
▶ Save and Print
Abandon edit
```

LocoScript first saves the document on disc, then puts up its Print menu. This menu is automatically set up to print one copy of the document you've just been working on, so you just need to press [ENTER].

```
Print document

Name:        EXAMPLE .LET
Group:       group 1
Drive:       A

✓ High quality
  Draft quality
  Number of copies:        1

▶ Print all of document
  Print part of document
```

At this point, you may see various messages as LocoScript checks the printer, paper and fonts selected in the document (known as the 'Intended' printer set-up) against the printer, paper and fonts it is currently set up to use (the 'Current' printer set-up).

If you set up the document for your PCW's built-in printer, you will probably just see a message telling you that it is about to print on this printer.

```
About to print:

Printer:     MATRIX
Paper:       A4              Portrait

▶ Proceed
  Cancel operation
```

Quickly check the details shown in this message – to check, for example, the type of paper LocoScript is expecting you to use (A4 in this case) – and then press [ENTER] to continue.

If you set it up for some other printer, however, you may very well see a message telling you that the 'Current and Intended printers do not match' which offers you the choice of either printing on your Current printer or on the Intended printer. Assuming that the printer you chose is attached to your PCW, move the cursor to the Change to intended option and press [ENTER]. You will then get a message telling you about the printer and paper LocoScript is about to use. Quickly check the details shown in this message (to check, for example, the type of paper LocoScript is expecting you to use) and press [ENTER].

Load a sheet of the correct type of paper into the printer (the printer's own manual will tell you how to do this if you are not sure) then press either the [EXIT] key (if you are using your PCW's built-in printer) or [PTR] followed by [⊞] if you are using some other printer. LocoScript should then start printing: when it has finished the page, you should be able to simply lift this out of the printer.

Sorting out the spacing

The document you print will probably be a bit disappointing to you: indeed, it will look rather a mess – especially at the top. However, this mess has both a very simple explanation and a very simple cure.

Jane Wellesley
Antiquarian Author
23 Shakespeare Close, North Heskdown, DR7 2AQ
Telephone (0422) 183566

The problem is that when we were setting the different fonts we wanted and the different sizes of text we required, we did nothing to ensure that the characters would be correctly spaced along each line or that the lines would be spaced far enough apart that they wouldn't overlap.

The spacing of the characters along the line is specified by the 'Character Pitch', while the spacing from line to line is specified by the 'Line Pitch' together with the 'Line Spacing'. (The Line Pitch sets the standard spacing for the lines, while the Line Spacing sets whether you want your text to be 'single spaced' or 'double-spaced' (or whatever) in much the same way as the Line Spacing lever on a typewriter.)

There are a number of possible settings for both the Character Pitch and the Line Pitch (as we explain in Chapter 7). But where you are using different fonts and different sizes of text in a document, there's only one setting to use for each of these – *Character Pitch PS* and *Line Pitch Auto*. Setting these throughout your document will prevent the mess you saw earlier because:

- *Setting Character Pitch PS ensures that the characters of your text are correctly spaced across the page by telling LocoScript to space each character according to its width.*

- *Setting Line Pitch Auto ensures that the lines of text are correctly spaced down the page by telling LocoScript to make the spacing between each line 20% larger than the largest character on the line (or as close to this as it can get).*

9402

To set these, open up EXAMPLE.LET for editing again (by pressing E followed by [ENTER]), then press [f2] to display the Layout menu, move the cursor to Change layout and press [ENTER] to go into the Layout Editor.

Character pitch			PS
10 12 15		17	√PS
√ Normal width			
Double width			
Point size			10
Line spacing			1
0 ½ √1 1½ 2 2½ 3			
CR extra spacing			0
√0 ½ 1 1½			
Line pitch			Auto
√Auto 5 6 7½ 8			

Once you are in the Layout Editor, press [f4] to display the Layout Editor's Size menu (which is identical to the one you used earlier). When this menu appears, move the cursor up to the second line of the menu and press [Space] until PS is ticked. Then move the cursor to the line of options below Line Pitch and then press [Space] until Auto is ticked.

Now press [ENTER] to close up the menu, then press [EXIT] to leave the Layout Editor and return to the document. You should see PiPS and Auto on the Information lines at the top of the screen, showing that you have selected the spacing you want. These settings will now remain in force throughout the document – provided you don't select different settings elsewhere in the document.

Finally...

Before closing up the document and seeing what effect these two settings have had on your printed document, there's one further thing that we want to show you – the effect of these settings on your screen display.

To see this, simply cursor down the document. The first few lines don't change but when you get into to main part of the letter, you will see LocoScript not just relaying the text but relaying the text in such a way that it goes beyond the right-hand edge of the screen.

This can seem very perturbing at first but it is actually nothing to worry about. The reason is simply that, now you have told LocoScript to space the characters according to their width, it can now fit more characters on each line. The characters on the screen are fixed at one particular size and can't be squashed up to show these extra characters. So LocoScript's only option is to let the text run into the right-hand margin on the screen. The text doesn't of course actually run into this margin as you will see if you now 'Save and Print' the document as before.

This time, the document should come out looking perfect!

Note: If the document looks fine except the parts of the table aren't aligned correctly despite being aligned on the screen, you have set up this table using spaces to line it up rather than tabs as we suggested. Using spaces to line up text doesn't work where you are using Character Pitch PS.

Replace each of your groups of spaces by a single press of the [TAB] key and you will find that this table is properly aligned – both on the screen and when its printed, whatever Character Pitch you use!

9308

Editing a document

One of the things that is very much easier to do on a word processor than on a typewriter is to produce a new version of a document that you have previously prepared. With a word processor, there's no need to start again from scratch – however complex the changes. Instead, you just call up the document, make the changes you require and then save and print the new document.

In this session of the tutorial, we look at the various techniques that LocoScript offers for modifying an existing document by looking at the steps we would use to produce a version of our example letter to go with Jane Wellesley's latest contribution to the 'British Garden Implements' series – 'British Rakes'.

Note: We assume that you have already got your PCW switched on and that the screen is showing LocoScript's Disc Manager Screen. If not, switch on (or reset your PCW) and load LocoScript now. (Turn back to Stage 1 of Session 1 if you are not sure how to do this.)

Opening the document for editing

To modify an existing document, you first need to display its current text on the screen. So the first step is to open our EXAMPLE.LET document for editing – just as we opened it for editing at the start of the previous session.

If you have come here straight from the previous session, all you need to do to open up EXAMPLE.LET again is check that the cursor is on this document, then type E (for Edit), and then press [ENTER].

But if you have switched off your PCW or done something else in the meantime, you will first need to insert your LocoScript 3 Examples disc (if you have a PCW8256/8512, insert this disc in your upper disc drive with Side 1 to the left) and press [f7] to signal the change of disc.

Then use the Cursor keys [↑], [↓], [←] and [→] to move the cursor EXAMPLE.LET, type E, check that EXAMPLE.LET is named in the menu that is displayed and press [ENTER].

```
Edit document
┌─────────────────────────┐
│ Name:    EXAMPLE .LET    │
│ Group:      group 1      │
│ Drive:      A            │
└─────────────────────────┘
```

The letter you have prepared over the previous two sessions should now be displayed on the screen, complete with all the styling codes that you inserted. We will now set about changing this letter in various ways.

Note: The new version of the document will replace the existing one. If you want to keep the old version of a document, the best thing to do is to make a copy of the existing file (we show you how to do this in Session 5) and then edit the copy.

Tutorial

Find and Exchange

Something you can do very easily using a word processor is replace one word, name or phrase for another throughout the whole of a document, thereby instantly converting text about one subject into text about another.

LocoScript has a 'Find and Exchange' facility specifically to enable you to make such changes.

To show you how this works, we shall use it to replace Wheelbarrows by Rakes throughout the document.

Before you make this exchange, you need the cursor at the top of the document so that you don't miss any of the places wheelbarrow is mentioned. (Exchanges are made down the document from the current position of the cursor.) So if you've moved the cursor away from the top, press [ALT] [SHIFT] and [PAGE] to get it back there.

Then with the cursor at the beginning of the document, press [EXCH] (ie. [SHIFT] + [FIND]) to display the Exchange menu.

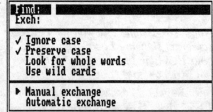

The top line of this menu (which the cursor is currently on) is for the word or phrase you want to replace – the 'Find text'. So type wheelbarrows here.

The next line of the menu is for the text you want to replace it by – the 'Exchange text'. So move the cursor down to the next line of the menu and type rakes.

That's set up the basic details of the exchange but before carrying it out, you need to consider whether you want to be selective about the instances of the Find text that LocoScript picks out for exchange.

If you scan the document (either on the screen or in its printed form) you will see that wheelbarrows appears as both wheelbarrows and as Wheelbarrows. What is more, you would like wheelbarrows to be replaced by rakes and Wheelbarrows by Rakes.

There's an option in the menu specifically for this – Preserve case. This tells LocoScript to give the word or phrase it inserts, the same combination of upper and lower case characters as the word or phrase that it is replacing (as far as this is possible). So you just need to make sure this is ticked, then move the cursor to the Automatic option at the bottom of the menu and press [ENTER]. LocoScript will then work through the document replacing wheelbarrows by rakes just as you require.

```
Find: wheelbarrows
Exch: rakes

√ Ignore case
√ Preserve case
  Look for whole words
  Use wild cards

  Manual exchange
▶ Automatic exchange
```

That's pretty much all there is to Find and Exchange.

9308

Copy, Cut and Paste

Another thing you can do very easily with LocoScript is re-order sections of your text – for example, taking a paragraph from the top of the document to the bottom in one easy move. Making such changes is often referred to as Cut and Paste editing.

The thing to remember about Cut and Paste editing is that you need to be very precise in where you place the cursor, both when you are selecting the section of text you want to move and when you are 'pasting it in' at its new position. If you are too casual in positioning the cursor, you can find yourself moving too little or too much or pasting the text in at the wrong place – all of which will take some effort to correct.

To show you how you do Cut and Paste editing in LocoScript, we shall move the paragraph starting 'I have arranged to produce camera ready copy' from the end of the letter and make it the second paragraph in the new version.

To start, you need place the cursor at the beginning of the text you are going to move ie. to the start of this paragraph. When the cursor is in place, press the [COPY] key – NOT the [CUT] key: the 'Cut' of this piece of Cut and Paste editing comes later. (Indeed, if you press [CUT] at this point instead of [COPY], you'll lose the text for good!)

Now move the cursor to the start of the text you want to leave behind – ie. to the Y of Yours faithfully... – and press [CUT]. As you do this, notice how the text between your two cursor positions becomes highlighted so that you can readily see how much text you are going to move.

```
→  Format→          210 x 210mm↵
→  Illustrations→   240 (2 per data page)↵
↵
(+Font1)I have arranged to produce camera ready copy direct to a laser printer f
word processor draft, and simply need to know if you wish any changes to be made
↵
Yours faithfully↵
↵
```

LocoScript then displays a message on the screen asking you to type 0...9 or A...Z.

```
COPY and CUT text:

type block 0..9
or phrase A..Z
or CAN to return to area select
```

For the sort of editing we're doing here, you always want to type a number – so type 0. This copies the text to 'Block 0' and then cuts it from the document. (Typing a different number would have copied the text to one of the other nine Blocks you can use to move text around your document.)

You now just paste this Block into the document at the new position you want for this text. So move the cursor up to the left-hand end of the line The details are:, press [PASTE] and then type 0 (the number of the Block containing the text you want to paste in here). LocoScript then pastes in the text you copied to this Block.

```
(–Italic)(*Font1)The Commissioning Editor↵
Daisy Publishers↵
124 High Street↵
North Heskdown↵
DR3 5EE↵
(RAlign)                                    10th June 1993↵
↵
Dear Sir,↵
(CEntre)          (*UL)(*Italic)(*Font2)(*PoinT14)British Rakes↵
↵
(*PoinT12)(–UL)(–Italic)(*Font1)Please find enclosed the manuscript of my guide
in outline last year, this (slim) volume will be suitable for inclusion in your
Implements"(–Italic) reference collection.↵
↵
(*Font1)I have arranged to produce camera ready copy direct to a laser printer f
word processor draft, and simply need to know if you wish any changes to be made
↵
the details are:↵
  →    (*Font2)Pages→       135↵
  →    Format→              210 x 210mm↵
  →    Illustrations→       240 (2 per data page)↵
  ↵
Yours faithfully↵
↵
↵
↵
```

*From the look of the screen, you will probably think all's well at this point but the
chances are that the text is no longer styled correctly. The problem with the Copy,
Cut and Paste we have just done is that as well as moving the text, you probably
also moved the Font code that set LX Roman again after the Sanserif of the table.
The fact that you have moved this code doesn't make any difference to the first part
of the letter where LX Roman was being used anyway – but its absence from the
bottom part of the document does make a difference because* Yours faithfully
and Jane Wellesley *are set to be printed in LX Sanserif.*

*To sort the styling out, either practice the Copy, Cut and Paste technique we've just
shown you by using it to move the Font code back after the table – or simply delete
the code from its new position and insert a fresh Font code by calling up the Style
menu as we showed you in the last session.*

```
(*PoinT12)(–UL)(–Italic)(*Font1)Please find enclosed the manuscript of my guide
in outline last year, this (slim) volume will be suitable for inclusion in your
Implements"(–Italic) reference collection.↵
↵
I have arranged to produce camera ready copy direct to a laser printer from my L
word processor draft, and simply need to know if you wish any changes to be made
↵
The details are:↵
  →    (*Font2)Pages→       135↵
  →    Format→              210 x 210mm↵
  →    Illustrations→       240 (2 per data page)↵
  ↵
(*Font1)Yours faithfully↵
↵
↵
↵
```

Further changes

The techniques of Find & Exchange and Cut & Paste are useful for major changes but the remaining changes usually have to be made by using the ⌫DEL and DEL→ keys to delete text you don't need and then re-typing.

Use this technique to change the date at the top of the letter to today's date, add the words 'As before' to the start of what is now the second paragraph, and to make the number of pages in 'British Rakes' 64.

```
(RAlign)                                              (Today's date)↵
↵
Dear Sir,↵
(CEntre)        (*UL)(*Italic)(*Font2)(*PoinT14)British Rakes↵
↵
(*PoinT12)(−UL)(−Italic)(*Font1)Please find enclosed the manuscript of my guide
in outline last year, this (slim) volume will be suitable for inclusion in your
Implements"(−Italic) reference collection.↵
↵
As before I have arranged to produce camera ready copy direct to a laser printer
LocoScript 3 word processor draft, and simply need to know if you wish any chang
made.↵
↵
The details are:↵
  →    (*Font2)Pages→     64↵
  →    Format→            210 x 210mm↵
  →    Illustrations→     240 (2 per data page)↵
↵
(*Font1)Yours faithfully↵
↵
↵
```

When you make the second of these changes, LocoScript won't simply absorb the extra words into the paragraph – at least, not to start with. Instead, it 'breaks' the paragraph by opening up a fresh line for words you are adding (in case you want to add a lot of text). To straighten out the paragraph again, you simply need either to press RELAY or to wait until you move the cursor further down the document again. LocoScript will automatically re-lay the paragraph the moment you move down to the next part of the document.

Saving (or abandoning) the changes

Having finished making these changes to the document, you can then choose whether to simply save the new version on disc, save it and print it – or throw the changes you've made away.

Whichever you want, the first step is to display the Exit menu, so press EXIT to display this now. You then choose what you want to happen to the document from this menu.

For the purposes of this tutorial, it doesn't matter which option you choose as long as you take one of the options that finishes work on the document (ie. not Save and Continue). So just move the cursor to the option you would like to take and press ENTER.

Disc Housekeeping

As well as creating, editing and printing documents, you also need to:

- *Keep yourself supplied with discs on which to store these documents*
- *Keep the files on these discs organised so that they are easy to find – by copying them (or moving them) from one disc to another; renaming them etc.*
- *Get rid of files you no longer need*
- *Last, but not least, make 'security' or 'back-up' copies of important files so that you don't lose all your hard work if something happens to the disc on which you have been storing your files – for example, someone spills coffee over it.*

These tasks are known collectively as 'Disc Housekeeping' and you can carry all of them out without leaving LocoScript 3.

All these actions are carried out from LocoScript's Disc Manager Screen so to start, you need to show this screen. If you haven't got LocoScript loaded or you are not sure how to display this screen, switch on (or reset your PCW) and load LocoScript now. (Turn back to Stage 1 of the first session if you are not sure how to do this.)

Formatting discs

One of your first requirements will be for 'Data discs' on which to store the documents and datafiles you prepare. It's easy enough to buy further discs but before a disc can be used to store documents or other data, its storage area has to be marked out electronically into a series of 'tracks' and 'sectors'. The process of marking this area out is known as 'formatting the disc'.

Formatting is also a good way of clearing an old disc of all the data it currently contains and making it ready to store fresh information.

The process is very straightforward as we shall now show you: you just pick the option to Format a disc and then follow the instructions on the screen. If you have a new disc that you need to format – or an old disc containing files that you no longer need – we suggest that you take the opportunity to format this disc now.

The first thing to do is to remove any discs that are currently in your disc drives and put them to one side – so that you cannot format these by mistake. You could lose valuable files that way.

Once you've removed these discs, press ⌜f2⌝ (⌜SHIFT⌝ + ⌜f1⌝) to display the Disc menu, move the cursor to Format disc and press ⌜ENTER⌝.

LocoScript responds by displaying a message similar to the following.

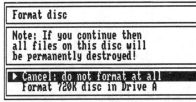

This principally gets you to confirm that you really want to format a disc (just in case you selected this option by mistake). But if you have a PCW with two disc drives, it also gets you to specify which of your two disc drives you are going to format the disc in. This is particularly important if, as on the PCW8512, your disc drives are of different types because you need to format the disc in the drive in which the disc is going to be used.

Make sure that the cursor is on the format option you want and press ⌜ENTER⌝.

LocoScript now asks you to insert the disc that's to be formatted, so insert this in the drive you said you would use and press ⌜ENTER⌝. If you are formatting a 3" disc in Drive A of a PCW8256/8512, make sure you insert this disc with the side you want to format to the left. *If a message now appears telling you that the disc is write-protected, release the disc from the drive, make sure that the write-protect holes on the disc are closed (there's a picture showing the position of these holes on page 9 of this book), re-insert the disc, check that the cursor in the message is on the* Disc write-enabled *option and press* ⌜ENTER⌝.

LocoScript now proceeds to format the disc. The message on the screen tells you how far this process has got.

> Format 720K disc in Drive A
>
> Formatting track 159

When LocoScript has finished formatting – and 'verifying' (ie. checking) – the disc, this message is replaced by one that asks you whether you want to format another or return to the Disc Manager.

> Formatting finished
>
> ▶ OK - return to Disc Manager
>   OK - format another disc

If you have been formatting a 3" disc in Drive A of a PCW8256/8512, it is a good idea having formatted one side of the disc to go on format the other side as well. So for you, we would recommend taking the option to Format another disc and then working through the steps again, this time to format the other side of the disc. In all other cases, it's simply a matter of whether you have any further discs that you want to format now.

If you have further discs to format, move the cursor to the Format another disc option, press ⌜ENTER⌝ and follow the instructions on the screen as before. If you don't, check that the cursor is on the option to Return to Disc Manager and press ⌜ENTER⌝ to continue with this Tutorial.

LocoScript 3 User Guide 39

Copying files

We are now going to show you how to make a copy of a file that you have stored on disc, which you then store either on the same disc or on a different disc. *(Note: The steps used to **move** a file from one group to another or from one disc to another are very similar to the ones we show you here. The only difference is in the option that you select from the menu.)*

Copying is used in all sorts of circumstances:

- *When you want to create a new version of a document without losing the old one*
- *When a printer file or a font file you require isn't on Drive M*
- *When you want to save a file you have created or modified on Drive M*
- *When you want to make a 'back-up' or 'security' copy of a file (though it's often easier to make a back-up of the whole disc as we describe later in this session)*

To show you the steps that you use, we are going to copy the EXAMPLE.LET document in group 1 of your LocoScript 3 Examples disc to the first group (group 0) on the disc you have just formatted – and we are going to make this copy assuming that you have one disc drive.

The special feature about copying from one disc to another when you only have one disc drive is that you can't make this copy directly. Instead you have to copy the file first to Drive M, then switch discs and copy the file from Drive M to the new disc. Otherwise the steps used for any copy are much the same. In fact, even if your PCW has two disc drives, you may still need to copy via Drive M if your disc drives are of different types – as they are on a PCW8512. (For further information, see the box on page 94 in the main part of this book.)

To start then, remove the disc you have just formatted from the disc drive, insert your LocoScript 3 Examples disc (ie. the disc containing the file that's to be copied) and press ⌐f7⌐ to tell LocoScript that the disc has changed. When LocoScript has finished re-writing the screen, you should be able to see the EXAMPLE.LET file in group 1.

The next step is to move the cursor to this file. (You always need to pick out the file you want to work on with the cursor.) Once the cursor is in place, press ⌐f3⌐ to display LocoScript's f3 File menu, check that the cursor is on the Copy file option at the top of this menu and press ⌐ENTER⌐.

```
▶ Copy file
  Move file
  Erase file
  Rename file
  Recover from limbo
```

LocoScript then asks you to pick out the destination for the copy – ie. the drive and group in which you want the copy to be made.

```
Pick destination:

select group and drive
then press ENTER
or CAN to abandon
```

The destination for this first stage simply needs to somewhere on Drive M so move the cursor across until it is in a group on Drive M and then press ⌐ENTER⌐.

LocoScript 3 User Guide

LocoScript then displays a 'Confirmation' menu, giving details of the file you've picked out to copy and of the new file that is to be created, which is automatically given the same name as the original file (though you can change this if you want).

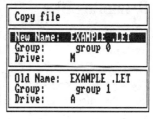

Check that the details shown in the menu are correct, then press ENTER. LocoScript then places a copy of EXAMPLE.LET on Drive M.

Now remove the LocoScript 3 Examples disc from the drive, insert the disc you formatted and press f7 to signal the change of disc – because you next need to copy this file from Drive M to your new disc.

As before, you now need to place the cursor on the file you're going to copy and then call up the f3 File menu. However, unless you've moved it, the cursor should still be on the EXAMPLE.LET file that you have just placed on Drive M. So you just need to check that the cursor is indeed on this file, then press f3, check that the cursor is on Copy file and press ENTER as before.

Once again, LocoScript responds by asking you to pick out the destination drive and group for the copy. The idea is to place the file in group 0 of the new disc but this time you can't select this by moving the cursor across the bottom part of the screen because this group is currently empty and so isn't listed in the lower part of the Disc Manager Screen. So what you do instead is hold down SHIFT and then use the ← → ↑ and ↓ Cursor keys to move the cursor at the top of the screen (the Group cursor) to this group.

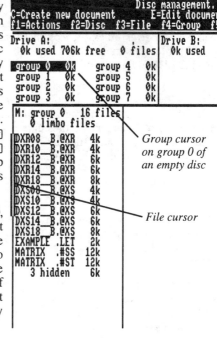

(When the Group cursor is on group 0, quickly look down at the File cursor at the bottom of the screen. You should see this has changed from a horizontal bar to a vertical bar overlapping one of the vertical divider lines in the lower part of the screen – simply to show that this part of the cursor isn't picking out any particular group at the moment.)

Press ENTER. LocoScript then displays its menu showing the details of the file it's going to copy (the EXAMPLE.LET file you placed on Drive M) and the new file it's going to create. Again, just check that the correct details are shown in the menu, then press ENTER. LocoScript then places a copy of the file on the new disc – and opens up a list for this group in the bottom part of the screen, because the group isn't empty any more.

LocoScript 3 User Guide   **41**

Renaming files

Another thing you might want to do when you are re-organising your discs is give some of your files new names.

To show you how you rename a file, we shall imagine that you want to change the name of the EXAMPLE.LET file you have just placed in group 0 of your newly formatted disc to RAKE.LET.

As always, the first thing to do is to insert the disc containing the files you want to work on. So remove the disc currently in your drive, then insert the LocoScript 3 Examples disc and press `f7` to signal the change of disc.

Next, move the cursor to the EXAMPLE.LET document, then press `f3` to call up the f3 File menu that's being used for all these individual file actions.

This time when the menu appears, move the cursor to Rename file and press `ENTER`. LocoScript then displays a menu giving the details of the file you've picked out, together with a slot for its new name.

The cursor is automatically placed on this slot, so all you have to do is quickly check that you've picked out the file you meant, then type the new name (RAKE.LET in this case) and press `ENTER`.

IMPORTANT: Only rename files that contain documents or datafiles. DO NOT rename any of LocoScript's files unless we specifically tell you to do this. In most cases, the names of these files are special and the files won't be found when they are needed if you change their names.

Erasing files

The other common action when you are tidying up your discs is to erase files that you no longer require – such as the document you've just renamed RAKE.LET.

Using LocoScript to erase a file is very easy. You place the cursor on the file you want to erase, press `f3` to call up the File menu, move the cursor to the Erase file option half way down the menu and press `ENTER` – first to take this option and then again to confirm that you want to erase the file that you have picked out.

Try using these steps to erase RAKE.LET.

Making back-up copies

Finally in this session, we are going to show you how to make reserve – or 'back-up' – copies of the files you don't want to lose. This back-up copy should always be on a different disc in case the disc is damaged.

The most straightforward way of making such back-ups is to copy the whole disc to another disc, which gives you a second disc with exactly the same information on it.

You have in fact already worked through the steps used to copy a disc when you prepared your LocoScript 3 Examples disc. But for practice, we shall now quickly take you through those steps again – this time to make a back-up copy of your LocoScript 3 Start-of-day disc because this is a useful thing to have.

(You will, of course, need a disc for the copy. If you don't have any new discs or any discs you could re-use because you no longer need their contents, we suggest you finish this session at this point for now and come back to these instructions later when you have a disc that you can use. **Note:** *There's no need to format a new disc before you copy another disc to it: LocoScript automatically formats the disc before it copies the files to it.)*

The first step in copying a disc is to remove the disc(s) currently in the disc drive(s) and put these to one side so that they don't get involved in the copy unnecessarily.

Then you want to make sure that the disc you want to copy (your LocoScript 3 Start-of-day disc in this case) is write-protected ie. that its write-protect holes are open. At the same time, check that the disc this is going to be used for the copy is write-enabled (ie. holes closed).

Now press ⬚f2⬚ (⬚SHIFT⬚ + ⬚f1⬚) to display the Disc menu, check the cursor is on Copy disc and press ⬚ENTER⬚. From then on, it is simply a matter of responding to the messages shown on the screen.

The first message asks you which type of disc you want to copy. On PCWs with one disc drive, you will just be offered the choice of cancelling the operation or copying one type of disc, with the cursor on the first of these options: so simply press ⬚↓⬚ once to move the cursor and then press ⬚ENTER⬚. On PCWs with two disc drives, you may be offered a choice of disc type to copy, the first being a Drive A-type disc and the second a Drive B-type disc. Because we are going to copy your Start-of-day disc, you need the Drive A option – so press ⬚↓⬚ once to move the cursor to the first of these options and then press ⬚ENTER⬚.

If you have a two-drive PCW, LocoScript will probably then tell you to insert the 'Source disc' (ie. the disc you are going to copy) in your Drive B and the 'Destination disc' (ie. your new disc) in Drive A. Simply insert your new disc in Drive A and your Start-of-day disc in Drive B as instructed and press ⬚ENTER⬚: LocoScript then proceeds to copy your Start-of-day disc to your new disc.

9402

If your PCW has one disc drive (or the disc types don't allow a direct copy), LocoScript instead asks you alternately for the 'Source disc' (the disc you are going to copy) and the 'Destination disc' (ie. your new disc) and copies the disc in a number of parts. Each time a message appears telling you that LocoScript is waiting for the Source disc, insert your Start-of-day disc and then press [ENTER]. Each time the message tells you that LocoScript is waiting for the Destination disc, insert your new disc and then press [ENTER]. Simply continue doing this until the copy is completed.

When the following message appears, the copy has been completed.

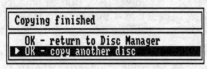

If you have another disc to copy (eg. a Start-up disc if the Installation program made you one of these), take the option to Copy another disc but otherwise just press [ENTER] to return to the Disc Manager.

Notes: (i) It's a good idea to make back-up copies of all your important discs, but if you have a PCW8256/8512, you should note that it isn't possible to make a copy of Side 2 of either your LocoScript 3 Master disc or of the Master disc of any other LocoScript product that has 'Installation data' on Side 2. This side of the disc has a special format which can only be read by the Installation program.

(ii) You can reduce the number of disc swaps that are required in making this copy by making more space on Drive M, for example by erasing some of the font files that are stored there. (You will, however, have to restore these files to Drive M before you print – for example by re-loading LocoScript.) Alternatively, you could add extra memory to your PCW, for example by adding the Locomotive Power Pack (see Appendix VI).

Setting up a Template

At the start of this Tutorial, you had to go to quite a bit of trouble both to arrange that the document you were preparing was set up for your printer and to put a stylish heading at the top of this letter. However, there's no need to go through so many steps every time you create a document. One of the features of LocoScript is that it is easy to create documents which are already set up as you want.

The key to this is LocoScript's Template system. Whenever you create a document, LocoScript automatically looks for a 'Template' to create this document from. This Template is simply a document with the special name TEMPLATE.STD. To create the new document, LocoScript makes a copy of the Template and then opens this new document for editing. (If no Template can be found, LocoScript creates the document instead from a very simple pattern for a document that is built into LocoScript itself.)

LocoScript can go on quite an extensive search for a Template to copy (described in Chapter 14) but the place it looks first is in the group that you have chosen to create the document in. So all you need to do to take advantage of this system is to set up a TEMPLATE.STD in each group for the type of documents that you want to store in that group.

Setting up the Template in full is outside the scope of this Tutorial (it is described in Chapter 14). But what we can do is produce a Template that gives you the effect of letterhead stationery from the EXAMPLE.LET document you prepared. You might even find this a useful Template to have!

Note: We assume that you have already got your PCW switched on and that the screen is showing LocoScript's Disc Manager Screen and the LocoScript 3 Examples disc. If not, switch on (or reset your PCW), load LocoScript, insert your Examples disc and press ⬚ *now. (Turn back to the start of Session 1 if you are not sure how to do this.)*

Creating the Template

A Template is just a document with the special name TEMPLATE.STD so you can create a new Template in just the same way as you create any new document (see Session 1). You just have to give it the special name TEMPLATE.STD.

But when as in this case you already have a document which has many of the characteristics that you need, it is far easier to make a copy of this document and then modify it to give you the Template you require.

So move your cursor to EXAMPLE.LET in group 1, press ⬚, check that Copy file is highlighted and press ⬚.

When the message appears asking you to pick out the destination for the copy, simply press [ENTER] to make the copy in group 1. LocoScript then displays a Confirmation menu with EXAMPLE.LET as the name for the new file. You now need to change this name – if for no other reason than you can't have two files called the same thing in one group. As the copy is to become a Template, we might as well give it the name TEMPLATE.STD now – so type this name and then press [ENTER]. LocoScript then makes a TEMPLATE.STD file from your EXAMPLE.LET.

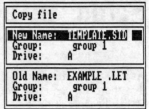

You now just need to press E, check the details shown in the menu and press [ENTER]. The Template is then displayed on the screen, ready for you to give it the features you want.

Setting the margins

One thing you might set are the margins.

To set these, press [f2] ([SHIFT] + [f1]) to display the Layout menu, then move the cursor to Change layout and press [ENTER]. LocoScript then puts you into the Layout Editor to work on the Template's Layout.

What you then do to set the margins depends on whether you want these to be a specific distance from the edge of the page or whether you are just interested in making the margins a few characters wider or narrower. Here we're going to imagine that you want the margins to be slightly wider than they currently are – say, by a couple of character positions on the Ruler line. What you do when you want to set the margins a precise distance from the edge of the page is explained in Chapter 8.

To make the left-hand margin a couple of characters wider, check that the cursor on the Ruler line at the top of your screen is up against the left margin marker (as shown below) and then press [⊞] a couple of times.

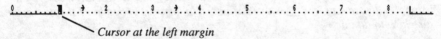

Cursor at the left margin

Each time you press [⊞], the left margin marker and the cursor should each move one position to the right, making the margin wider. If you move the margin too far to the right, press [⊟] instead to move it step by step back to the left. (If instead a tab marker is placed on the Ruler line and the cursor stays still, the cursor wasn't up against the margin: press [⊟] to clear away this tab, use the [←] and [→] Cursor keys to re-position the cursor and then try again.)

To make the right-hand margin similarly a couple of characters wider, press the Space bar to move the cursor to the right margin marker and then press [⊟] a couple of times to move this margin a couple of positions to the left (again making the margin wider). This time if you move the margin too far, use the [⊞] key to move it back to the right.

LocoScript 3 User Guide

Note: Pressing $\boxed{\text{Space}}$ *when the cursor is at the right margin takes the cursor to the left margin, giving you an easy route to the left margin if, after moving the right margin, you decide you want to change the left margin again.*

Setting the main font and text size

While you are changing the Template's Layout, it's a good idea to set the main font you will want to use in the documents. If this font is available at different sizes, you should also set the main size that you will want to use together with Character Pitch PS and Line Pitch Auto – for the reasons we explained in Session 2. Setting these things here will save you setting them at the start of the individual documents. *(If you have already left the Layout Editor (ie. it doesn't still say* Editing layout *on the top Information line), press* $\boxed{\text{f2}}$, *move the cursor to* Change layout *and press* $\boxed{\text{ENTER}}$ *to bring you back into the Layout Editor. If your PCW bleeps as you press* $\boxed{\text{f2}}$, *you're still in the Layout Editor.)*

The menus used to set these things in this layout are the same as those used to set the font, the size etc. in the documents themselves – the f3 Style menu for the font; the f4 Size menu for the size and the two pitches. Moreover you use these menus in exactly the same way.

Suppose you will be wanting to use 12pt LX Sanserif for the majority of your text. To set LX Sanserif, you simply press $\boxed{\text{f3}}$ to display the Style menu, tick LX Sanserif and press $\boxed{\text{ENTER}}$ – just as you did in Session 2. The only difference is that the menu is somewhat shorter because Italic is the only text style that you can set within a Layout.

To set the other details, press $\boxed{\text{f4}}$ ($\boxed{\text{SHIFT}}$ + $\boxed{\text{f3}}$). The Character Pitch should already be set to PS and the Line Pitch to Auto because we set these in the Layout in Session 2. So all you need to do is set the Point size to 12 and press $\boxed{\text{ENTER}}$ – again just as you did in Session 2.

* Once these details have been set, press $\boxed{\text{EXIT}}$ *to leave the Layout Editor and return to the document.*

Note: If your printer has good quality fonts built-in, these will be quicker to print than the LX fonts. So you may find it best to use a built-in font for the bulk of your text and leave the LX fonts for special effects like headlines and small print that your printer's own fonts can't provide.

Setting up the letterhead

All that's needed to give the effect of letterhead stationery is for it to include your name and address, positioned and styled in whatever way you want – and the easiest way to get this is by modifying the text the Template has inherited from the EXAMPLE.LET document.

9402

The first step is to remove the main part of the letter, which you plainly don't want in every document you create.

This is easily done. Just move the cursor to the start of the Commissioning Editor's address (Line 9) and press [CUT]. Then press [PAGE] to move the cursor to the bottom of the page and press [CUT] again. LocoScript then cuts this text out of the Template.

Now all that's left to do is to replace Jane Wellesley's details by your own name and address – by editing the text between the codes. (It is, of course, important to ensure that you don't delete the codes because it is these that set the styling for the name and address.)

(If the codes are shown at the moment, press [f8] to display the Options menu, use [+] to tick the Codes option and press [ENTER].)

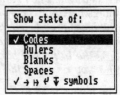

When you have set up your name and address to your satisfaction, press [EXIT] followed by [ENTER] to save your Template to disc.

Showing that it works

To finish this session, we'll quickly show that the effort you have put into this Template will indeed give you documents that automatically have all the features you've set.

To see this, just keep the File cursor in group 1, type C and press [ENTER] to create a new document.

The address that automatically appears when this document is opens on the screen should convince you that the new document indeed does have all the features you have put into the Template.

*Notes: (i) Templates only provide the pattern for **new** documents created in the same group. Adding a Template or changing the existing Template doesn't change any documents already in the group.*

(ii) As well as setting up Templates in individual groups, it is useful to set up a 'general-purpose' Template in group 0 (or the SYSTEM group) of your Start-of-day disc – particularly, if the main printer you use isn't your PCW's built-in printer. By setting up this Template for your preferred printer, you can arrange that all your documents are created ready set-up for this printer even where there isn't a Template in the group. (Chapter 14 explains how this works.)

Reference Section
Part I: Basics

Chapter 1

Everyday actions

This chapter describes:

- *How to load LocoScript 3*
- *How to configure your system for larger characters and/or "Sticky" Shift keys*
- *How to get back to the central point of operations – the Disc Manager Screen*
- *How to pick out the file you want to work on or the group you want to work in*
- *How to use LocoScript's menus*
- *How to abandon an action you've started*

1.1 Loading LocoScript

Before you can use LocoScript 3 to prepare a document, you need to load the LocoScript 3 program into your machine and start it running – as follows:

1. Check there are no discs in the drives, then switch your PCW on.

2. If you have a Drive B Start-up disc, insert this in Drive B. Then insert your Start-of-day disc in Drive A. (On a PCW8256 or 8512, insert this disc with Side 1 to the left.)
You should then see a pattern of horizontal lines as the PCW reads from the disc. If nothing happens, press the Space bar: this prompts the PCW to start reading the disc.

3. If the message Insert next disc *appears, remove the disc from Drive A, replace it by the next Drive A Start-up disc in the sequence the Installation program prepared for you and press* [ENTER]. *Repeat this each time the message appears.*

4. If a message appears offering to write an updated SETTINGS.STD file to your Start-of-day disc, check that your Start-of-day disc is in Drive A and then press [ENTER] *to accept the option to write the file to the disc in Drive A.*

5. When the Disc Manager Screen (similar to that shown on page 51) appears, remove the disc(s) from the drive(s). LocoScript has now been loaded.
If you see a very different display or the screen flashes or your PCW bleeps, you probably haven't put a LocoScript Start-of-day disc in the drive – but wait until your PCW has finished reading from the disc (ie. until the light on the disc drive stops flashing) before removing the disc and trying again with a different disc. (If you continue to have problems, consult the Troubleshooting section of this book.)

IMPORTANT: Once the program has been loaded, the Start-of-day disc – and any additional Start-up discs you have – has done its job: it won't be needed again until you need to load LocoScript 3 again. Indeed, this is precisely why it is called the Start-of-day disc. All the rest of your work is with 'Data discs', which you use to store the documents that you prepare. You shouldn't store any documents on your Start-of-day disc or on any Start-up discs. (Preparing a Data disc is described in Section 5.1.)

Chapter 1: Everyday actions

LocoScript 3 User Guide   **49**

9308

> • *If your machine is already on, you don't have to switch it off and switch it on again before you can load LocoScript 3. Instead, insert your Start-of-day disc in Drive A, any Drive B Start-up disc in Drive B and then use the special three-key combination* [SHIFT] [EXTRA] *and* [EXIT] *to 'reset' your machine. This is equivalent to switching off and switching on again but is better for your machine.*
>
> *Note: Resetting completely clears your computer's memory – so always check that everything important is saved on disc before you reset your machine. This applies in particular to files and documents you have stored on Drive M.*

1.2 Special configuration options

LocoScript includes three special configuration options which you can select by ticking the appropriate options in the Disc Manager Screen's f8 Options menu. (How you tick an option is explained in Section 1.4.)

• *Magnified text display – in which documents are displayed in double-height, double-width characters as you edit them.*

To select this, tick `Large edit characters` in the f8 Options menu.

Note: The magnification only affects text that is being edited. Messages on the screen, menu options, document names etc. remain their normal size. The text is also printed at its normal size.

• *'Sticky' Shift keys – which allows key combinations involving two or more keys to be typed by pressing the keys in sequence rather than together.*

To select Sticky Shift keys, either tick `'Sticky' shift keys` in the f8 Options menu or hold down the [SHIFT] key as you load LocoScript from your Start-of-day disc. A * should appear in the top right-hand corner of the screen to show that the 'Sticky Shift keys' option has been selected.

As you type a key combination, you should see a * followed by letters representing the Shift keys you press (S for [SHIFT], A for [ALT] etc.) in the top right-hand corner of the screen – unless this part of the screen is showing another message such as Num.

• *No key repeats – ie. the PCW doesn't automatically repeat keys that are held down for any length of time.*

To select this, tick `Disallow key repeats` in the f8 Options menu.

> *Note: You can save the settings you have made here for use the next time you load LocoScript by saving your current Settings file on your Start-of-day disc (as described in Section 12.1). Equally, you should note that if you save a new copy of the Settings file for some other reason (eg. because you have just added a new font or a new Paper Type), you will also save the current setting of each of the above three options.*

1.3 Displaying the Disc Manager Screen

The Disc Manager Screen is the screen that shows you the files and documents that are available for you to work on. It is also the central point of operations within LocoScript. As a general rule, you need to return to the Disc Manager Screen between, say, editing one document and editing a different document or printing the same document.

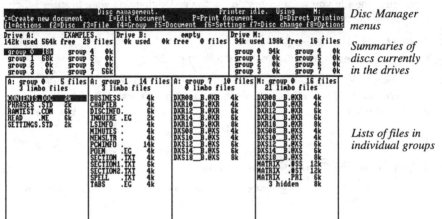

Disc Manager menus

Summaries of discs currently in the drives

Lists of files in individual groups

The Disc Manager Screen is displayed immediately after you have loaded LocoScript. At other times, you can get back to the Disc Manager Screen as follows:

1. Finish whatever you are doing at the moment. For instance, if you have a menu on the screen, close this up by pressing [CAN].

2. Press [EXIT]. *(*[EXIT] *is always the key to press to signal to LocoScript that you want to leave the job you're currently doing.)*

3. If a menu is displayed, select the appropriate option and press [ENTER].

4. If this doesn't return you to the Disc Manager Screen, then press [EXIT] *again.*

Disc Manager Display options

The Disc Manager normally doesn't show you either 'Hidden' program files or 'Limbo' files containing past versions of your documents (though it does show you how many of these files you have in each group). To display these files alongside the other files on the Disc Manager Screen:

1. Press [f8] *to display the Options menu (see opposite).*

2. Tick the appropriate options in this menu (eg. by using [⊞]*), and then press* [ENTER].

The screen is then re-written with the additional files displayed. Hidden files (other than the 'system' files on Drive M) are shown marked H; Limbo files are shown marked lim.

9308

1.4 Selecting files and groups

The files on each disc are organised into groups, of which there are eight on each disc. How you use these groups is entirely up to you, but the idea is to use them to keep similar documents together. Indeed, LocoScript's system of Templates for new documents positively encourages this (see Chapter 2).

You select the file you want to work on or the group that you want to store a file in by moving the cursor to it on the Disc Manager Screen – as follows:

1. Display the Disc Manager Screen.
(Turn to Section 1.3 if you are not sure how to do this.)

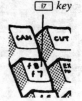

[f7] key

2. Insert the disc containing the file or group of files you require and then press [f7] to tell LocoScript that you have changed the disc in the drive.

The Disc Manager Screen is then updated to show the range of files this disc contains.

3. To pick out the file you want to work on:

Use the [↑] [↓] [←] and [→] Cursor keys to move the band of highlighting in the lower part of the Disc Manager Screen (the 'File cursor') to the name of this file.

• *To pick out a particular group on this disc (eg. to store a document in it):*

If the group already has files in it: Move the File cursor into the list of files for this group in the lower part of the screen.

If the group is currently empty: Move the 'Group cursor' in the upper part of the screen to its name by holding down [SHIFT] as you press [↑] [↓] [←] and [→].

Cursor on group containing files

Cursor on an empty group

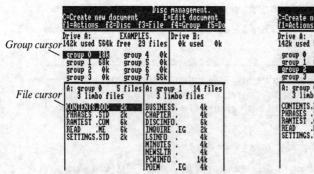

Group cursor

File cursor

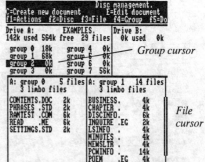

Group cursor

File cursor

IMPORTANT: The disc that contains any file that is being worked on must remain in the disc drive all the time that this file is in use. So before removing any disc from a disc drive and replacing it by another, ALWAYS check whether this drive is listed in the 'Using' message on the top Information line of the screen. If the drive is listed, you must not change the disc.

1.5 Using the menus

At each point within LocoScript, you are offered a choice of menus covering the different actions currently available to you. These menus are summarised on the third Information line at the top of the screen.

To display any of these menus, you simply press the function key [F1]...[F8] written alongside the name of the menu on these Information lines.

What you do once the menu has been displayed depends on the type of menu it is. There are essentially three types of menu, though several menus are made up of a combination of these basic types:

• *Commands menus giving a list of alternative actions: Pick the option you want from such a menu by placing the cursor on it and pressing* [ENTER].

This option will be marked with a ▶ or a ♦. If it is marked with a ▶, LocoScript will simply carry out the action you have selected; if it is marked with a ♦, LocoScript will carry out this action but then return to the menu so that you can either select another command from the menu or repeat the same command. (You could think of the diamond as a pair of arrows back to back, going off to carry out your command and then coming back to the menu.)

Note: Where there are one or two 'Command options' at the bottom of a menu, you don't always need to move the cursor to select the action you require. If the option you want is already marked with a ▶, you can take it simply by pressing [ENTER].

• *Settings menus showing you the current settings of particular aspects of either your LocoScript system or the text you are preparing : Make any changes you want to these settings and then press* [ENTER] *to go ahead with the new settings.*

These settings can either be simple values or selections from lists of options.

To set a value, place the cursor on the relevant line of the menu, type the value you want and press [ENTER].

To select from a list of options, move the cursor to the option you require and press either [+] or the Space bar. To clear a previous selection, you position the cursor on the option and press [-] or the Space bar.

If the settings you make affect other settings in the menu, LocoScript will make the necessary adjustments for you.

[+] *(Set) key*   [-] *(Clear) key*

• *Confirmation menus showing the details LocoScript is about to work with, eg. the name of the document you have picked out to edit: Make any changes that are required to the details that are shown and then press* [ENTER] *to go ahead.*

To change the details shown, move the cursor to the relevant line of the menu and then edit the current information as if it were text – but with the added facility that you can clear away existing text by pressing [-].

9308

Moving the cursor around a menu

There are a number of ways of moving the cursor in a menu:

- *Pressing the Cursor keys.*
- *Pressing* ⌈SHIFT⌉+⌈↓⌉ *to move the cursor directly to the last line of the menu. Similarly, pressing* ⌈SHIFT⌉+⌈↑⌉ *moves directly to the first line of the menu.*
- *Pressing* ⌈TAB⌉ *to move the cursor to the next Command option in the menu.*
- *Typing the capital letters in the option name to move the cursor directly to this option.*

The last two techniques can't however be used when the cursor is on a line of a menu that accepts text, like the Find and Exch lines in the Find and Exchange menus. In such cases, anything you type is taken as part of the required text.

1.6 Abandoning actions

Mistakes are always possible. The ways out of trouble are as follows:

⌈CAN⌉ *key*

• *If you call up a menu you don't want* (or you have got to a stage in the process at which there is a menu on the screen that you want to get out of), press ⌈CAN⌉. This closes up the menu. However, don't press ⌈CAN⌉ when there is an error message on the screen: **always** select one of the options listed in the error message.

⌈STOP⌉ *key*

• *If LocoScript has started an operation you don't want* – for example, moving you from one end of the document to the other or replacing one word for another throughout your document – the general procedure is to press ⌈STOP⌉, wait for LocoScript to pause and then press ⌈STOP⌉ again. The first ⌈STOP⌉ makes LocoScript pause; the second abandons the action.

If however you want LocoScript to stop printing, the key to press is ⌈PTR⌉. When you press ⌈PTR⌉, LocoScript stops sending any more to the printer and puts you into Printer Control State from where you can sort out paper jams, abandon printing etc. (See Chapter 4.) **Note:** Printing may continue for some time after you press ⌈PTR⌉, depending on the type of printer you are using.

• *If you want to abandon the changes you have been making to a document*, press ⌈EXIT⌉ to finish work on the document and then select the Abandon edit option in the Exit menu. The new version is then thrown away: it doesn't replace the previous version stored on disc. LocoScript doesn't touch the version stored on disc until after the new version has been successfully stored.

In fact, all is not lost if you change your mind about discarding the old version after saving the new version – or accidentally select the wrong option in the Exit menu. LocoScript doesn't actually erase discarded documents from the disc until it needs the space to store a new document: instead it puts them into a special 'Limbo' state. This gives you the chance to recover any documents you discard accidentally (see Section 5.5).

Creating documents

New documents are created by taking the 'Create document' option offered at the Disc Manager Screen. When you select this option, LocoScript creates a new file and opens it for editing.

This chapter describes:

- *How to pick out where the new document is to be stored*

- *How to create a new document and set its name*

- *How the Editor Screen is laid out and what information is displayed on the screen*

- *How to type all the different characters LocoScript 3 provides, including accented letters*

- *How to insert ready-prepared text into a document*

- *How to count the number of words in a document*

- *How to save the document you prepare*

The new file is actually created by copying a special 'Template' document because this enables you to start typing your document right away. You don't have to start by specifying the details that LocoScript needs to know before it can start processing your text – the type of paper you want to use, the margins, the typeface, the line spacing, to name but a few – because the new document automatically inherits this information from the Template that is copied.

The document that is copied is known as a Template because it acts as the 'pattern' for the new document. Which Template document is used in any particular instance depends on which group you choose to create the document in and on the range of Template documents that you have set up. The system is explained in Chapter 14.

In the absence of any specific Template documents, LocoScript creates the document from a very simple outline for a document, held within the LocoScript program itself.

2.1 Creating a new document

New documents are created at the Disc Manager Screen – that is, the screen which displays the contents of your discs. The steps are as follows:

1. Display the Disc Manager Screen.

(Turn to Section 1.3 if you are not sure how to do this.)

2. Decide where you want to store the new document.

The new document needs to be stored on a Data disc. (Section 5.1 explains how to prepare Data discs.) Documents can be created on Drive M but only as a temporary measure because Drive M is wiped clean when you switch your PCW off or reset it.

Which group to store the document in depends on the type of document you wish to create. If you have a Template for this type of document, you will save yourself a great deal of effort in setting up this document if you create it in the group that contains this Template (or in one from which this Template is picked up). *(See Chapter 14 for more information about Templates.)*

3. Insert the disc on which you want to store the new document and press ⬚.

If your PCW has disc drives of different types (as for example on a PCW8512), be sure to place your disc in the drive for which the disc has been formatted.

Note: This disc will need to stay in the drive all the time you are working on your new document.

4. Move the cursor into the group on this disc in which you want to store the new document.

If this group already contains other files, you can pick it out by moving the File cursor (the band of highlighting in the lower part of the screen) into the list for this group – using the Cursor keys ⬚ ⬚ ⬚ and ⬚.

If the group is currently empty, you will need to hold down [SHIFT] at the same time as pressing the Cursor keys in order to move the Group cursor to this group in the upper part of the screen.

Group cursor

File cursor

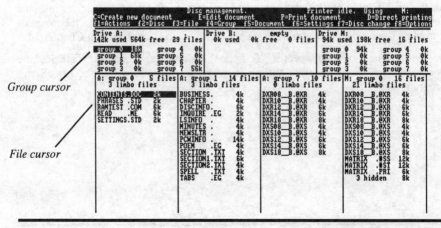

5. Press the C letter key.

(C for Create should be easy to remember but C=Create new document is also written on the second Information line to remind you.)

6. Check that the correct drive and group are given in the menu that's shown.

If the wrong group or drive is shown in the menu, either press [CAN] to clear away the menu, re-position the cursor and then press C again or edit the details shown. *(To select a different group, cursor to the Group line of the menu and type the name of the group you wanted (or its number, if the group doesn't have a special name); to select a different drive, cursor to the Drive line of the menu and type the letter of the drive you want.)*

7. Type the name you want for the new document.

What you type writes over the DOCUMENT.nnn name that LocoScript has given the document. You will see a small cursor move along the line as you type. When you type the full stop, LocoScript automatically makes the rest of the main part of the name blank and transfers the small cursor to the extension so that the next thing you type is the first character of the extension. Finally, press the Space bar once or twice to clear the remaining characters of the DOCUMENT.nnn name.

If you spot a mistake in the name you have typed, then correct it exactly as you would correct text. In particular, you don't have to rub out all the way back to the mistake – you can just position the small cursor with the Cursor keys where you need to make the change and make the correction in the normal way.

8. Press [ENTER] to proceed.

LocoScript then clears away the Disc Manager Screen and opens up its Editor Screen, ready set up for the document you are going to create.

What to call the document:

Document names have a main part of up to eight characters, to which you can add an 'extension' of up to three characters separated from the main part by a full stop. You can use a variety of characters in this name (see Appendix III) but in general it is best to use A...Z and 0...9. You can't put any spaces in this name.

It's a good idea to choose something that will remind you about the contents of the document. For example, you might call your account of the treasure hunt your club held in May TREASURE.MAY or TRHUNT.MAY.

The name is always given in capitals but don't worry about typing capitals – *whenever LocoScript needs something to be in capital letters, it automatically translates any lower case letters you type into capitals.*

9308

Chapter 2: Creating documents

2.2 The Editor Screen

The main features of the screen on which you prepare documents are:

- **The Information lines:**

The document you are editing

The font, Line Spacing etc. you're using

Number of lines per page

The Drive(s) currently in use

Page number

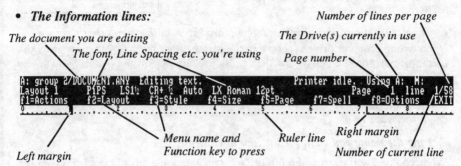

Menu name and Function key to press

Ruler line

Right margin

Left margin

Number of current line

Note: The number of lines per page and the number of the current line both count *'Standard'* lines (spaced at 6 lines per inch). The actual number of lines on your page and the actual line number may well be different from those shown here.

- **The Ruler line (immediately below the Information lines):**

This shows you where the margins and tabs are. The default Ruler line is set up for standard A4 paper, with margins approximately 1" from each side of the page and no tabs. (Chapter 8 describes how to adjust the margins and how to set up some tabs.)

Note: The marks on the Ruler line don't count inches: instead they count characters spaced at the current 'Scale Pitch'. The markings therefore show you how many characters you can fit between the margins or between two tab positions *when your Character Pitch matches the Scale Pitch*. If you use a different Character Pitch (see Section 7.2), the number of characters that will fit will also be different.

- **The Text cursor:**

This is used to mark where in the text you are working – in particular, where anything you type will appear on the screen.

- **End-of-page lines:**

These mark the points in your text where one page ends and another begins. A long document will have a number of End-of-page lines spread through it, but a new document or a short document will only have one End-of-page line – immediately under the last line that has been typed.

The pattern in the End-of-page line tells you how many blank lines there are at the bottom of the page it finishes. Use this to work out if you can add a short paragraph to a page without moving any of the text over to the next or how many blank lines to put at the beginning of a short document so that it is neatly centred on the page.

Lines of text on the page

Blank lines at the bottom of the page

Display options

There is a quite lot of information that can be displayed on the Editor screen alongside the actual text of a document – for example, the styling codes you have inserted in the document and details of different margins and tabs you have used.

LocoScript offers you the choice of how much of this 'extra' information is displayed alongside your text while you are working on a document. The menu used to control this is the f8 Options menu. Each option of this menu refers to a different piece of extra information you can display. If an option is ticked, the information will be displayed; if the tick is 'Cleared', the information associated with this option won't be displayed. With all the options cleared, the screen shows only the characters that will be printed.

Two of the options – Blanks and Spaces – allow you to see the difference between spaces you have typed and blanks that LocoScript puts into the screen display in order to lay out the text. If Spaces is ticked, all the places you have typed a space will be marked by ∴. If Blanks is ticked, all the unused parts of the screen are shown as dots: this includes the blanks LocoScript inserts immediately following a Tab.

Spaces as blobs

```
This.means.that.it.has.the.specific.job.of.processing.text.-.helping.you.to.
make.whatever.changes.you.want.to.the.text.you.type.and.wrapping.the.words.
you.type.around.in.special.codes.that.specify.how.the.text.should.be.laid.
out.and.styled.when.you.come.to.print.it.↵
↵
Computers.are.good.at.manipulating.the.information.in.their.memory.-.and.
```

Blanks as dots

```
.......This means that it has the specific job of processing text - helping you to ...
.......make whatever changes you want to the text you type and wrapping the words ....
.......you type around in special codes that specify how the text should be laid .....
.......out and styled when you come to print it.↵................................
.......↵.........................................................
.......Computers are good at manipulating the information in their memory - and ......
```

To set the extra information to be displayed in the document you are working on:

1. Press ⬚f8⬚ *to display the Options menu.*

2. Tick the information you want displayed (eg. by using ⬚⊞⬚*); clear the tick against the information you want hidden (eg. by using* ⬚⊟⬚*).*

3. When the options are set as you require, press ⬚ENTER⬚*.* LocoScript then rewrites the screen – taking account of the options you set.

Note: The combination of the display options that are being used when you save a document is also saved with the document and re-appears the next time you edit the document.

2.3 Typing text

Typing text is basically a matter of pressing the keys or the combination of keys for the characters you want and pressing ⌜RETURN⌟ when you specifically want to start a new line eg. at the end of a paragraph. Pressing ⌜RETURN⌟ inserts a Carriage Return, shown on the screen as ↵. (Note: You don't have to press ⌜RETURN⌟ at the end of each line because LocoScript automatically wraps the text at the right-hand margin for you.)

The only complication is in typing some of the more exotic characters that LocoScript supports.

LocoScript 3 handles a very wide range of characters, including Greek and Cyrillic letters – more than there are key combinations on the keyboard to use. (There's a full list of these characters in Appendix III.) To allow you to type all these characters, LocoScript uses the keys of the keyboard six times over, corresponding to the six keyboard layouts shown in Appendix III, and a different approach is taken for typing the Greeks, Cyrillics and Symbols covered by the second three layouts to that taken to type the 'Standard' characters covered by the first three layouts.

Typing Standard characters

The characters covered by the 'Normal', 'Alt' and 'Extra' layouts are typed just as you would expect:

The 'Normal' characters, which are the characters engraved on the keys, are typed by pressing the keys either on their own or with ⌜SHIFT⌟ held down.

The 'Alt' characters (which include characters like © and special language characters like ß) are typed by holding down ⌜ALT⌟ at the same time as pressing the keys either on their own or with ⌜SHIFT⌟ held down.

The 'Extra' characters (which are mainly accents, of which more below) are typed by holding down ⌜EXTRA⌟ at the same time as pressing the keys. (Note: In this case, you never press ⌜SHIFT⌟ as well.)

Typing Greeks, Cyrillics and Symbols

To type the characters from the 'Greek', 'Cyrillic' and 'Symbol' layouts, the keyboard has to be put into different modes known as 'Supershifts' which select different sets of keyboard layouts to work with. For example, the Greek Supershift substitutes the 'Greek' layout for the 'Normal' layout and the 'Normal' layout for the 'Alt' layout. (The 'Extra' layout in fact stays available in all the different Supershifts.)

The different Supershifts are selected by holding down ⌜ALT⌟ and pressing a function key: ⌜ALT⌟+⌜f3⌟ selects the Greek Supershift; ⌜ALT⌟+⌜f5⌟ selects the Cyrillic Supershift; and ⌜ALT⌟+⌜f7⌟ selects the Symbol Supershift. The keyboard then continues to use the keyboard layouts of the selected Supershift until you either select a different Supershift or return to the 'Normal' Supershift by pressing ⌜ALT⌟+⌜f1⌟. (The Supershift you are currently using is also shown in the top right-hand corner of the screen – as Gre, Cyr or Sym.)

9308

The result of all this is when you want to type Greek characters (for example), you press [ALT]+[F3], and type as much Greek as you want by pressing the keys (with or without [SHIFT] as appropriate) – typing any accents and breathing marks that you want from the 'Extra' keyboard as described below. Then when you want to type Latin script characters again, you either press [ALT]+[F1] to put the keyboard back into the Normal Supershift, or if you just want to type a few Latin script characters, you can type them instead by holding down [ALT] as you type.

Typing accented characters

LocoScript supports a wide range of accents, any of which can be added to any of the characters it supports by typing first the accent and then the character. (If you just want the accent on its own, type the accent and then press [ENTER].)

The accents are all on the 'Extra' keyboard layout (though there are also a few on the Greek layout), so to type the accent you just need to hold down [EXTRA] and press the appropriate key for the accent you require. For example, to type an acute accent, you need to hold down [EXTRA] and then press the E key. So to type an é, you need to hold down [EXTRA] and press E and then press the E key again to give you the é you require.

Notes: (i) If you want to type a number of 'Shifted' characters, start by pressing the 'Shift Lock' key (which works just like the Shift Lock on a typewriter). Alternatively, if you want to type a number of capital letters, press [ALT] + [ENTER]. LocoScript then converts any lower case letters you type into capital letters – until you press [ALT] + [ENTER] again. (It also shows Caps *in the top right-hand corner of the screen.)*

(ii) If you want to include raised or lowered characters eg. in a technical formula, it's possible to type some of these characters directly from the 'Symbol' layout (see below) but in general the thing to do is to make these characters Superscripts and Subscripts. Putting these into your text is covered in Section 6.3.

(iii) Whether zeroes are slashed or unslashed is defined by the Layout for the text, alongside such things as whether you want dot or comma as decimal point marker (see page 141). Note: Zeroes typed by pressing [ALT] *0 are always unslashed.*

IMPORTANT:

Being able to type a character is no guarantee that you can print it: you can only print a character if the font or printwheel you are using supports it. For instance, the LX fonts supplied as standard with LocoScript 3 give you the characters from the Basic Symbol Set, while the 9512 daisy-wheel printer gives just gives the characters on the petals of the printwheel that is fitted in the printer – plus characters such as ≠ that can be produced from combinations of these characters.

To print the full range of characters, you need to use a suitable printer and either:

• *the additional LX Symbol pack (this will give you the best quality results)*
• *or the Standard and Sans Serif fonts supplied for the PCW matrix printer*
• *or fonts from the LocoFont, LocoFont 24 or LocoFont BJ packs*

If your text contains a character that isn't available on your printer, LocoScript will leave a blank when you print so that you can fill this in later by hand.

308

2.4 Inserting pre-prepared text

If the text you want to include in a LocoScript document is already stored in another document – even one prepared using a different word-processor (provided this is held in a suitable form) – you shouldn't have to re-type this. What you can do instead is insert this document into your LocoScript document as follows:

1. Place the cursor at the point in your LocoScript document where you want this text to be inserted.

2. Press ⌐f1⌐ to display the Actions menu, move the cursor to Insert text *and press* ⌐ENTER⌐.
LocoScript then displays the Disc Manager Screen for you to pick out the file you want to insert.

3. Move the cursor to the file you want to insert and press ⌐ENTER⌐.

4. Check that the menu displayed shows the file you wanted and then press ⌐ENTER⌐.
LocoScript then proceeds to insert the contents of the file into your document.

- *Note:*

(i) Only the following can be inserted in this way: another LocoScript document; a document held as an ASCII file (see Chapter 16); or a LocoSpell User dictionary. (Inserting a User dictionary inserts an alphabetical list of the words in that dictionary.)

(ii) LocoScript inserts the whole of the chosen file. If you don't need the whole file, you can press ⌐STOP⌐ followed by ⌐STOP⌐ again to stop the insert once the text you have got the text you require and then get rid of anything you didn't want eg. by using the Cut and Paste techniques described in Section 3.4. Alternatively, if the text you want is in a LocoScript document, don't use this Insert technique: instead, copy the text you want to a Block and then paste that Block into your new document as described in Section 3.4.

2.5 Counting the number of words

Any time that you are working on a document, you can count the number of words it contains as follows:

1. Press ⌐f7⌐ to display the Spell menu.

2. Select Count words *with the cursor and press* ⌐ENTER⌐.
LocoScript then counts all the words in the document and displays the answer in a message on the screen. When you have noted the number of words, press ⌐ENTER⌐ to clear away the message and continue.

Note: If you have the LocoSpell spelling checker, then each time you check the spelling of a document, this will tell you the number of words in the text that has been checked.

2.6 Saving the new document

While you are working on a document, your current text is only held in memory. To preserve this, the document needs to be saved on disc – not just when you have finished preparing the text but also while you still working on it so that you don't lose the work you have done so far if there's a power cut. (We suggest saving your work often – at least about once an hour – to avoid accidentally losing it.)

The first step is to press ⌈EXIT⌉. This displays an Exit menu offering the following choice of actions:

```
▶ Finish edit
  Save and Continue
  Save and Print
  Abandon edit
```

Finish edit – which saves your document on disc and returns you to the Disc Manager Screen.

Save and Continue – which saves your document on disc then returns you to where you were working in the document. *(This is the option to take when you want to preserve the work you have done so far.)*

Save and Print – which saves your document on disc and returns you to the Disc Manager, but then immediately puts you straight into the menu that is used to print it out (see Chapter 4).

Note: The Save and Print option isn't included if there isn't a printer connected to your PCW or the printer isn't connected properly – or it is already printing.

Abandon edit – which throws away all the work you have done, then returns you to the Disc Manager Screen. Nothing is saved on disc.

To take the option you want, simply place the cursor on this option and press ⌈ENTER⌉.

As LocoScript saves your document, you will see the light on one of your disc drives flash on and off as your document is written onto the disc – unless you have chosen to save your document on Drive M. Then you won't see your document being written onto the disc but you will see a message like this, reminding you to copy the document you have saved on Drive M to one of your discs as soon as possible. Drive M is wiped clean the moment your computer is switched off or reset and anything stored there is lost – so never put off copying anything important to a floppy disc.

```
WARNING: Files saved on drive M

Before switching off, copy :

the result of your edit

▶ OK
```

Press ⌈ENTER⌉ to clear the message off the screen.

• *When you return to the Disc Manager Screen, the File cursor will always be on the document you have just been working on. LocoScript always leaves the cursor in place so that you can easily work with the same document again.*

9308

Chapter 3

Editing a document

This chapter describes how to edit a document – that is, take a document that is already stored on disc and change it. It will show you:

- *How to open a document for editing*

- *How to move the Text cursor from one place to another in a document*

- *How to make small-scale insertions and deletions*

- *How to duplicate, move or delete sections of text ('Cut and Paste' editing)*

- *How to replace one word or phrase for another throughout a document (using 'Find and Exchange')*

- *How to throw away the changes you made*

3.1 Opening a document for editing

When you want to change a document you've already prepared or just look at its contents, you need to select it on the Disc Manager Screen (ie. the screen that lists the contents of your discs) and then open it for editing. The steps are as follows:

1. Display the Disc Manager Screen.
If you are not sure how to display this screen, turn to Section 1.3.

2. Insert the disc on which the document is stored and press [▤].
If your PCW has disc drives of different types (as for example on a PCW8512), be sure to place the disc in the drive for which the disc has been formatted.

Note: This disc will need to stay in the drive all the time you are editing the document because LocoScript will be reading it and writing to it while you work.

3. Move the File cursor to the document you want to work on.
Don't worry if the document isn't displayed at the moment: just keep pressing [→] and [←] until the group in which you stored the document is displayed. The groups are displayed in the order Drive A (first to last), Drive B (first to last) and then Drive M (first to last). The only reason the group you want won't be displayed is if you didn't put the right disc in the drive!

4. Press the E *letter key, check the details shown in the menu that's displayed and then press* [ENTER].
(Remember E for Edit – or check the second Information line when you are unsure.)

9308

LocoScript then clears away the Disc Manager Screen and puts up the Editor Screen, with the document you have selected already in place. An example of the screen display is shown below. This is the first 28 lines of the document – 28 lines being the most that can be displayed on the screen at any one time. The cursor is right at the top of the document.

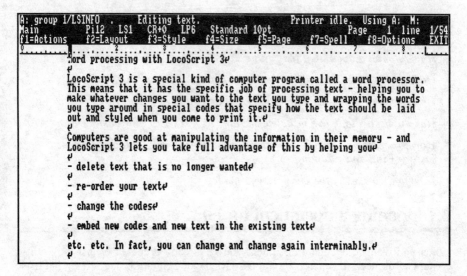

3.2 Positioning the cursor

Before you can change the text at a particular point in your document, you have to move the cursor there.

LocoScript lets you to move the cursor from character to character or from word to word, from line to line, from page to page or even from one end of the document to the other. It also lets you jump straight to a particular page or a particular point in the document. The steps used are described in the following sections.

You can also move the cursor directly to a particular word by telling LocoScript to 'Find' this word. The steps used in this case are given in Section 3.5.1.

Note: When you make a small move, the text of your document stays on the screen – perhaps scrolling a little to bring the part of the document you want onto the screen. When you make a big move – for example, from the top to the bottom of the document, the screen is completely re-written when the new section of your document is displayed. You also see a message summarising the move you are making.

• *To abandon a movement that you have started to make, press* [STOP]*, wait for LocoScript to pause and then press* [STOP] *again.*

[STOP] *key*

　　　　　　　　　　　　　　LocoScript 3 User Guide

9308

3.2.1 Using the Cursor keys

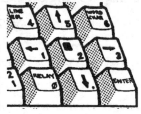

One way of moving the cursor, is to use the four Cursor keys ⬅, ➡, ⬆ and ⬇.

These keys are mainly used to move the cursor over the part of the document you can see at the moment. But keeping these keys pressed when the cursor reaches the edges of the screen makes the text of the document 'scroll' so that you can see the next part of the document.

Holding down SHIFT and/or ALT at the same time as pressing a Cursor key gives a different type of movement. With SHIFT, the cursor moves in the direction you expect but in very much larger steps. With ALT, the cursor doesn't move but the text on the screen does so that the cursor still finishes at a new place in your document.

3.2.2 Using the Textual Movement keys

Moving the cursor from the end of one line to the beginning of the next or from one end of a document to another is not particularly easy with the Cursor keys. A very much better way of making these moves is by using your PCW's 'Textual Movement keys' which are gathered in a group above the Cursor keys.

The Textual Movement keys all have names that suggest the sort of movement pressing the key will produce. PAGE moves to the beginning of the next page; DOC moves to the end of the document; WORD moves to the beginning of the next word; LINE moves to the beginning of the next line; etc. etc. The only one which you might not readily understand is EOL – which moves the cursor to the End Of the Line.

Most of these keys have two Textual Movements engraved on them – for example, there's a key with both DOC and PAGE on it. If you just press this key, you will get the 'PAGE' action. To get the 'DOC' action, you have to hold down the SHIFT key as you press the key. In every case, the movement with SHIFT held down is a 'large' version of the movement without SHIFT – in accordance with a general rule of LocoScript that holding down SHIFT produces a similar but bigger movement of the cursor.

Pressed on their own or together with SHIFT, these keys move the cursor forward through the document. When you want to move backwards through the document, hold down ALT at the same time as pressing the key or the key combination. The cursor is then moved the corresponding distance back through the document.

Note: To LocoScript, paragraphs are blocks of text that are separated from each other by a blank line or by extra spacing after the Carriage Return (see Chapter 8). Addresses, for example, are therefore usually treated as single paragraphs.

9308

3.2.3 Moving straight to a particular page

You can move the cursor directly to a particular page by using the Find page option in the f5 Page menu. The steps are as follows:

1. Press ⌐5⌐ *to display the Page menu.*

2. Check that the cursor is on the Find page *option.*

3. Type the number of the page you want and press ⌐ENTER⌐.

So, for example, to go to page 3 of a document, you would press ⌐5⌐, type 3 and press ⌐ENTER⌐.

```
▶ Find page        ????
─────────────────────────
End page here
Last line of page
─────────────────────────
Keep current line with:
     ?? lines above
     ?? lines below
```

LocoScript then moves the cursor to the start of your chosen page. As it does this, a message appears on your screen telling you about the move LocoScript is making.

3.2.4 Using Unit markers

Unit markers are simply codes, represented on the screen by (UniT), that you can put into your document to mark particular positions such as the start of a section. Once these markers have been inserted in the document, you can move directly to the next marker by pressing the ⌐UNIT⌐ key (⌐SHIFT⌐+⌐PARA⌐).

*   *To insert a Unit code:*

Position the cursor where you want the marker, press ⌐⊞⌐ *and type* UT *(or use the associated Set menu – see Section 6.4).*

Note: As well as being a marker, this code has the action of a carriage return – so you will typically insert the Unit code in place of the ↵ that immediately precedes the section you want to pick out.

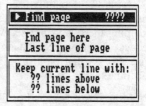

⌐UNIT⌐ *key*

*   *To move forward to the next Unit marker, press* ⌐UNIT⌐ *(*⌐SHIFT⌐+⌐PARA⌐*).*
If there isn't another Unit marker, then the cursor is simply left at the end of the document.

*   *To move to the preceding Unit marker, press* ⌐ALT⌐+⌐UNIT⌐.
If there isn't such a marker, the cursor is simply left at the start of the document.

3.3 Making small changes

When the changes you want just involve deleting or inserting odd words or letters:

1. Position the cursor where you want to make the change.   *The Delete keys*

Remember, the true position of the cursor is given by its left-hand edge.

2. Use [DEL→] *and* [←DEL] *to rub out characters you don't want.*

3. Type in any new characters that are required.

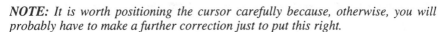

NOTE: It is worth positioning the cursor carefully because, otherwise, you will probably have to make a further correction just to put this right.

*The only time this is difficult is when you want to add something to a table of information. The problem with a table is that it contains a lot of 'blanks' which **look** exactly like spaces you type but aren't really part of the document at all. The margins around your text are also full of these blanks. When the cursor is on a group of these blanks, LocoScript could insert what you type in a very different place to the one you expect. If you find yourself getting confused, we suggest setting the Display options so that you can see the difference between blanks and spaces as described in Section 2.2.*

Relaying after making changes

Paragraphs typically look distorted after you have changed them. In particular, if you insert new text at the beginning of a paragraph, LocoScript automatically opens up a new line for this text, producing a break between the new text and the old.

One way of correcting the layout is to press [RELAY]. This makes LocoScript relay the current paragraph now. Alternatively, you can simply carry on making your corrections because LocoScript automatically ensures:

[RELAY] *key*

- Everything is correctly laid out up to the last character you typed.

- The layout of your document is correct up to the point you have moved to by pressing one of the Textual Movement keys.

- Each paragraph is re-laid as you move the cursor into the next paragraph.

This means that after you change a paragraph, you can cursor around the paragraph without the text moving but the moment you type something, press a Textual Movement key to move forwards through the document or move into the following paragraph, the text is instantly re-laid up to your current working position.

LocoScript also checks, and if necessary corrects, all aspects of layout – the line breaks, the page breaks, etc. etc. – as it saves your document. This means that, whatever state you leave your document in while you are editing it, it will always be neatly arranged on the page when you come to print it out or when you next edit it.

3.4 Copying, moving and deleting sections of text

The techniques described in Section 3.3 are used where you want to change a few letters or a few words. LocoScript can also help you make really quite drastic changes to a document:

- *Duplicating sections of text*
- *Moving sections of the text from one place in your document to another*
- *Deleting sections of text*

Such changes are often referred to as 'Cut and Paste editing'.

3.4.1 The common factor

Duplicating, moving and deleting sections of text all work with a block of text which you first mark out and then store as a 'Block'. (You can have up to 10 Blocks in use at the same time, each storing a different piece of text.)

The different operations of duplicating, moving and deleting text come from the different actions you can take once you have marked out the block of text you are interested in.

The first choice is whether to retain the original text in the document. To retain it, you make a 'Copy' of this text – rather like you might make a copy in your notebook of a paragraph out of a book. Otherwise you 'Cut' it out – as you might take a Press cutting and stick it in your notebook. The second choice is whether to 'Paste' the text in at some other point in the document.

- *Duplicating is making a Copy of the original which you then Paste in where you want the second copy of this text.*
- *Moving is Cutting out the original and then Pasting it in at its new location.*
- *Deleting is Cutting out the original and not pasting it back in.*

The steps needed to carry out each of these actions are given in the following sections.

Copying and Moving text between documents

LocoScript 3 (unlike LocoScript '1') *doesn't* forget the contents of its Blocks when you finish work on the document. Instead it remembers the text you store in any Block until you either clear the Block (see opposite); store something else in the Block; or switch off or re-set your machine.

This means that, as well as using the Blocks to copy and move text within a document, you can also use them to copy and move text between documents. You simply have to edit the document containing the text you require, copy or cut this text to a Block, then switch over to editing the second document and paste in the Block where you need it.

NOTES:

Positioning the cursor: It is important to position the cursor carefully at every stage of these operations because you can't change this position later – *except by pressing* [CAN] *and starting all over again.* Remember, the left-hand edge of the cursor marks its true position.

You may well find it easiest to position the cursor exactly where you want it if you use the Textual Movement keys (see Section 3.2.2 above).

We also recommend setting the Display options so that the screen shows both the styling codes you have inserted and where you have typed carriage returns, tabs etc. This will allow you to see precisely what codes etc. you are removing from their position and/or inserting at the new position – and hence what adjustments in the styling you have to make both where you are taking the text from and where you are inserting it in order to get the results you want.

Marking out the section of text: LocoScript automatically highlights the section you mark out. (You will still be able to see the cursor because this blinks.)

Remember to go beyond any final space or carriage return you want to include.

Don't worry if you overshoot: just move the cursor back again to the right position. (The highlighting will shrink back, too. It always just marks the section between the first character you marked and the current position of the cursor, wherever that is on the screen.)

Pasting the Block of text back in: There's no need to paste in a Block immediately after you have copied text to it, nor does pasting in the text 'use up' the Block: indeed, you can paste in as many copies as you like both in the current document and in other documents. LocoScript continues to remember this text until you tell it to remember another piece of text as this Block or you switch off or reset your machine.

Seeing what you have stored as Blocks: If you ever forget which Blocks out of the 10 you are using and what you are using them for, press [f1] to bring the Actions menu onto the screen, move the cursor to Show Blocks and press [ENTER].

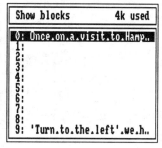

The menu that appears lists the Blocks –together with the first few words of the text stored in each Block that you have used. Press [ENTER] when you have finished looking at the list to tell LocoScript you are ready to proceed.

• *If you don't need any of the Blocks shown, you can get rid of it (and give yourself a bit more room on Drive M) by moving the cursor to the Block in the above menu and pressing* [–].

9308

3.4.2 Duplicating a section of text

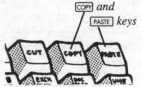
COPY and PASTE keys

To duplicate a section of text within a document, you first 'Copy' it to a Block and then you 'Paste' in a copy of this Block. The steps are as follows:

1. Place the cursor at the beginning of the section of text you want to copy and press [COPY].

A message then appears, (to start with, both in the middle of the screen and on the third Information line), telling you to move the cursor to the end of your chosen section of text.

2. Move the cursor to the end of the section you want to copy – and press [COPY] *again.*

LocoScript then puts up another message in the middle of the screen and more permanently on the third Information line, asking you to type one of the numbers 0...9 or a letter. (The letters refer to LocoScript's Phrases feature: see Chapter 15.)

3. Type the number of the Block you want to store the text in.

4. Place the cursor where you want to insert the copy of the text, press [PASTE] *and then type the number of the Block in which you stored the text.*

Example: Duplicating the first verse of POEM.EG

To duplicate the first verse of POEM.EG (one of the documents on the LocoScript 3 Examples disc) at the end of the poem, open this document for editing (as described in Section 3.1) and then check that the cursor is right at the beginning of this document (for example by pressing [ALT] + [DOC]).

When the cursor is at the start of the document, press [COPY]. Then move the cursor to the beginning of the second verse of this poem (for example by pressing [PARA]) and press [COPY] again.

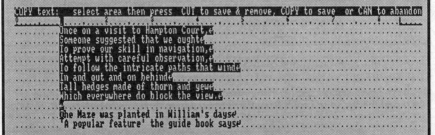

When the message appears asking you to type a number or a letter, type 0 (for example). Then move the cursor to the end of the document (for example by pressing [DOC]). When the cursor is in position, press [PASTE] and type 0 to insert a copy of the first verse at the end of the document.

3.4.3 Moving a section of text

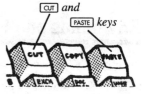

CUT *and*
PASTE *keys*

Moving a section of text is just like duplicating a section of text except that instead of 'Copying' it to a Block, you 'Cut' it to a Block. The steps are therefore as follows:

1. Place the cursor at the beginning of the section of text you want to copy and press COPY.

2. Move the cursor to the end of the section you want to copy – and press CUT.

Pressing CUT tells LocoScript both to store a copy of the text and to remove the original from the document.

3. Type the number of the Block you want to store the text in.

4. Place the cursor where you want to insert the copy of the text, press PASTE *and then type the number of the Block in which you stored the text.*

3.4.4 Deleting a section of text

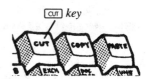

CUT *key*

LocoScript has two ways of deleting a block of text.

Method 1

The first – and the safer one – is to go through all the steps of moving a block of text from one place to another except for pasting in the block in the new position. In other words, you:

1. Place the cursor at the beginning of the section of text you want to copy and press COPY.

2. Move the cursor to the end of the section you want to copy – and press CUT.

3. Type the number of the Block you want to store the text in – but never paste this Block in again (unless you decide you want this text after all!).

Method 2

The other method is similar but less safe because there is no way that you can restore the text if you change your mind. The steps are as follows:

1. Place the cursor at the beginning of the section of text you want to copy and press CUT.

2. Move the cursor to the end of the section you want to copy – and press CUT *again.*

The text you have just deleted has gone for good.

9308

3.5 Finding and Exchanging

LocoScript's Find and Exchange facilities let you:

- *Move the cursor to a particular word or phrase, when you don't even know which page it is on: this is the Find part of the operation.*

- *Replace one word or phrase for another throughout all or part of a document: this is the Exchange part of the operation.*

You might use this where you have prepared a document about a product under its development name but now need to substitute the actual name it is going to have.

3.5.1 Finding a particular word

Finding a word or a phrase is the efficient way of moving the Text cursor when you don't have any clear idea where the word or phrase you want to move to is. You give LocoScript the word or phrase to look for and it searches the document for this, starting at your current working position. The steps are as follows:

1. Make sure the cursor is positioned higher up the document (ie. nearer the beginning) than the word you want to find – because the search is carried out forwards through the document.

2. Press FIND. *LocoScript then displays its Find menu.*

 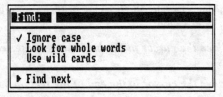

3. Replace any 'Find text' already in the Find slot at the top of the menu with the word, part of word or phrase you want LocoScript to Find.

Either edit this text exactly as you would normal text or press ⌈·⌉ to clear away the old text and then type your new text.

Note: The Find text you set can be up to 30 characters long, and can include carriage returns (↵) and tabs (→), but it can't include any word-processing codes.

4. Set the options you want LocoScript to apply in its search (see Section 3.5.3).

5. Press ENTER *to take the* Find next *option at the bottom of the menu.*

LocoScript then searches forwards through the document, trying to match the Find text against the document. If it finds a section that matches the Find text, LocoScript puts the cursor on the first character of the section. If no matching section is found, it leaves the cursor at the end of the document.

Finding another example of the same text

Because LocoScript automatically keeps the Find text you last used, all you need to do to search for another example of this text is:

• *Press* [FIND] *followed by* [ENTER].

3.5.2 Exchanging one word for another

Exchange is the quick and reliable way of changing one word or phrase into another throughout a document.

Exchange is essentially the Find facility described above with the added feature that it doesn't just search for a phrase, it also replaces that phrase with new text. You should notice a number of similarities between Find and Exchange.

Like Find, Exchange always works forwards through the document from your current working position so you must start with the Text cursor higher up the document than the first word you want to change.

The exchange can be carried out either manually or automatically. In a Manual exchange, LocoScript stops each time it finds an example of the text you've given it to search for and asks you to specify whether this particular example is to be replaced. In an Automatic exchange, LocoScript simply replaces each instance of this text it finds – though you can limit the exchange to just the current page or the current paragraph if you wish.

The steps are as follows:

1. Make sure the cursor is positioned higher up the document (ie. nearer the beginning) than the first word you want to exchange – because the search is carried out forwards through the document.

2. Press [EXCH] *(ie.* [SHIFT] *+* [FIND]*). LocoScript then displays its Exchange menu.*

3. Replace any 'Find text' already in the Find slot at the top of the menu with the word, part of word or phrase you want LocoScript to Find.

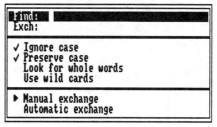

Either edit this text exactly as you would normal text or press [▫] to clear away the old text and then type your new text.

Note: The Find text you set can be up to 30 characters long, and can include carriage returns (↵) and tabs (→), but it can't include any word-processing codes.

4. Replace any 'Exchange text' already in the Exch slot with the word, part of word or phrase you want LocoScript to insert instead.

This text too can be up to 30 characters long, and include carriage returns (↵) and tabs (→), but not word-processing codes.

5. Set the options LocoScript is to apply to this exchange (see Section 3.5.3).

6. If you want the Find text to be automatically replaced by the Exchange text, *move the cursor to* Automatic exchange *at the bottom of the menu and press either:*

> ENTER *to carry out the exchange to the end of the document;*

> PAGE *to carry out the exchange to the end of the current page; or*

> PARA *to carry out the exchange to the end of the current paragraph.*

- **If you want to confirm each exchange before it is made,** *check that* Manual exchange *is selected (ie. has the* ▶ *beside it) and then press* ENTER .

LocoScript then searches forwards through the document, trying to match the Find text against the document. When it finds a section of the document that matches the Find text, it stops and displays a message both in the middle of the screen and on the Information lines, prompting you to press either the ⊞ key, the ⊟ key or CAN. (If the message is covering the piece of text LocoScript has picked out for exchange, just wait a moment for the message to be cleared away.)

```
Match found:

press + to exchange and continue
- to simply continue
or CAN to abandon
```

Press ⊞ to make the exchange and carry on to the next example; press ⊟ to simply carry on to the next example; or press CAN to abandon the exchange.

Example: Replacing disk by disc in DISCINFO

The DISCINFO document on the LocoScript 3 Examples disc contains both disc and disk.

To make all the disks into discs, open this document for editing (as described in Section 3.1), check that the cursor is right at the beginning of this document (for example by pressing ALT + DOC) and then press EXCH (SHIFT + FIND) to display the Exchange menu.

Press ⊟ to clear away any existing Find text and type the word disk.

Move the cursor to the Exch line of the menu, press ⊟ to clear away any existing Exchange text, type the word disc.

Check that Manual exchange is selected and then press ENTER .

Each time LocoScript picks out the letters disk in the document, either press ⊞ to make the exchange and carry on to the next example; press ⊟ to simply carry on to the next example; or press CAN to abandon the exchange.

3.5.3 The Find and Exchange options

The Find and Exchange menus include a series of options which you can use to specify more about the examples of the Find text that you want LocoScript to pick out and, if you are carrying out an exchange, how the replacement should be made.

You need to tick the options you want and clear the ticks against any options you don't want. The options are explained below.

The options you select for one Find and Exchange operation are automatically carried over to the next, so that there's nothing to set when you want to carry out a series of similar exchanges.

Note: To tick any of these options, place the cursor on the option and press either ⊞ or the Space Bar. To clear the tick against an option, place the cursor on the option and press either ⊟ or the Space Bar.

Ignore case

Ticking this option tells LocoScript to pick out places where the same spelling is used but not necessarily the same combination of capital and small letters. For example, if you tick Ignore case when searching for disc, LocoScript will pick out Disc as well as disc. When this option isn't ticked, LocoScript will only pick out examples written exactly as in the Find text (ie. just disc).

Preserve case (Exchange only)

Ticking this option tells LocoScript to copy (as far as possible) the current use of capital and small letters in making the replacement. Specifically, it means:

– if the old word is all in lower case letters, the replacement word should be as well

– if the old word is entirely in capitals, the replacement word should be in capitals as well, and

– if the old word starts with a capital letter, then so should the replacement word.

For example, if the current word is Disc and the exchange text is disk, LocoScript will insert Disk if Preserve case is ticked but disk if this option isn't ticked.

Look for whole words

Ticking this option tells LocoScript to reject places where your Find text forms part of a longer word. For example, if you tick Look for whole words when searching for disc in the DISCINFO document, LocoScript will reject words like discretion and discuss which would otherwise be picked out.

Note: Words like discs which have the search word as their root will also be rejected if you tick this option. When you ask for Whole Words, LocoScript takes you literally and just gives you precisely what you asked for.

Use wild cards

This option allows you to give LocoScript the 'pattern' of a word or a phrase to look for rather than the exact words.

The key to creating this pattern is the 'Wild card' character ?. When you tick Use wild cards, LocoScript doesn't take ?s in the Find text literally but instead understands them as standing for any character. So if, for example, you wanted LocoScript to search for either disc or disk, then you could tell LocoScript that you want it to find words that match the pattern dis *(some letter)* by giving the Find text as dis? and ticking Use wild cards. If Use wild cards wasn't ticked, LocoScript would look for dis?.

Note: You can only specify wild cards in the text you give LocoScript to find. Any ?s in the Exchange text will simply be put into your document.

3.6 Throwing away unwanted changes

To throw away the changes you have made and go back to the last version of a document you saved:

1. Press EXIT *to tell LocoScript that you want to finish work on this document (the current task).*

2. Select the option to Abandon edit *and press* ENTER .

LocoScript then clears away the document on the screen and returns you to the Disc Manager Screen. It doesn't save anything on disc.

* *To display the version of the document you last saved, simply press* E *followed by* ENTER *to open the document for editing again.*

9308

Chapter 4

Printing

Producing documents on a word processor is pointless unless you also know how to print them out. So this chapter describes:

- *how to tell LocoScript which document you want to print out, how much of the document you want to print and how many copies*

- *how to abandon a document you've started printing by mistake*

- *how to feed the paper either line by line or through to the top of the next sheet*

- *and last, but by no means least, what to do when you run into problems, such as the paper becoming jammed.*

It also describes the special steps you need when you want to use a sheet feeder that's added as an optional extra to your printer and the option of Direct printing in which you use your PCW very much like a typewriter.

Note: LocoScript allows you to print your documents on a wide variety of printers, other than your PCW's built-in printer. You need to add extra software to use a different printer (provided by the LocoScript 3 Printer Support Pack) and you have to tell LocoScript which printer you want to use, but other than that the steps are just as described here. The special steps involved in using an 'External' printer are described in the External Printers Guide, provided in the Printer Support Pack.

Printer Control State

Printer Control State is the part of LocoScript from which you check up on or change anything to do with the printer you are using.

[PTR] *key*

To go into Printer Control State, just press the [PTR] key on your PCW's keyboard (though if there is a menu on the screen, you will need to finish with this menu first).

To leave Printer Control State, just press [EXIT] to return to whatever you were doing before.

When you are in Printer Control State, the Information lines at the top of the screen show which printer LocoScript is currently expecting you to use and its current state eg. which document is currently being printed (if any). There is also a list of the menus available to change any aspect of the printer set-up.

If something goes wrong when you print a document, the first thing to do is to press [PTR] to go into Printer Control State. Firstly, this stops LocoScript from sending any more text to the printer. Just as importantly, the information at the top of the screen will probably tell you what is wrong. (For more information, see Section 4.6.)

LocoScript 3 User Guide 79

The files needed to print

Before it can print on a printer, LocoScript needs the various printer files that support this printer and its fonts to either be loaded into memory or to be available in group 0 (or the 'SYSTEM' group) on Drive M – as follows:

1. The file or files needed to drive the printer itself.

The main file needed to drive any printer is the file called *printername*.PRI. For example, to use the PCW8256/8512/9256/PcW10's built-in matrix printer, you need MATRIX.PRI, while to use the inkjet printer supplied with some models of the PcW9512+, you need INKJET.PRI – unless you are using LocoFont BJ, in which case you need the two files LQ24.DRV and 24INKJET.PRI.

If you use an 'External' printer, you will need a .DRV file to work alongside the .PRI file. Normally, the .DRV file you will need is INSTALL.DRV but if the printer is used in 'Download mode', you will need LQ24.DRV instead.

If you have more than one printer on your system, you should be able to see these files on Drive M but if you only have one printer, these files could have been simply loaded into memory and you won't be able to see them.

2. Character Shape files (.@xx files) to support any LX fonts you use.

Which Character Shape files you need is explained in Appendix II of this book.

3. Character Set files (.#xx files) to support any other fonts that you use (and the different sizes of these fonts you use).

For example, if you have used the Old English font on the PCW matrix printer, you will need the MATRIX.#OE file; while if you have used any 'LS' fonts on the 9512+ bubblejet printer, you will need one or more 24INKJET.#xx files.

The sole exception is the Courier font on the 9512+ Inkjet printer which is supported by the INKJET.PRI file. There's no .#xx file for this font.

Note: If you have followed all our instructions correctly, these files should all have been placed on your Start-up discs by the Installation program and either loaded into memory or copied to Drive M from these discs as part of the process of loading LocoScript. If any of the files are missing, copy them from wherever they are stored to group 0 (the 'SYSTEM' group) on Drive M by hand for the moment but then investigate why these files were missing. Is the problem, perhaps, that you haven't got room on Drive M for all the files that you would like to load – in which case, the answer is either to reduce the number of files on your Start-up discs or to expand your PCW's memory.

IMPORTANT: *Don't erase any printer files from Drive M while a document is being printed. Even if a printer file isn't being used at the moment, LocoScript may be expecting to call on it at any moment.*

4.1 Printing a document

IMPORTANT: *Before you can print a document (or carry out any of the other actions in this chapter), you must have a printer connected to your PCW. Moreover, this needs to have been plugged into your PCW **before you switch your PCW on**.*

There are four main stages to printing a document:

• *Picking out the document you want to print*

• *Specifying which pages you want to print, how many copies you want etc. etc.*

• *Sorting out (with LocoScript) which printer and paper you are going to use*

• *Finally, actually printing the document*

Notes: (i) If your printer has its own power switch, make sure that the printer is switched on and that it is 'on-line' before you pick out the document to print.

(ii) You can use LocoScript for other jobs while the document is printing. You could, for example, create a new document or edit a document you prepared before. However, the disc holding the document you are printing must be left in the drive.

Stage 1: Selecting the document to print

In the main, you pick out the document you want to print from the Disc Manager Screen (that is, the screen that lists the contents of your discs) as follows:

1. Display the Disc Manager Screen.
(See Section 1.3 if you are not sure how to do this.)

2. Insert the disc on which the document is stored and press 🔟.

3. Move the File cursor to the document you want to print and press P.
(Remember P for Print – or check the second Information line if you are unsure.)

LocoScript then displays its Print menu, ready for you to specify such things as how many copies you require. (If instead you see a message saying the printer is 'active', LocoScript hasn't finished the last document you asked it to print: it may be simply waiting for you to load more paper. Just leave this message on the screen while the previous document is finished (the message will disappear of its own accord) – or, if you don't want this, abandon printing as described in Section 4.3.)

• *If you want to print the document you have been working on, take the* Save and Print *option from the Exit menu when you finish work the document. LocoScript first saves the document and then displays the Print menu ready for you to specify the number of copies etc. (If the* Save and Print *option isn't offered, LocoScript is still printing the last document you asked it to print – which you either need to finish or to abandon (see Section 4.3).)*

Stage 2: Specifying the number of copies etc.

The lower part of the Print menu allows you to set the quality of printing; the number of copies; and the range of pages you want to be printed.

When the menu first appears, the options are set so that if you simply want to print a copy of the whole document at the print quality you last used, you just have to press ENTER and then go on to Stage 3 of this procedure. *(LocoScript menus are always set up ready to carry out the task you are most likely to want.)*

Note: Be sure to set the print quality and the number of copies you want *before* you select the range of pages you want to print.

High or Draft Quality

Dot-matrix printers like that supplied with the PCW8256/8512/9256/PcW10 and inkjet printers like the one supplied with some models of the PcW9512+ offer the choice of producing 'High Quality' output slowly or 'Draft Quality' output typically about three times as fast.

In general, it's best to choose High Quality for finished documents but Draft Quality for print-outs while you are still working on the document.

Simply tick the quality you want – for example by placing the cursor on it and pressing ⊞. *(The tick next to the other option is automatically cleared for you.)*

Note: The option you pick has no effect on a daisy-wheel printer such as the one supplied with the PCW9512 or on a laser printer because these can only produce one quality of print.

The number of copies

LocoScript lets you print up to 99 copies of your document at a time.

To specify the number of copies you want, move the cursor to Number of copies, *type the number you want and then press* ENTER.

Note: LocoScript will print one copy of all the pages you select, then another set – thereby automatically giving you collated copies. It doesn't print all the page 1s and then all the page 2s etc. etc.

The range of pages

The bottom section of the menu allows you to specify whether you want to print the whole of the document or just part of it.

To print the whole of the document:

Check Print all of document *is selected (marked with the ▶) and press* ENTER.

If you only want to print part of the document:

Select Print part of document *and press* ENTER.

LocoScript then displays a second menu, with slots for the page numbers of the first and the last page you want printed – currently filled in with the numbers of the first and last pages in the document.

If you don't want to start at the first page of the document, *check the cursor is on* From page, *type the number of the first page you require and press* ENTER.

If you don't want to print through to the last page, *move the cursor to* To page, *type the number of the last page you require and press* ENTER.

Then press ENTER *again to tell LocoScript to go ahead.*

Note: If you only want to print one page, you need to set this page's number on both the From page line and the To page line.

```
Print document

Name:      PCWINFO .
Group:        group 1
Drive:     A

✓ High quality
  Draft quality
Number of copies:       1

    Print all of document
 ▶ Print part of document

Print part of document

Name:      PCWINFO .

First page              1

 From page              1
 To page                3

Last page               3
```

Stage 3: Sorting out the printer set-up that will be used

Before printing, LocoScript compares the printer, fonts and paper for which the document has been prepared (see Chapter 12) against the printer set-up it is currently primed to work with, in case these are different. Doing this allows LocoScript to draw your attention to any differences between these two set-ups, and where possible, to switch over to the printer set-up you intended to use for the document.

It checks first whether the document is set up for the printer LocoScript is expecting to use. It then checks whether the fonts specified in the document are available on this printer (or if you are using a daisy-wheel printer, that the printwheel currently fitted matches the Character Set and Character Style specified in the document). Lastly, LocoScript checks whether the printer is currently set up for the paper for which the document has been laid out.

If you always use the same printer set-up, LocoScript probably won't find any differences and so goes straight on to Printing the document (Stage 4). But if there are any differences, you will see messages such as this telling you what is specified in the document and what LocoScript is currently set up to use. If your Intended selection is marked with a ?, it means this isn't available on your system (or it is different in some way).

```
Document and current printer do not match
Current is not the intended printer

Current is: MATRIX
Intended:    BJ130E

 ▶ Use the current printer
   Change to printer intended for document
   Cancel operation
```

9308

The messages give you the choice of using the Current set-up, changing to the 'Intended' set-up (if this is possible) or cancelling printing. In general, you will get the best results if you print on the 'Intended' printer. If you print the document on another printer, you won't necessarily have access to the same fonts and typesizes and so the printed result won't be as good, though it should always be quite adequate for a draft copy (which is all the 'Use Current' option is intended to be used to produce). The compromises that are made when you 'Use Current' are explained in Part III of the LocoScript 3 External Printers Guide.

Move the cursor to whichever option you require and press [ENTER].

Note: If you opt to change to the Intended set-up, you must also make the corresponding changes to your printer itself eg. fitting the 'Intended' printwheel and loading the 'Intended' paper. You should also note that this then becomes the Current printer set-up ie. the set-up LocoScript expects you to use until you tell it otherwise.

Stage 4: Printing the document

Once the printer set-up has been checked, LocoScript may go straight ahead and print – or you may first see an 'About to print' message such as that shown here. In particular, you will always see such a message for the first document you print after loading.

```
About to print:

Printer:        MATRIX
Paper:          A4              Portrait

▶ Proceed
  Cancel operation
```

The purpose of this message is to tell you what LocoScript is expecting to use so that you can ensure that the printer is set up to match. If your printer isn't set up to match, your document will probably contain wrong characters or even complete gibberish. It also tells you which type of paper LocoScript is expecting you to use, because if there's a different type of paper in the printer and you print on this, your text may well be printed in the wrong place on the paper or even off the paper and onto the platen of your printer.

When the printer is set up correctly, press [ENTER] *to clear away the message.*

If Paper please now appears at the top of the screen, load some of the correct paper into your printer, adjust its position and then press either [EXIT] (if you are using the 8256/8512/9256/PcW10 matrix printer or the 9512 daisy-wheel printer) or [PTR] followed by [⊞]. *(The printer's own manual or, in the case of the built-in printer, your PCW's manual should tell you how to load paper.)*

The document should then start to print.

Note: If you print on single sheet stationery fed into the printer by hand, you will need to load a fresh sheet of paper at the end of each page – prompted either by a Paper Please message or by the printer's own 'Paper out' message. But if you use a sheet feeder (or continuous stationery), you should only see the Paper Please message again when you run out of paper in the printer. (If you get the Paper Please message at the end of every page, LocoScript isn't set up to expect a sheet feeder: see Section 4.2 opposite.)

4.2 Using a sheet feeder

Printing on single sheet stationery is much easier when you can use a sheet feeder to feed the paper for you – and indeed, many printers either have a built-in sheet feeder or offer a sheet feeder as an optional extra. In particular, sheet feeders are available as optional extra for both the 9512/9512+ daisy-wheel printer and the 9512+ inkjet printer, though not for the PCW matrix printer.

Paper fed into a printer from a sheet feeder isn't handled in quite the same way as paper fed by hand, so LocoScript needs to know when a sheet feeder is being used.

If the sheet feeder is built into the printer:

There shouldn't be any problem as LocoScript should automatically be set up to expect you to use this. (If you like, you can check this is the case by pressing [PTR] to go into Printer Control State and looking at the Information lines. If LocoScript is expecting you to use a sheet feeder, Sheet feeder should appear on the second Information line at the top of the screen.)

If the sheet feeder is an optional extra:

When you want to go over to using the sheet feeder:

1. Fit the sheet feeder to your printer and make any settings that are required on the printer itself.
There may be an option switch that you need to set or you may need to change some of the 'front panel' settings on the printer. See your other manuals for details.

2. Press [PTR] to go into Printer Control State and check that the correct printer and paper are selected (shown on the second Information line).

3. Press [f8] to display the Options menu and use [⊞] to tick the Sheet feeder ***option in this menu.***

4. Press [ENTER] to close up the menu, and then [EXIT] to leave Printer Control State.

When you want to feed paper some other way:

You need to clear this Sheet feeder setting.

The formal way to do this is to clear the tick beside the Sheet feeder option in the f8 Options menu in Printer Control State. However, simply setting up LocoScript for a continuous type of stationery is sufficient (eg. when the Intended paper is continuous). Because sheet feeders can only handle single sheet stationery, LocoScript responds by displaying an Alert message which gives you the option of confirming that the sheet feeder has been removed and the printer is now set up for continuous stationery. If you take this option, LocoScript clears the Sheet feeder setting for you.

4.3 Abandoning printing

It is always possible that after setting LocoScript off printing, you decide either that you don't want to print this document or that you don't want so many copies after all. For example, you may decide that you only want eight copies instead of 10.

In either case, you need to go into Printer Control State and 'abandon printing'.

If you decide you didn't want to print after all:

1. Press ⌐PTR⌐ *to go into Printer Control State.*
LocoScript stops printing the document as soon as it can: depending on the printer you are using, printing may stop as soon as the end of the current line or it may go on for some time.

2. Press ⌐f7⌐ *to display the Document menu.*

3. Move the cursor to Abandon printing *and press* ⌐ENTER⌐.

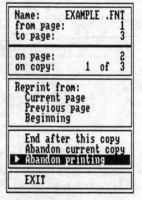

```
Name:      EXAMPLE .FNT
from page:            1
to page:             3

on page:             2
on copy:      1  of  3

Reprint from:
   Current page
   Previous page
   Beginning

   End after this copy
   Abandon current copy
 ▶ Abandon printing

   EXIT
```

If you decide you don't want all the copies you asked for:

1. Wait until LocoScript starts printing the last copy you want and then press ⌐PTR⌐ *to go into Printer Control State.*
LocoScript stops printing the document as soon as it can: depending on the printer you are using, printing may stop as soon as the end of the current line or it may go on for some time.

2. Press ⌐f7⌐ *to display the Document menu.*

3. Move the cursor to End after this copy *and press* ⌐ENTER⌐.

(The third option, Abandon current copy, is typically used when you have run into a problem such as the paper jamming in the printer: see Section 4.6 below.)

4. Move the cursor to the Exit *option and press* ⌐ENTER⌐ *again.*

Important: Before you can print any more of the current document or select another document to print, you must leave Printer Control State. Do this by pressing ⌐EXIT⌐.

Resetting the printer

Resetting the printer re-initialises it. Should you ever need to do this:

1. Press ⌐PTR⌐ *to enter Printer Control State (if you aren't already in this).*

2. Press ⌐f1⌐ *to display the Actions menu and take the option to* Reset printer.

4.4 Adjusting the paper in the printer

There are four adjustments you can make to the paper in the printer (or to LocoScript's view of the paper) from within LocoScript.

- *Feed the paper through the printer a line at a time*

- *Feed the current sheet out of the printer*

- *Reset LocoScript's idea of where the 'Top of form' is on continuous stationery (eg. after a paper jam)*

- *Reset LocoScript's idea of the left-hand edge of the paper by setting the Left Offset*

4.4.1 Feeding the paper line by line

Note: If your printer has a Line Feed button, we suggest you use that rather than the steps given here.

To advance the paper one or more lines through the printer:

1. Press PTR *to go into Printer Control State.*

2. Press f1 *to display the Actions menu and move the cursor to* Feed one line.

3. Press ENTER *as many times as are needed to move the paper the required number of lines.*

4. Press EXIT *followed by* ENTER *to leave the menu and then* EXIT *to leave Printer Control State.*

```
      Feed to top of form
   ▶ Feed one line
      Set top of form
      Reset printer
      EXIT
```

4.4.2 Feeding the current sheet out of the printer

Note: If your printer has a Form Feed button, we suggest you use that rather than the steps given here.

To feed the current sheet out of the paper and to the top of the next page:

1. Press PTR *to go into Printer Control State.*

2. Press f1 *to display the Actions menu, move the cursor to* Feed to top of form, *and press* ENTER.

3. Press EXIT *followed by* ENTER *to leave the menu and then* EXIT *to leave Printer Control State.*

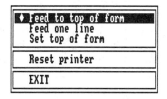

```
   ▶ Feed to top of form
      Feed one line
      Set top of form
      Reset printer
      EXIT
```

308

4.4.3 Resetting 'Top of Form'

Because LocoScript can't 'see' the paper in the printer, it automatically maintains an idea of how far down the current page it has got. This doesn't go awry on single sheet stationery because it is automatically reset every time fresh paper is loaded but it can go adrift on continuous stationery – particularly after a paper jam.

When this happens, you should adjust the paper so that the printer is ready to print on the first line of a new page and then reset the Top of Form as follows:

1. Press PTR *to go into Printer Control State.*

2. Press F1 *to display the Actions menu, move the cursor to* Set top of form *and press* ENTER .

3. Press EXIT *followed by* ENTER *to leave the menu and then* EXIT *to leave Printer Control State.*

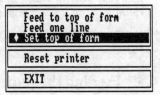

4.4.4 Setting the Left Offset

The Left Offset moves the start position for each line of text to the right of the printhead's natural start position.

It has two main uses. Firstly, it allows you to adjust for the position of the tractors on the printer's tractor feed when these are being used to feed continuous stationery through the printer (see Section 12.6). Secondly it allows you to set the start position for the different pieces of text you print using Direct Printing (see Section 4.5 opposite).

To set the Left Offset:

1. Press PTR *to go into Printer Control State.*

2. Press F6 *to display the Left Offset menu.*

3. Either: Type the Left Offset that is required as a number of tenths of an inch and then press ENTER *twice.*

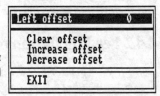

Or: Move the cursor to Increase offset / Decrease offset *as appropriate and press* ENTER *as many times as are needed to set the Left Offset you require. Then press* EXIT *followed by* ENTER *to leave the menu.*

Note: This works best on the PCW matrix and daisy-wheel printers which respond to each press of the ENTER key as if you were moving the printhead directly. Other printers, including the 9512+ inkjet printer, don't move the printhead to show you the Offset you have set.

4. Press EXIT *to leave Printer Control State.*

9308

4.5 Direct printing

When you have a pre-printed form to fill in, you don't have to go back to using the typewriter you parked under the stairs. Instead, you can use your PCW as if it were a typewriter by using LocoScript in its Direct Printing mode – with the added advantage that you can perfect and style the text before it goes onto the form.

Note: Direct Printing works best when you are printing on the 8256/8512/9256/ PcW10 matrix printer or the 9512 daisy-wheel printer. It can also be used on the 9512+ inkjet printer and on external printers, but it is not quite to easy to position the printhead ready for printing on these printers.

Starting Direct Printing

1. Load the paper on which you want to print in the normal way.

2. Display the Disc Manager Screen.

(Turn back to Section 1.3 if you are not sure how to do this.)

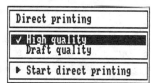

3. Press the D letter key, tick the print quality you require, and then press [ENTER] to confirm that you want to go ahead.

(D for Direct Printing should be easy to remember but, as usual, it is written on the second Information line in case you need to check.)

LocoScript then displays its Editor Screen (see Section 2.2) for you to prepare the text you want to print.

Positioning the paper ready to print

Before setting up the text to print, you need position the printhead where you want this text to be inserted.

To get the right position down the page:

- *On the PCW matrix and daisy-wheel printers (and other similar printers), turn the Paper Feed Knob on the side of the printer*

- *On the 9512+ inkjet printer and other similar printers, press the Line Feed (LF) button on the printer repeatedly*

- *Alternatively, press [PTR] to go into Printer Control State and use the* Feed one line *option in the f1 Actions menu to move the paper as described in Section 4.4.1 above.*

To get the right position across the page:

- *<u>Either:</u> Go into Printer Control State and set the Left Offset as described in Section 4.4.4 above (Note: This works best on the PCW matrix and daisy-wheel printers because these respond directly to the Left Offset you set.)*

- *<u>Or:</u> Take the* Change layout *option from the f2 Layout menu and set the Left Margin where you want printing to start (as described in Section 8.2).*

Inserting the text

1. Type the text you want at the current position up to, <u>but not including</u>, any ↵.
It is important not to press [RETURN] until you have finished preparing this text because pressing [RETURN] sends this text to the printer.

Alternatively, if the text you require is stored as a Block (see Chapter 3) or a Phrase (see Chapter 15), just Paste this in. (Note: While it is important that you shouldn't press [RETURN] at this stage, it doesn't matter if the text you paste in includes ↵s. Indeed, a neat way of ensuring that you have the same address on an envelope as you have in a letter is to copy the address in the letter to a Block and then paste this Block in when you use Direct Printing to prepare the envelope.)

2. Correct any mistakes you make exactly as if you were preparing a document.

3. Set the Layout and Styling you want for this text.
– again, exactly as if you were preparing a document (ie. see Chapters 6 – 10), except you don't get the option to use a different font.

4. Move the cursor to the end of the text (eg. by pressing [PAGE]) and then press [RETURN].
LocoScript immediately clears the screen and prints what you typed, starting at the Left Offset you set. When it has finished you can prepare another line or paragraph.

Note: If you simply want to leave one or more blank lines, just press [RETURN] the appropriate number of times. However, the blank lines won't be printed immediately: instead they are 'saved up' for printing with the next section of text.

Finishing

- *Press [EXIT], pick the option you want from the menu that is displayed and press [ENTER].*

Either option will return you to the Disc Manager Screen. The difference between them is that Finish Direct Printing will print any text you still have on the screen before returning you to the Disc Manager, whereas Abandon Direct Printing will throw this text away.

You are then returned to the Disc Manager Screen. Nothing of what you have done is recorded on disc.

4.6 Dealing with printer problems

Printers are unfortunately prone to problems because they need to have everything set right before they work correctly. However, these problems are usually straightforward to correct.

This section looks at the three main things that can go wrong when you try to print a document – and explains what steps to take:

- *Nothing is printed*
- *The paper jams in the printer*
- *The printer stops printing before the end of the document*

(Further assistance is given in the Troubleshooting sections of both this guide and the External Printers Guide supplied in the LocoScript 3 Printer Support Pack.)

4.6.1 Nothing is printed

1. If your printer has its own control buttons, check that it is switched on and that it is set on-line.

2. Check that there is paper in the printer.

3. Press the [PTR] key to go into LocoScript's Printer Control State and read the message on the second Information line.

4. If this says 'Waiting for paper', simply press [⊞] to 'resume printing'. Printing should now start.

If some other message is shown, consult either the Troubleshooting section of the LocoScript 3 External Printers Guide (if you have a copy of this) or the Troubleshooting at the back of this book.

If you still can't get your printer to print, consult your dealer because it is likely that the printer itself is faulty.

4.6.2 The paper jams in the printer

1. Press [PTR] to put LocoScript into its Printer Control State.
Printing will stop as soon as possible. (If you are really desperate, switch the printer off, wait a few seconds and then switch it back on again.)

2. Clear out the old paper and reload with fresh paper.

3. Check the page number shown on the Information lines at the top of the screen (which tells you how far LocoScript had got through printing the document) and then note the page number of the last page that was printed successfully.
LocoScript may well have sent several further pages of text to the printer after the problem happened.

4. Press ⌐f7⌐ to display the Document menu.

This normally gives you a choice of three places to reprint from – or of abandoning printing this document, or this copy, altogether. However the Previous page option is only included when it is appropriate.

```
Name:      PCWINFO .
from page:              1
to page:                3

on page:                3
on copy:       1 of   1

Reprint from:
♦ Current page
  Previous page
  Beginning

  Abandon printing

  EXIT
```

5. To print from the beginning of the current page (as shown on the Information lines):

Check the cursor is on Current page and press ⌐ENTER⌐. Then move the cursor to the EXIT option at the bottom of the menu and press ⌐ENTER⌐ again.

To print from a previous page:

Move the cursor to Previous page and press ⌐ENTER⌐ as many times as are needed to 'wind' the page number on the Information lines back to the page you require. Then move the cursor to the EXIT option at the bottom of the menu and press ⌐ENTER⌐ again.

To print from the beginning of the document:

Move the cursor to Beginning and press ⌐ENTER⌐. Then move the cursor to the EXIT option at the bottom of the menu and press ⌐ENTER⌐ again.

(To abandon printing, *move the cursor to either* Abandon current copy *or to* Abandon printing *as appropriate and press* ⌐ENTER⌐.)

6. When LocoScript displays a message reminding you to re-position the paper, check that the paper is correctly positioned, and then press ⌐ENTER⌐.

7. Press ⌐EXIT⌐ to leave Printer Control State.

LocoScript then starts reprinting the document from the point you picked out.

4.6.3 The printer stops printing

If the printer stops printing in the middle of a document, the chances are that the printer has spotted the end of the paper you are feeding into it, and has stopped so that there is no risk of accidentally printing on the platen. If you are working on single sheet stationery, just follow the usual procedure for loading fresh paper but *if you are using continuous stationery*:

1. Press ⌐PTR⌐ to enter Printer Control State.

2. Press ⌐f1⌐ to bring the Actions menu onto the screen.

3. If the menu includes the option to Finish current page, *move the cursor to this option and press* ⌐ENTER⌐. *Then press* ⌐EXIT⌐ *to leave Printer Control State.*
LocoScript will then finish printing the current page.

When it stops again, load fresh paper into the printer.

Chapter 5

Disc Housekeeping

From time to time, as well as creating and editing documents, you also need to:

- *Prepare new discs (or old discs you no longer need) ready for storing files*

- *Make 'Back-up' copies of your discs*

- *Check whether a disc is OK if you think it might have been damaged*

- *Re-organise the contents of your discs – erasing files you no longer want; moving others to other discs*

- *Give new names to files, groups or even discs*

All these actions can be carried out from the Disc Manager Screen – that is, the screen that is used to display the contents of your discs. You don't need to leave LocoScript to carry out any of these actions. (If you are not sure how to display this screen, turn to Section 1.3.)

This chapter describes how to carry out each of these actions. It also describes

- how to recover from 'Limbo' the previous version of a document or a file you have erased by mistake, and

- how to set up and inspect brief information about a file

- how to call up the Disc Manager without leaving your current document.

Disc capacity

Each of your discs can only hold so much data, specified by its capacity – typically expressed as a number of 'k'. (1k of data is roughly equivalent to 1000 characters.)

You can find out the capacity of your discs (and of Drive M) from the boxes summarising the contents of your drives in the upper part of the Disc Manager Screen. Among the information given about each drive is the amount of storage space on the disc that is already being used and the amount of free space on the disc. This part of the screen also shows the amount of space taken up by the files in the different groups on the disc, while the lower part of the screen shows the size of each individual file as number of k, written after the filename.

It's always worth checking how much free space there is on a disc before you try to store a new file on it. Otherwise you can waste a lot of time and go through a lot of unnecessary trauma trying to create a document or store a copy of a file on a disc when there isn't enough room for it.

You also need to be aware of how much free space you have on your disc before you edit a document. Although your edited document will replace the current one, for safety the new version is stored before the old version is deleted – so you need space on the disc for the new version before you start editing the document.

Different types of disc

Depending on which model of PCW you have, your disc drives will accept different types of disc or discs formatted in different ways. On a PCW8512, you even have two 3" disc drives which accept discs formatted in different ways.

The possibilities are as follows:

- *3" discs with the two sides formatted separately (also known as CF2 discs or 180k discs)*

These discs can store about 170k of information on either side of the disc and can be read in any 3" disc drive. But they can only be written in Drive A of either a PCW8256 or a PCW8512.

- *3" discs with the two sides formatted together (also known as CF2DD discs or 720k discs)*

These discs can store about 700k of information but they can only be read or written in either the PCW9512's Drive A or a PCW8512's Drive B.

- *3½" discs*

These discs can also store about 700k of information and they can be read or written in any 3½" disc drive, such as the disc drives on the PcW9256, the PcW9512+ and the PcW10.

The various Disc Housekeeping actions described in this chapter all need the discs to be used in a suitable drive.

In general, any disc needs to be placed in a drive in which the disc can be *written*, but when you are copying from a disc, you can simply use this disc in a drive in which it can be *read*.

So in particular, you can copy *from* a 180k 3" disc placed in Drive B of a PCW8512 but you can only copy *to* this disc when it is placed in Drive A of either a PCW8256 or a PCW8512.

Note: It is possible to replace the 3" drives on the older PCWs by 3½" drives. For further information, please contact our Sales Department. (The address is given at the font of this book.)

5.1 Preparing Data discs (Formatting)

Before anything can be stored on a disc, you need to 'Format' it: that is, mark out the storage area on each side of the disc electronically into the appropriate pattern of tracks and sectors.

Formatting is also a good way of clearing out the contents of an old disc that you don't want any more and making it ready to store new files. But do check first that you don't need any of the files currently on this disc: these files can't be recovered after you have formatted the disc.

The steps used to format a disc are as follows:

1. Display the Disc Manager Screen.
(Turn to Section 1.3 if you are not sure how to do this.)

2. Remove any discs currently in your disc drive(s) and put them to one side.
– so that there's no risk of formatting these discs by accident. (Anything that was stored on a disc cannot be recovered after the disc has been formatted.)

3. Press ⌷f2⌷ *(*⌷SHIFT⌷+⌷f1⌷*) to call up the Disc menu, move the cursor to* Format disc *and press* ⌷ENTER⌷*.*

4. When the message appears asking which type of disc you want to prepare, select the appropriate Format option and press ⌷ENTER⌷*.*

If your disc drives are of different types (as they are on a PCW8512), be sure to pick the option that means that the disc will be formatted in the drive in which it will used (or at least written to).

5. When the message appears asking you to insert the disc that is to be formatted, check that the write-protect hole(s) on this disc are closed (see page 9). Then insert the disc in the drive specified in the message and press ⌷ENTER⌷*.*

If you have opted to format a 3" disc in Drive A of a PCW8256/8512, make sure that you insert this disc with the side you want to format to the left.

LocoScript then proceeds to format the disc. A message on the screen tells you how this is progressing.

6. When the disc has been formatted (and the new format verified), LocoScript displays a message giving you the choice of formatting another disc or returning to the Disc Manager. Simply pick the option you want and press ⌷ENTER⌷*.*

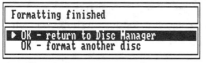

Note: If you have been formatting a 3" disc in Drive A of a PCW8256/8512, only one side of this disc has so far been formatted so you will probably want to take the format another disc option and work through Steps 4 – 6 again, this time to format the other side of the disc. (Other types of disc are formatted as a whole and so don't need any further formatting.)

5.2 Making back-up copies of discs

As well as keeping your discs organised, it is important to ensure you have a reserve – or 'back-up' – copy of every document you care about losing. This back-up copy should always be on a different disc in case the disc is damaged, eg. by someone scratching the disc.

The most straightforward way of making such back-ups is to make a copy of the whole disc on another disc – ie. a second disc with exactly the same information on it.

The steps to use to copy a disc are as follows. As the disc is copied, you will see messages referring to the 'Source disc' and the 'Destination disc'. The Source disc is the disc you want to copy; the Destination disc is the disc you want to make the copy on.

Note: The number of stages in which the copy is made depends on the amount of space free on Drive M. This means you can reduce the number of stages that are needed by adding extra memory to your PCW (eg. by adding the Locomotive Power Pack) or by erasing files that you don't need from Drive M before you make the copy.

1. Display the Disc Manager Screen.
(Turn to Section 1.3 if you are not sure how to do this.)

2. Take out the discs currently in the disc drive(s) and put them to one side.

3. Check that the disc you want to copy is write-protected (ie. the write-protect hole(s) open) but the disc on which you want to make the copy is write-enabled (holes closed).
(There is a picture showing the positions of these holes on page 9.)

4. Press ⌐f2¬ *(*⌐SHIFT¬+⌐f1¬*) to display the Disc menu, check that the cursor is on* Copy disc *and press* ⌐ENTER¬*.*

5. LocoScript then displays a message checking that you want to copy a disc and getting you to specify the type of disc that you want to copy. Move the cursor to the appropriate Copy disc *option and press* ⌐ENTER¬*.*

6. LocoScript then displays a message telling you where to insert the Source disc for the copy and, if appropriate, where to insert the Destination disc. Insert these discs as instructed, check that the cursor is on the 'Disc now in drive' *option and press* ⌐ENTER¬*.*

If you have a two-drive PCW, LocoScript may now simply copy all the contents of your Source disc to your Destination disc. (A message on the screen shows how this copy is progressing.)

If you have a single-drive machine (or your second drive can't be used in making the copy), LocoScript will copy a section of the Source disc into memory, then ask you to insert the Destination disc so that it can write this section to the new disc. That done, LocoScript will ask for the Source disc again so that it can copy the next section of the disc – and so on until the copy has been completed. Each time one of these messages appears, remove the disc currently in the drive, insert the disc requested in the message and then press ENTER.

Note: If you are copying a 3" Drive A disc on a PCW8256/8512, be sure to insert both this disc and your Destination disc with the side you want to copy to the left.

7. When the copy has been completed, LocoScript puts up another message asking you whether you want to copy another. Simply pick the option you want and press ENTER.

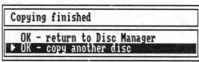

Note: If you have been copying a 3" Drive A disc on a PCW8256/8512, only one side of this disc has so far been copied. If you need to copy the other side as well, take the copy another disc option and work through Steps 5 – 7 again, this time to copy the other side of the disc. (Other types of disc are copied as a whole.)

Note: You don't need to format a new blank disc before you make a copy of a disc onto it. The disc is automatically formatted as part of the process of copying the disc.

5.3 Verifying discs

If you are concerned that a disc may have been damaged, then you can readily test whether this is the case by 'Verifying' the disc. This checks that the disc is correctly formatted.

Note: There is no need to verify discs that you have just formatted: LocoScript automatically verifies any disc that it formats.

1. Display the Disc Manager Screen.
(Turn to Section 1.3 if you are not sure how to do this.)

2. Press f2 *(*SHIFT+f1*) to display the Disc menu, check that the cursor is on* Verify disc *and press* ENTER.

3. LocoScript now asks you to confirm that you want to verify a disc and which drive you will be using: select the appropriate option and press ENTER.

4. LocoScript then asks you to confirm that the disc you want to verify is in the drive. Check that this is the case and then press ENTER.
LocoScript then checks the formatting of the disc in the selected drive.

5.4 Copying, moving and erasing files

Copying, moving and erasing files are essential parts of Disc Housekeeping.

Although these seem three very different actions, they are in fact very similar. In each case you start by picking out the file on the Disc Manager Screen with the File cursor; then you press ⬚ to bring the File menu onto the screen and select the action you want from this menu. If the action you choose involves making a copy of the document, you then pick out the group you want to store the copy in (see Section 1.4). Finally, LocoScript puts up a summary of the action you have picked out so that you can confirm everything is correct before it goes ahead.

The following sections describe Copying, Moving and Erasing files in more detail.

5.4.1 Copying files

There are a number of reasons why you might want to copy a file:

- – To give yourself a copy of this file on a particular disc (eg. a temporary copy on Drive M).
- – To give yourself a starting point for a new document. (It can be easier to create a new document by editing a copy of an existing one than to start from scratch.)
- – To give yourself a back-up copy.

The steps used are essentially the same whether you want to make the copy on the same disc as the original file, or on a different disc. The only difference is that when you are copying from one disc to another, you need to insert each of these discs in a suitable disc drive before you start to make the copy – or if that's not possible, to make the copy via Drive M (see Step 3 below). When the copy is being made on the same disc, you just have the one disc that you need to insert.

1. Display the Disc Manager Screen.
(Turn to Section 1.3 if you are not sure how to do this.)

2. Insert the disc containing the file that is to be copied in a drive in which this disc can be read.

3. If the copy is to be made on a different disc, insert this disc in a drive in which it can be written (if this is possible).

If this isn't possible, you will need to copy the file first to one of the groups on Drive M, then switch the disc in the disc drive, press ⬚ and copy the file from Drive M to its true destination. Note: There's an example of copying via Drive M in Session 4 of the Tutorial (page 40).

4. Press ⬚ to signal the change of discs.

5. Place the cursor on the file that you want to copy.

6. Press ⬚ to display the File menu, check that the cursor is on Copy file *and press* ENTER.

7. When the message appears asking you to pick out the destination for the copy, move the cursor to the group in which you want the copy to be made and press [ENTER].

```
Pick destination:

select group and drive
then press ENTER
or CAN to abandon
```

If this group already contains any files, you can simply move the File cursor to the list of files in this group. If the group is empty, hold down [SHIFT] as you press the Cursor keys to move the Group cursor to the group you require.

```
Copy file

New Name:    PCWINFO .
Group:        group 0
Drive:       M

Old Name:    PCWINFO .
Group:        group 1
Drive:       A
```

8. Check the details shown in the Confirmation menu, change the name of the New file (if you want to do this) then press [ENTER].

When you press [ENTER], LocoScript first checks whether there is already a file with this name in the Destination group. If there isn't, LocoScript goes ahead and copies the document but if there is, it puts up the following Alert message telling you this:

```
ERROR in:  Copy file

New name already exists

▶ Replace with the new file
  Choose another name
  Cancel operation
```

Replace with the new file is selected for you because, in most cases, this will be what you want. However, you should only select this option if you are sure you don't want this other version – because LocoScript has to delete the existing file before it can make the copy.

If you don't want to lose the old file, select Choose another name and press [ENTER]. You then get the chance to pick out the group and the name for the new file all over again.

(If you don't want to make the copy after all, select Cancel operation and press [ENTER]: LocoScript returns you to the Disc Manager Screen.)

For example, to create a copy of the PCWINFO document in group 2 of the LocoScript 3 Examples disc:

Insert the LocoScript 3 Examples disc and press [f7] to signal the change of disc.

Now move the File cursor to PCWINFO on Drive A. When the File cursor is over the document name, press [f3] to bring the File menu onto the screen.

Check that the cursor is on Copy file, then press [ENTER].

When the message appears asking you to pick out the destination for this copy, hold down [SHIFT] and then use the Cursor keys to move the Group cursor to group 2 on Drive A. When the Group cursor is over the right group, press [ENTER]. LocoScript then puts up a menu summarising the copying operation you have picked out.

Check the details shown in this menu, then press [ENTER] to make the copy.

LocoScript 3 User Guide   **99**

5.4.2 Moving files

Moving files from one place to another – either to a different disc or to a different group on the same disc – is a very powerful tool in re-organising your discs.

Moving a file is very much like copying a file, except that after the copy has been made, the original file is erased. As a result, the steps used to move a file are just like those used to copy a file – ie. as follows:

1. Display the Disc Manager Screen.
(Turn to Section 1.3 if you are not sure how to do this.)

2. Insert the disc containing the file that is to be moved in a drive in which this disc can be read.

3. If the file is to be moved to a different disc, insert this disc in a drive in which it can be written (if this is possible).
If this isn't possible, you will need to move the file first to one of the groups on Drive M, then switch the disc in the disc drive, press [f7] and move the file from Drive M to its true destination.

4. Press [f7] to signal the change of discs.

5. Place the File cursor on the file that you want to move.

6. Press [f3] to display the File menu, move the cursor to Move file *and press* [ENTER].

```
Copy file
▶ Move file
  Erase file
  Rename file
  Recover from limbo
```

7. When the message appears asking you to pick out the destination, move the cursor to the group to which you want the file to be moved and press [ENTER].
If this group already contains any files, you can simply move the File cursor to the list of files in this group. If the group is empty, hold down [SHIFT] as you press the Cursor keys to move the Group cursor to the group you require.

8. Check the details shown in the Confirmation menu, change the name of the New file (if you want to do this) then press [ENTER].

In general, LocoScript then simply goes ahead and moves the file. But if there is already a file with this name in the Destination group, it will display an Alert message offering the same choice of Replace with the new file; Choose another name; or Cancel operation that was offered when copying files (see opposite). Simply select the option you want and press [ENTER].

IMPORTANT: If you move a document to Drive M, you should immediately copy it to another disc. If you don't, you risk losing this document altogether – though a copy of the file will initially be retained on the original disc as a 'Limbo' file which can if necessary be recovered (see Section 5.7).

5.4.3 Erasing files

An important part of tidying up is to erase documents and files you no longer need.

Of course, you must be certain that you don't need a document or file before you decide to delete it. If you are at all unsure about whether you need a file, leave it alone – because the chances are that you will need it after all. This applies in particular to files on Drive M and on your Start-of-day disc: if you don't know about these files, don't delete them because they are probably important to LocoScript.

The steps used to erase a file are as follows. Once again, the steps are very like those of copying or moving a document:

1. Display the Disc Manager Screen.
(Turn to Section 1.3 if you are not sure how to do this.)

2. Insert the disc containing the file you want to erase in a drive in which this disc can be written and press ⌐f7⌐ to signal the change of disc.

3. Place the cursor on the file that you want to erase, then press ⌐f3⌐ to display the File menu, move the cursor to Erase file *and press* ⌐ENTER⌐ .

4. Check the details given in the menu that is displayed are correct, then press ⌐ENTER⌐ *– or* ⌐CAN⌐ *to abandon the action.*

LocoScript then removes the file from the list of files on your disc – but it doesn't actually erase it from the disc altogether. Instead, it puts the file into a state of 'Limbo' to give you the chance of recovering documents that you throw away by accident (see Section 5.5 overleaf).

Erasing a file fully

If a document contains confidential information, you might not want to leave it in Limbo after it has been erased – because it would be easy for someone else to recover it. Instead, you will want to erase the document fully as follows:

1. Erase the file in the normal way (see above).

2. Press ⌐f8⌐ *(*⌐SHIFT⌐+⌐f7⌐*) to display the Options menu, use the* ⌐⊞⌐ *key to tick* Show Limbo files *and then press* ⌐ENTER⌐ .
LocoScript then rewrites the screen, listing Limbo files as well (marked lim).

3. Place the File cursor on the Limbo file you want to erase.

4. Press ⌐f3⌐ *to display the File menu, move the cursor to* Erase file *and press* ⌐ENTER⌐ .

5. Check that the correct file has been picked out, then press ⌐ENTER⌐ .

LocoScript then erases the document completely: it can't now be recovered – at least, not by normal means!

5.5 Recovering files from Limbo

When you erase a file or move it to another disc, LocoScript removes the file from the list of files on your disc – but it doesn't actually erase it from the disc altogether. Instead, it puts the file into a state of 'Limbo' – as a 'Limbo file' – and it stays in Limbo until the space on the disc it is occupying is needed for another file. The previous version of any document you edit is also held in Limbo on your disc.

LocoScript has this Limbo state as a safety net for you – so that you can recover documents that you throw away by accident or lose in the process of moving (eg. by moving a file to Drive M but forgetting to move it on to another disc).

When you realise you have thrown away the wrong file, you need to recover it from Limbo as soon as possible. The longer you wait, the more likely it becomes that the file has been removed completely. If space is needed for a new file, LocoScript removes files from Limbo – oldest first – until enough room has been made.

1. Display the Disc Manager Screen.
(Turn to Section 1.3 if you don't know how to do this.)

2. Press ⬚ f8 *(* SHIFT *+* f7 *) to display the Options menu, tick* Show Limbo files *(eg. using* ⬚ *) and then press* ENTER *.*

LocoScript then rewrites the screen, listing Limbo files as well (marked lim).

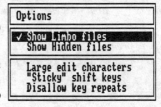

Limbo file

3. Place the File cursor on the Limbo file you want to recover.
This will still have its original name.

4. Press ⬚ f3 *to display the File menu, move the cursor to* Recover from limbo *and press* ENTER *.*
LocoScript now displays a menu giving details of the Limbo file you have picked out and the name it will have when it is recovered. Normally, this will be the old name but if there is another document of this name in the group, LocoScript will leave the name blank for you to type in a new name.

5. Check that the correct file has been picked out, set a new name for the recovered file (if necessary) then press ENTER *.*
LocoScript then brings your document back from Limbo.

5.6 Giving discs, groups and files new names

Another improvement you can make to the organisation of your discs is to ensure that everything has a name that makes it easy to pick out.

Discs, groups and files can each be given new names – by using the Rename option in the appropriate menu (ie. the Disc menu to name a disc, the Group menu to name a group and the File menu to rename a file).

In general, the characters you can use in these names are the capital letters A...Z and the numbers 0...9, but there's a full list of the characters you can use in Appendix III.

5.6.1 Naming a disc

Discs can be given names just like file or document names – with a main part of up to eight characters, then a dot and an optional extension of up to three characters.

To give a disc a new name:

1. Display the Disc Manager Screen.
(Turn to Section 1.3 if you are not sure how to do this.)

2. Insert the disc that you want to name in the drive in which it is used and press [f7] *to signal the change of disc.*

3. Place the cursor in one of the groups on this disc, then press [f2] ([SHIFT]+[f1]) *to display the Disc menu, move the cursor to* Rename disc *and press* [ENTER].

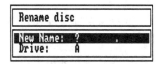

4. When the menu appears, type the new name for this disc and press [ENTER].
Don't worry about typing this name in capitals (LocoScript automatically converts any lower case letters you type into capitals).

Pressing [ENTER] names the disc. Now, whenever this disc is put in the drive, you will be able to tell which disc it is just by looking beside the drive name at the top of the Disc Manager Screen. (It's a good idea to write this name on the disc label as well.)

Disc name

5.6.2 Naming a group

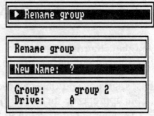

Groups can be given names of up to eight characters, which can also be changed any time you like – including back to its original group *n* name.

1. Display the Disc Manager Screen.
(Turn to Section 1.3 if you don't know how to do this.)

2. Insert the disc containing the group you want to name and press ⌜f7⌝ *to signal the change of disc.*

3. Check that the cursor is on this group, then press ⌜f4⌝ *(*⌜SHIFT⌝+⌜f3⌝*) to display the Group menu, check that the cursor is on* Rename group *and press* ⌜ENTER⌝.

4. When the menu appears, type the new name for this group and press ⌜ENTER⌝.
Don't worry about typing this name in capitals (LocoScript automatically converts any lower case letters you type into capitals).

This gives the group the new name – as you can see both where the contents of the disc are summarised and at the top of the column showing the names of the documents in this group.

Note: To clear a group name (ie. return the group to a simple numbered group), move the Group cursor to this group, select Erase file *in the f3 menu, type the name* group-name.GRP *in the menu that appears and press* ⌜ENTER⌝.

5.6.3 Renaming a file

1. Display the Disc Manager Screen.
(Turn to Section 1.3 if you don't know how to do this.)

2. Insert the disc containing the file you want to rename and press ⌜f7⌝ *to signal the change of disc.*

3. Move the File cursor to the file, then press ⌜f3⌝ *to display the File menu, move the cursor to* Rename file *and press* ⌜ENTER⌝.

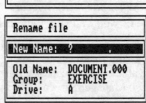

4. When the menu appears, type the new name you require and press ⌜ENTER⌝.
Don't worry about typing this name in capitals (LocoScript automatically converts any lower case letters you type into capitals).

The file is now renamed.

Note: The only files you should rename are documents and datafiles that you have set up yourself. DO NOT rename any of LocoScript's program or support files (eg. printer files, font files etc.) except where our instructions explicitly tell you to do this. Most of these files have special names and the files won't be found when they are needed if you change their names.

5.7 Seeing information about files

Associated with every file is a brief description which you can 'inspect' from the Disc Manager Screen. This description will tell you more about the file than is possible to deduce simply from its name. In particular, the descriptions of documents and datafiles include three lines of text known as the Identity text which you can set up yourself.

5.7.1 Inspecting files

```
▶ Inspect document
  Set first pages
  Set total pages
```

To see the information that's held about any file:

1. Display the Disc Manager Screen.
(Turn to Section 1.3 if you don't know how to do this.)

2. Place the cursor on the file you want to inspect and press [f5] ***to display the Document menu.***

3. Check that the cursor is on Inspect document ***and press*** [ENTER].

```
Name:       CONTENTS.DOC
Group:        group 0
Drive:      B

LocoScript 3 document
Details of the contents
of your product pack
                      Apr 93

First page            1
Last page             1
Total pages        ????
```

LocoScript then displays the information it has about the file you have picked out.

4. When you have finished looking at this information, press either [ENTER] ***or*** [CAN].

5.7.2 Setting up a document's Identity text

A document's Identity text is a description of up to three lines of 30 characters which you can record about the document. It can be set up either from the Disc Manager Screen or while you are working on the document.

(*Note:* Similar descriptions can be set up about LocoMail and LocoFile datafiles – using much the same steps.)

To set the Identity text from the Disc Manager Screen:

1. Place the cursor on the file and then 'inspect' it as described above (ie. press [f5] ***to display the Document menu, check that the cursor is on*** Inspect document ***and press*** [ENTER] ***).***
LocoScript then displays the information it currently has about the file you have picked out. The part of the description that we are interested in here are the three lines towards the bottom of the display.

2. To set up the text you require, edit each line of the Identity text separately – moving from line to line either by moving the cursor or by pressing [RETURN].
Note that any characters that are moved off the right-hand end of the display are simply lost. There is no wrapping of the text from line to line.

Note: Not all the characters that you can type can be used in this description: in particular, you cannot use any Cyrillic characters or many of the Mathematical symbols. A list of the characters you can use is given in Appendix III.

3. When you have finished setting up the Identity text, press ⌈ENTER⌉ *to record the new text and close up the display.*

To set the Identity text while you are editing the document:

1. Press ⌈f1⌉ *to display the f1 Actions menu.*

2. Move the cursor to Edit identity *and press* ⌈ENTER⌉.

3. Set up the individual lines of the Identity text as described above and then press ⌈ENTER⌉ *to record the new text and close up the display.*

5.8 Using the Disc Manager whilst editing

Occasionally, you will need access to the Disc Manager Screen while you are editing a document. You do this as follows:

1. Press ⌈f1⌉ *to display the Actions menu.*

2. Move the cursor to Disc manager *and press* ⌈ENTER⌉.

LocoScript then displays the Disc Manager Screen and gives you access to all the Disc Manager menus, as you can see by looking at the Information lines. But it hasn't abandoned work on the document you are editing – it has just put it on one side for the moment, as you can confirm from the top Information line which will be displaying the message like A:group 1/PCWINFO. Disc management whilst editing.

You can now carry out most of the actions that you normally carry out from the Disc Manager Screen – such as Copying, Moving, Deleting and Renaming. You can even start printing one of your other documents.

However, a number of actions aren't possible. In particular, you can't edit another document and you can't do anything that directly affects the document you are currently editing. You can't, for example, copy it, move it, rename it or print it and you must not remove the disc holding this document from the drive and replace it by another. If you need to move any files off this disc onto another (for example, to make some more space on the disc) and you have a single-drive machine, you must move these initially to Drive M and only move them to your other disc once you have finished editing the document.

When you have finished using the Disc Manager, press ⌈EXIT⌉. *LocoScript then returns you to the document you were editing.*

Part II

Text Layout

Part I of this User Guide described how to put text into a document and how to change it once it is there. In this part of the book, we look at how you style the text and how you lay it out on the page. This covers:

- *The font (or typeface) used for the text – plus the typesize (especially if the font you've chosen can be printed at more than one size)*

- *The print style used for the text – bold, italic, underlined etc.*

- *The spacing of the characters along the line and from line to line*

- *The positions of the margins and tabs*

- *Positioning the text centrally or to the right; indenting it; or justifying it (to give it a straight right-hand edge as well as a straight left-hand one)*

- *Controlling the Line Breaks and Page Breaks within your text*

These aspects of your text are primarily defined by the 'Layout' that is being used for the text. This sets the underlying selection of font, typesize, spacing, margins and tabs for this section of the text – that is, the font etc. that are used at the beginning of the section and the ones that you go back to when additional stylings are turned off. (Each document automatically has two Layouts – one for the main body of the text and another for Headers and Footers – but more can be added if they are needed, as we explain in Chapter 8.)

On top of the Layouts, LocoScript has a whole series of 'word-processing codes' which allow you to style parts of the text in different ways – putting some into a different font or a different typesize, putting others into bold or italic etc. etc. LocoScript has codes to change pretty much any aspect of the Layout from the font that is used to the positioning of the text between the margins. The only aspects of the Layout which can't be changed by inserting codes are the margins and tabs and various related issues such as the scale of the Ruler line at the top of the screen.

The various different codes used to style your text are inserted either from menus or by a quick keystroking technique which is introduced in the first chapter of this part (Chapter 6). The underlying styling set by a Layout is controlled from a 'Layout Editor' which is called up from the f2 Layout menu.

One thing to remember about LocoScript's word-processing codes, however, is that they are all cancelled by any Layout codes you insert. So if you want a particular styling to continue into an area with a new Layout, you either need to set this styling in this Layout or to repeat the various codes that are required after the Layout code.

0308

Font and print style

If you simply type text into a document, this will all be printed in the same font (or typeface) and in a plain (upright) print style – and as a result, the document will look rather dull. Using different fonts and print styles can radically improve the appearance of a document.

LocoScript lets you use up to four different fonts in any document and to switch between these at will. It also lets you enhance the text further by using print styles such as bold, italic and underlining. This chapter explains:

- *How to select the different fonts and print styles used in your text*

- *How to set the underlying font, and*

- *How to substitute one font for another throughout a document*

It also describes the special features of printing a document that uses multiple fonts.

Note: Most fonts look best when the characters are 'proportionally spaced', particularly when the font can be printed at different sizes. To arrange this, you need to set the Character Pitch to PS. Chapter 8 describes how to do this.

We also suggest working with 'Codes shown' so that you can readily see which fonts and print styles you have selected in your document. In general, this styling isn't shown on the screen – only when the document is printed. Showing codes is one of the Display options you have while editing a document (see Section 2.2). To select it, you simply have to tick the Codes *option in the f8 Options menu.*

> **IMPORTANT:** The range of fonts and print styles you can use in your documents depends on the printer you use.
>
> If your printer supports LocoScript 3's LX fonts, you will be able to use a mixture of these fonts together with whatever other fonts are available on this printer. You will also be able to use the full range of print styles – at least in the LX fonts.
>
> On other printers, however, you may be restricted to one font: you may also be limited in the range of print styles you can use. In particular, if you use a daisy-wheel printer (such as that supplied with the PCW9512 and some models of PcW9512+), you can only change font by switching to a different printwheel: changing printwheel isn't practical in the middle of a document so you are automatically restricted to one font per document. However, you can choose which font this is – by following the steps given in Section 6.5.

Font availability

There are certain conditions which need to be met before a font can be either selected in a document, or used in printing. The rules are as follows:

- *First and foremost, the font must be recorded in the Settings file.*

Recording the font in the Settings file is an integral part of installing any font, so all your fonts should be properly recorded if you have followed the Installation procedure correctly. The only things that may have prevented the font from being recorded are:

- if you already have 15 fonts recorded for your printer (15 is the maximum number you can record)
- if you failed to save a copy of the new Settings file on your Start-of-day disc at the end of the Installation procedure (You will be able to tell that this has happened if you see a message telling you that your Settings file is out-of-date when you load LocoScript.)
- if you have exceeded the maximum amount of information that the Settings file can hold, which is possible but very unlikely

- *Before a font can be selected in a document:*

It simply has to have been recorded in the Settings file as described above.

- *Before a font can be used in printing:*

The font has to have been recorded in the Settings file, *and* the relevant font file(s) must either have been loaded into memory or be in group 0 (sometimes called the 'SYSTEM' group) on Drive M.

Where you are using one of LocoScript 3's LX fonts, the files you need on Drive M are the various *Character Shape* (.@xx) files to cover both the range of characters used in the document and the different point sizes at which these characters are to be printed. (Section II.2 explains which Character Shape files you need.)

Where you are using any other font, you need the corresponding *Character Set* (.#xx) file on Drive M.

In general, any font that has been installed on your Start-up discs should be available whenever you want it. Any font file in group 0 on your Start-up discs is automatically copied to Drive M when you load LocoScript. The only difficulty comes where you have only a limited amount of space on Drive M, when you may need to arrange that the correct group of files are in group 0 of Drive M when you need them – if necessary, by copying the files there yourself.

6.1 Using different fonts in your text

Note: This section describes how to switch from one font (or typeface) to another within a document. If your printer doesn't allow you to use a mixture of fonts in your documents, you should ignore this section.

Text is initially put into the font specified in the Layout – that is, the overall set of rules that are applied in laying out this text. If you want any text to be in a different font, you specify this by inserting 'Font codes' – one at the beginning of this text selecting the font you require and another at the end specifying the font to be used for the following text. (We describe how to set the font in the Layout in Section 6.4.)

(+Font*n*) *code*

further devices. For example, we will be describing later how you can use this port to attach another printer to your PCW.

Section 1: The Devices (-Font) *code*

* The Keyboard's role is purely to take information and instructions from

---

Most Font codes have the form (+Font*n*) where *n* is the Font number 0...3 to which the font has been assigned in the document's Document Set-up (see Part III): for example, (+Font2) selects Font number 2. There is also a (-Font) code which tells LocoScript to go back to the Font set in the Layout. (The reason these record the Font number rather than the name is that it gives you a quick way of changing all the font selections if you switch over to printing the document on another printer. It also means you can readily exchange one font for another throughout the whole of a document – for example, if you extend the range of fonts you have on your printer (eg. by adding one of the LocoFont packs). The steps used to make such global changes are given in Section 6.5.)

The main way of inserting these codes is by picking out the font you want to use – by name – from the f3 Style menu. (The steps are given opposite.) But there is also a quick keystroking method of inserting these codes, described in Section 6.3, which you can use to insert both (+Font*n*) codes and (-Font) codes – though you do need to know the Font number for the font you require. (The Font codes inserted via the Style menu are all of the (+Font*n*) form.)

Note: The font you choose doesn't change the appearance of the text on the screen, though if you are using Character Pitch PS (as we recommend), it could well change where the line breaks appear in the text (see Section 7.2). Showing codes as described in Section 2.2 will, however, let you see what Font codes you have inserted, while looking at the Information lines will show you (among other things) the font used at the current position of the cursor.

You should also remember that a Font code is cancelled by any Layout code that follows it in the document. So if you want a font to continue to be used 'the other side' of a Layout code, you need either to follow the Layout code with another Font code or to set this font as part of the Layout (as described in Section 6.4).

LocoScript 3 User Guide

Which fonts to use

There are several things to think about in choosing the fonts to use in a document:

- *The different sizes of text you intend to use – particularly for headlines and small print. (The 10 or 12pt text typically used for the bulk of a document can be printed in almost any font.)*

- *The characters you will want to print – because each font typically only offers a selection of the characters LocoScript supports. (Only the PCW matrix Standard and Sans Serif fonts, the LocoFont fonts, and the LX fonts offer the full range of characters – the latter with the extra files provided in the LX Symbol pack.)*

- *The different print styles you intend to use – because some fonts are only available in a limited range of print styles.*

- *The overall appearance that you want for the text – eg. formal, modern, decorative etc.*

If you are still left with a choice of fonts to use, the other thing to consider is *speed*. Fonts that are built into a printer typically take less time to print than fonts that are 'downloaded to the printer' (as the LocoFont fonts and LX fonts are).

Note: You may well get the best results from using your printer's built-in fonts for the main part of the text but the LX fonts for headlines and small print where you need different sizes.

To select a different font

1. Position the cursor where you want to change over to the new font.

2. Press ⌈f3⌉ *to display the Style menu.*

3. Tick the font you require and press ⌈ENTER⌉.
LocoScript then inserts the code (+Font*n*) where *n* is the Font number of the font you selected. This puts the text following the code into your chosen font.

(There is an example showing these steps in use overleaf.)

```
Underline
Word underline
Bold
Double strike
Italic
Superscript
Subscript
Reverse

0: Standard
1: Sans serif
2: LX Roman
✓ 3: LX Sanserif
```

Note: If the font you want is not listed in the menu but there's a slot available for a further font (shown as a line of dashes), tick this slot instead. When you press ⌈ENTER⌉, LocoScript will display a message telling you that no font has been defined for this Font number. Press ⌈ENTER⌉ to this message. LocoScript then displays a list of the fonts available on your printer. Simply pick out the font you want with the cursor and press ⌈ENTER⌉ to both add it to the list of fonts used in the document and select it in the document. (If there isn't a slot available, the only way to make your chosen font available is to follow the steps given in Section 6.5 to change the range of fonts used in the document.)

Example: Putting the title line of PCWINFO into LX Sanserif

The components of your PCW

Your PCW has three obvious components – a Monitor Unit (with the screen and disc drive), a Keyboard and a Printer – but the way to think about it is as a processor, which actually does all the computing (such as working out equations like x=x1+b2), to which are attached a number of electronic 'Devices' whose job is either to supply the processor with information and instructions, or to receive information from the processor, or in some cases, both.

Edit the PCWINFO document, place the cursor at the start of its title line and press the f3 key to display the Style menu. When this menu is displayed, move the cursor down to the entry for LX Sanserif near the bottom of the menu, press [⊞] to tick this and then press [ENTER]. LocoScript then inserts a (+Font1) code at the beginning of the line.

Now move the cursor to the end of the title line and press the f3 key again. This time move the cursor to the entry for LX Roman, then press [⊞] followed by [ENTER] as before. LocoScript then inserts a (+Font0) code at the end of the line.

```
(+Font1)The components of your PCW(+Font0)§
↵
Your PCW has three obvious components ⊣ a Monitor Unit (with the screen and
disc drives), a Keyboard and a Printer ⊣ but the way to think about  it  is
as a processor, which actually does all the computing (such as working  out
equations like x=x1+b2), to which  are  attached  a  number  of  electronic
'Devices' whose job is either to supply the processor with information   and
instructions, or to receive information from  the  processor,  or  in  some
cases, both. ↵
↵
```

The (+Font1) code at the start of the title line selects LX Sanserif which is then used for the text up until the (+Font0) code at the end of the line which selects LX Roman for the remaining text – as you can confirm by moving the cursor to the different parts of the text and seeing which font is shown on the Information lines.

9308

6.2 Using different print styles

LocoScript supports a wide range of different print styles:

- **Bold**
- **Italic**
- **Double-strike**
- **Underlining** – *both full underlining (in which spaces are underlined) and word underlining (in which spaces aren't underlined)*
- **Superscript/Subscript**

*Note: The Style menu from which these are selected also includes a 'Reverse' option. This is not a print style but a **screen** style that allows you to highlight sections of a document so that they stand out as you edit it. It doesn't make the text white on black when it is printed.*

Where you want to use these different styles in a document, you need to insert a pair of styling codes – one 'turning on' the chosen style at the beginning of the text you want to affect, the other 'turning it off' at the end of this text. The codes that turn the different styles on all start (+...), while those that turn them off all start (-...). For example, the (+Bold) code that turns Bold on while (-Bold) turns Bold off.

```
                    further devices. For example, we will be describing later how you can use this
(+Bold) code        port to attach another printer to your PCW.
                    Section 1: The Devices          (-Bold) code

                    * The Keyboard's role is purely to take information and instructions from
```

{The codes can be inserted either from the f3 Style menu (as described below) or by using quick keystroking techniques described in Section 6.3.

Note: The print style you set for a piece of text doesn't change its appearance on the screen. Showing codes as described in Section 2.2 will, however, let you see what styling codes you have inserted, while looking at the Information lines will show you the styling that is selected at the current position of the cursor.

You should also note that these styling codes are cancelled by any Layout code that follows them in the document. So if you want a particular print style to continue to be used 'the other side' of a Layout code, you need to follow the Layout code with another code selecting this style.

*IMPORTANT: Selecting a print style in your document does not guarantee that the text will be printed in that print style: the crucial factor is whether the printer you use can produce that style in the font you've selected. It can also depend on the size of text you've selected and whether you've opted for High Quality or Draft Quality printing. For example, on the PCW matrix printer, 15 or 17 pitch text in the Standard and Sans serif fonts isn't be printed bold in High Quality because the result would just look smudged. **Note:** If you use an external printer, you can find out which print styles it supports by printing the EFFECTS document provided on Printer Support Pack Disc 1 on this printer.*

To set the print style:

1. Position the cursor where you want to change over to a different print style.

2. Press ⌨f3 *to display the Style menu.*

3. Tick or clear the tick beside the different print styles offered in the menu until you have the combination of print styles you require. Then press ⌨ENTER.

LocoScript then inserts the appropriate code (+...) and (-...) codes needed to set the print style you have selected.

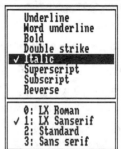

Note: If you tick a style that conflicts with an existing selection, LocoScript will automatically clear the earlier selection. For example, if you tick Superscript, LocoScript automatically clears Subscript. Similarly, if you tick Underline, it will automatically clear Word Underline.

Example: To underline the title of the PCWINFO document:

> The components of your PCW
>
> Your PCW has three obvious components – a Monitor Unit (with the screen and disc drive), a Keyboard and a Printer – but the way to think about it is as a processor, which actually does all the computing (such as working out equations like x=x1+b2), to which are attached a number of electronic

Edit the PCWINFO document, place the cursor at the start of this title line and press the f3 key to display the Style menu. When this menu is displayed, move the cursor Underline and press ⌨ to tick this. Press ⌨ENTER. LocoScript then inserts a (+UL) code at the beginning of the line.

Now move the cursor to the end of the title line and press the f3 key again. Again place the cursor on the entry for Underline but this time press ⌨ to clear the tick beside this. Press ⌨ENTER as before. LocoScript then inserts a (-UL) code at the end of the line.

> (+UL)The components of your PCW(-UL)↵
> ↵
> Your PCW has three obvious components – a Monitor Unit (with the screen and disc drives), a Keyboard and a Printer – but the way to think about it is as a processor, which actually does all the computing (such as working out equations like x=x1+b2), to which are attached a number of electronic

The (+UL) code at the start of the title line turns on full underlining up until the (-UL) code at the end of the line which clears this styling for the remaining text – as you can see on the screen (once the document has been re-laid: see Chapter 3).

Chapter 6: Fonts and print style

6.3 Using quick keystroking to style text

The menus provide a reliable way of inserting the various word-processing codes but they slow down experienced users. So LocoScript also allows you to insert the codes you require by typing special sequences of keystrokes. Once these keystrokes have been learnt, this becomes easily the quickest way of inserting codes.

The quick keystroking uses the PCW's ⊞ and ⊡ keys and the capital letters in the codes themselves as follows:

- *If the code 'turns on' a particular effect, you type* ⊞ *followed by the capital letters in the code.*

- *If the code is used to 'turn off' an effect or to revert to the styling set in the Layout, you type* ⊡ *followed by the capital letters in the code.*

- *If the code includes a specific value, you type* ⊞ *followed by the capital letters in the code as before. Then you type the required value into the single-line menu that appears and press* ENTER *to clear away the menu.*

Note: If you accidentally type the wrong letter while keystroking a code, what to do depends on what happens:

– If your PCW bleeps, just type the letter you meant to type.

– If the wrong code is inserted, press ←DEL and start again.

– If neither of these happen, press ←DEL and type the letter you meant to type.

If you don't know which keys to press

If you don't know which the letters to type for a particular code, press ⊞ *or* ⊡ *as appropriate and then wait. After a short pause, a menu will appear.*

There are two forms of this menu, known as the Set menu (shown when you press ⊞*) and the Clear menu (shown when you press* ⊡*). What they offer is simply an alphabetical list of the codes you might wish to insert (though you may need to scroll the menu to see all the codes that are available). You just need to move the cursor to the one you want, type any value that is required (signalled by ?s in the menu) and press* ENTER *.*

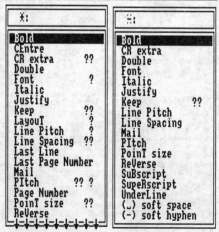

The cursor can be moved to the code you want by pressing the cursor keys. It can also be moved by typing the capital letters in the code name, in which case the menu automatically shrinks to show just the options that fit the letters you have typed so far. This makes it very easy to see when you have typed enough because, at that stage, you will have got down to a menu with just one entry.

LocoScript 3 User Guide

Print Style keystrokes

Style	Code to set	Keystroking	Code to clear	Keystroking
Bold	(+Bold)	⊞B	(-Bold)	⊟B
Italic	(+Italic)	⊞I	(-Italic)	⊟I
Double-strike	(+Double)	⊞D	(-Double)	⊟D
Full underlining	(+UL)	⊞UL	(-UL)	⊟UL
Word underlining	(+Word)	⊞W	(-UL)	⊟UL
Reverse (Screen effect only)				
	(+ReV)	⊞RV	(-ReV)	⊟RV
Superscript	(+SupeR)	⊞SR	(-SupeR)	⊟SR
Subscript	(+SuB)	⊞SB	(-SuB)	⊟SB

Example: Putting the title line of PCWINFO into LX Sanserif

LX Sanserif is Font number 1 in the PCWINFO document, so to get the required result, you want a (+Font1) code selecting LX Sanserif at the start of this line and a (-Font) code returning to the original font (LX Roman) at the end of the line.

```
└────┘.....:.....:.....┐.....4.....:.5▊....:.....6.....:....7.....:....8....L.
      (+Font1)The components of your PCW(-Font)≗
      ↵
      Your PCW has three obvious components ‐ a Monitor Unit (with the screen and
      disc drives), a Keyboard and a Printer ‐ but the way to think about it is
      as a processor, which actually does all the computing (such as working out
      equations like x=x1+b2), to which are attached a number of electronic
      'Devices' whose job is either to supply the processor with information and
      instructions, or to receive information from the processor, or in some
      cases, both. ↵
      ↵
      In the case of your PCW, the processor is housed in the Monitor Unit and
      the devices are a Keyboard, a Screen, a Printer and Disc Drives. Your PCW
      also has a slot on the back known as a 'Port' which can be used to attach
      further devices. For example, we will describing later how you can this
      port to attach another printer to your PCW.↵
```

So the first step is to edit the PCWINFO document, place the cursor at the start of its title line and type ⊞ F (F being the only capital letter in the required code). Then when the one-line menu appears, type 1 (for Font number 1) and press [ENTER] to insert the required (+Font1) code.

Now move the cursor to the end of the title line and type ⊟ F to insert the required (-Font) code.

9308

6.4 Setting the underlying font

Note: This section describes how to set the 'main' font used in a document that is set up for printing on a printer which allows you to use multiple fonts. If you are restricted to one font per document, you should ignore this section and follow the instructions in Section 6.5 instead.

Underlying any section of text is the font set in the Layout. Ideally, this should be the font you want for the majority of the text in that section – firstly because it is automatically selected at the start of the section that uses this Layout, and secondly because it means that you can select this font simply by typing ⌷F to insert a (-Font) code.

To set this font, you simply need to call up the Layout Editor to work on this Layout and then select the font you require in the Layout Editor's version of the f3 Style menu. The following steps are the ones used to set the font in a Layout that is already in your document, such as the one used right at the start of the document – but the only difference in setting the font in a Stock Layout (see Chapter 13) or when you are setting up a new Layout code (see Section 8.3) is in the steps used to call up the Layout Editor, which are given in the appropriate section of this book.

Note: As well as setting the font, you can also make the underlying print style italic rather than upright.

1. Edit the document and place the cursor in the part of the document that is controlled by the Layout you want to change.

2. Press ⌷ *to display the Layout menu, select* Change layout *with the cursor and press* ⌷ENTER⌷ *to go into the Layout Editor.*
The information at the top of the screen shows the current settings of the Layout you picked out to change.

```
 New layout
▶ Change layout
 Layout exchange
 Layout replacement
 Centre
 Right align
 Set justification
```

3. In the Layout Editor, press ⌷ *to display the Style menu and tick the required font. (You can also tick or clear the Italic print style option at the top of the menu if you want.)*

```
      Italic
✓ 0: LX Roman
  1: LX Sanserif
  2: Standard
  3: Sans serif
```

4. Press ⌷ENTER⌷ *to finish with the Style menu.*

5. Make any other changes you require to the Layout and then press ⌷EXIT⌋.

6. Save the document on disc to preserve the changes you have made.

6.5 Changing the fonts used in a document

Changing the fonts used in a document (eg. because you have switched to printing the document on a different printer) is extremely easy. You simply have to replace the old font by the new one in the 'Font table' that forms part of the document's Document Set-up (see Part III). The new font is then automatically substituted for the old one throughout the whole document – thanks to the way LocoScript records the Font number in the document rather than the Font name.

1. Edit the document you want to change, press ⌐f1⌐ *to display the Actions menu and take the* Document setup *option to go into its Document Set-up.*

2. Once you are in Document Set-up, press ⌐f6⌐ *to display the Printing menu.*

3. Check that the correct printer is shown towards the bottom of the menu. If a different printer is shown, place the cursor on the Printer *line of the menu, press* ⌐ENTER⌐, *tick the correct printer in the menu that's shown and then press* ⌐ENTER⌐ *again to return to the main menu.*

4. The upper section of this menu shows the fonts that are currently selected. Move the cursor to a font that you wish to exchange and press ⌐ENTER⌐.

5. When the list of fonts appears, tick the font you wish to use instead and then press ⌐ENTER⌐. *(The line of dashes lets you set this Font number back to the 'No font' state.)*

6. Repeat Steps 4 and 5 to replace other fonts if required.

7. When you have exchanged all the fonts you want, move the cursor to the EXIT *option at the bottom of the menu and press* ⌐ENTER⌐ *to return to Document Set-up.*

8. Finally, press ⌐EXIT⌐ *followed by* ⌐ENTER⌐ *to leave Document Set-up and then save the edited document on disc.*

Setting the font where you are restricted to one font per document

The steps used to set the font used when your printer restricts you to just one font per document are similar to the ones used when you can use many fonts. The only difference is at Steps 4 – 6 where instead of setting a number of fonts, you specify the 'Character Set' and the 'Character Style' that are to be used. On a daisy-wheel printer, the Character Set specifies the family to which the printwheel belongs (characterised by the arrangement of characters on the petals of the wheel) while the Character Style defines the typeface and design pitch of the printwheel that you will be using. On other printers, the Character Set on its own picks out the printer's built-in character set that is to be used: the Character Style setting can be ignored.

Note: Before you can use a new printwheel, you need to record a Character Style for it in your Settings file. The steps to use are given in Appendix V.2.

9308

6.6 Printing documents that use multiple fonts

Printing a document that uses a number of fonts and typesizes is just like printing a document that uses the same font and the same typesize throughout (as described in Chapter 4).

The main difference is in the range of printer files LocoScript calls on in order to print the document – but you won't normally be aware of this because they are simply called up from Drive M as and when they are required. The only time the number of files used may matter is when you are short of space on Drive M. (There's full information on the files needed to print on page 80.)

The other difference is in some of the messages that may be displayed as LocoScript goes through the process of checking the 'Current' printer set-up against the 'Intended' printer set-up recorded in the document. In particular, you may see a message similar to the following:

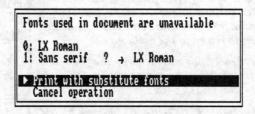

```
Fonts used in document are unavailable

0: LX Roman
1: Sans serif   ?  →  LX Roman

▶ Print with substitute fonts
  Cancel operation
```

If you see this message, it means that one or more of the fonts you have used in your document are not available on Drive M.

The fonts that are missing are the ones marked ? in the list that is shown and the font that LocoScript has picked out to use instead is shown alongside. Either take the 'Print' option to print with this font instead – or take the 'Cancel' option to return to the Disc Manager to sort out why this font is missing (see page 223 in the Troubleshooting section).

Chapter 7

Size, pitch and spacing

An important feature of LocoScript 3 is that you can use different sizes of text in your documents (as long as you use a suitable font). You can also set the spacing of the characters both along the line and from line to line to suit the size of characters you are using and any other requirements you may have.

The results you can achieve can be quite impressive – as you can see from the examples shown on pages 5 and 6 of this User Guide.

The common factor in setting these aspects of your text is the f4 Size menu, which is available both for setting different sizes and spacing within your text and for making these settings within a Layout.

This chapter explains:

- *How to select different sizes and spacings eg. for headings or for individual paragraphs, and*

- *How to set the underlying size and spacing used for your text*

Note: The size of text and the spacings you set in your document will not change the appearance of the text on the screen, except for changing where the line breaks and the page breaks are in your text. Characters shown on the screen don't become any larger (or smaller) and lines of text don't space out on the screen when you increase the line spacing. (Few enough lines of text can be shown on the screen as it is!)

We therefore suggest working with 'Codes shown' so that you can readily see what sizes and spacings you have set in your document. Showing codes is one of the Display options you have while editing a document (see Section 2.2): to select it, you simply have to tick the Codes option in the f8 Options menu. You can also use the Information lines to tell you what sizes and spacings are being used at the current cursor position.

The other point to remember is that all types of styling code are cancelled by any Layout code that follows them in the document. So if you want a particular size or spacing to carry on 'the other side' of a Layout code, you either need to follow the Layout code with a fresh set of codes selecting the size and spacing you want or to set these are part of the Layout (as described in Section 7.4).

7.1 Using different sizes of text

Important: You can only use different sizes of text where the font(s) you are using are available in more than one size. If the printer you use doesn't support LocoScript 3's LX fonts (see Appendix II) and doesn't offer any of its own fonts at multiple sizes, you can ignore both this section and the Point Size setting in the f4 Size menu – though you might find it interesting to read about how LocoScript handles different sizes. Note: If you have a matrix printer, there's an alternative sizing effect you can get by setting different Character Pitches: this is described in Section 7.2.

The size of characters at any point in a document is given by their 'Point Size'. This specifies the height in 'points' – the standard units used by commercial printers. This height is typically measured from the top of a capital letter to the bottom of a letter like p or g, though there is some variation between different typefaces. The capital letters usually occupy about three-quarters of this height. 1 point is ½z", so a Point Size of 12 (or 12pt) means an overall height of '½z" or ⅛" and capital letters around ⅛" high.

Height recorded as the Point Size

LocoScript lets you set Point Sizes between 6pt and 72pt. But it is best to only set sizes that the font you are using is available in because those are the only sizes that can be printed. If you set some other size, LocoScript will lay out your document for the size you've specified but when you come to print the document, it can only insert characters of the nearest size that is available. As it prints, LocoScript will do its best to adjust the spacing on the line for the characters that are actually used but depending on what was specified and what's available, the result can be anything from very short lines or widely spaced words to lines so long that you lose some of the text off the right-hand end. Limiting yourself to the sizes that are actually available will always give the best results.

The main fonts that can be printed at different sizes are LocoScript 3's LX fonts, though some of the fonts built into external printers can also be printed at more than one size. In particular, the 'scalable' Times and Univers fonts on HP LaserJets and compatible printers and the Times and Sans Serif fonts on 'ESC/P2' printers can be printed at different sizes. Other fonts, including the various LocoFont fonts we provide for the PCW matrix printer, for the PcW9512+ Bubblejet printer and for other 'Download' printers, are only available at one size, which is taken to be 10pt.

Setting different sizes

Initially the text in your document will be whatever size is set in the Layout – that is, the overall set of rules that are applied in setting out this text. (We describe how to set the size in the Layout in Section 7.4.) Where you want any section of the text eg. a heading or a footnote to be printed at a different size, you specify this by inserting a 'Point Size' code immediately before each piece of text you want in a different size.

(+PoinT36) *code*

Newbell & Company

(+PoinT14) *code* — Chartered Surveyors and Land Agents

(+PoinT10) *code* ———— 25 High Street, Draperston

(+PoinT8) *code* — Tel: (0125) 776432 Fax: (0125) 774611

Point Size codes generally take the form (+PoinT*n*) where *n* is the size (in points) you want for the following text, though there is also a (-PoinT) code which puts the size back to that set in the Layout. These codes can be inserted either from the f4 Size menu or by using quick keystroking (see Section 6.3). The steps used are given overleaf.

```
0...........1..........2.........3.........4.........5.........6.........7.L......8..
       (CEntre)(+PoinT36)(+Bold)(+Font1)Newbell & Company(-Bold)↵
       (CEntre)(+PoinT14)Chartered Surveyors and Land Agents↵
       (CEntre) (+PoinT10)(-Font)25 High Street, Draperston↵
       (CEntre)(+PoinT8)Tel: (0125) 776432 Fax: (0125) 774611↵
       (-PoinT)↵
       ↵
```

Note: You can set any Point Size between 6 and 36pt in steps of 1pt or between 38 and 72pt in steps of 2pt, but you are strongly advised to set only those Point Sizes you have available in your chosen font. (There is a list of the sizes provided by the supplied LX font files in Appendix II, while you can find out which sizes of text are supported by the other fonts you have by 'inspecting' the identity text of the various .#xx that you use with your printer – see Section 5.7.)

You should also note that the size you set doesn't change the appearance of the text on the screen, though it may well change the line breaks and the page breaks within the text. You may also find that your lines of text appear either very short or very long on the screen, often breaking into the right-hand margin. This is nothing to worry about. It is purely a screen effect brought about by the change in the number of characters that can be fitted along each line of text – as we explain in the next section.

308

Using the Size menu:

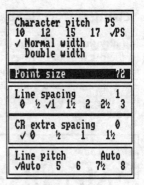

1. Position the cursor where you want to change to a different character size.

2. Press ⌜f4⌟ *to display the Size menu.*

3. Move the cursor to the Point size *line of the menu, type the Point Size you require and press* ⌜ENTER⌟.
Note: If you try to set a Point Size LocoScript doesn't support (eg. 71pt), this will be automatically 'rounded down' to the next smaller valid setting (70pt).

4. Press ⌜ENTER⌟ *again.*

Using quick keystroking:

1. Position the cursor where you want to change to a different character size.

2. Press ⌜⊞⌟, *type* PT *followed by the Point Size you require and press* ⌜ENTER⌟.

Where you want to go back to the Point Size set in the Layout:

1. Position the cursor where you want to go back to the size set in the Layout.

2. Press ⌜⊟⌟ *followed by* PT.

IMPORTANT:

As well as setting the size of characters you want to use, you also need to arrange that there is sufficient space for these characters both along the line of text and from line to line down the page. The way to ensure this is by setting the Character Pitch to PS (see Section 7.2) and the Line Pitch to Auto (see Section 7.3). Setting Character Pitch PS ensures that the characters are correctly spaced along the line of text, while setting Line Pitch Auto ensures that the lines of text are correctly spaced from each other. With other settings of the Character Pitch and the Line Pitch, you could find that the characters overlap each other.

You can make these settings alongside the Point Size in the Size menu but we recommend you to set them in the Layout so that you can be guaranteed that your text is correctly spaced throughout. The steps to use are given in Section 7.4.

7.2 Using different Character Pitches

The Character Pitch defines how the characters are spaced along the line. However if you are using a built-in font on a matrix printer or a font from either the LocoFont, LocoFont 24 or LocoFont BJ sets, you can also look on the Character Pitch as a styling effect because, with these fonts, the characters that are printed are automatically adjusted to suit the spacing you have set (as shown below). In particular, you can use the Character Pitch to produce 'Double width' characters in these fonts. (Where the character shapes don't get adjusted to suit the Character Pitch setting, selecting Double width gives you double-spaced characters.)

Standard effect
Character Pitch PS
Character Pitch 10
Character Pitch 12
Character Pitch 15
Character Pitch 17

With Width Adjustment
Character Pitch PS
Character Pitch 10
Character Pitch 12
Character Pitch 15
Character Pitch 17

Character Pitch PSD
Character Pitch 10D
Character Pitch 12D
Character Pitch 15D
Character Pitch 17D

Characters can either be spaced 'Proportionally' (represented by Character Pitch PS) or at a 'Fixed pitch' (Pitches 10, 12, 15 and 17). When Proportional spacing is used, each character is spaced according to its width: thus narrow characters like i and l take up less space on the line than wide characters such as M and W. When a Fixed pitch spacing is used, the characters are evenly spaced along the line regardless of their shape – at the spacing defined by the Character Pitch setting. For example, a Character Pitch of 10 means a character every ⅒" (giving 10 characters per inch).

In general we recommend setting Character Pitch PS even where the font you are using is described as a 'Fixed pitch font'. Using Character Pitch PS guarantees that the characters are always correctly spaced for their widths: if the font is a Fixed pitch font, you will still get the required Fixed pitch effect because the characters are all the same width.

You should certainly set Character Pitch PS where the font or printwheel is described as 'PS'. Using one of the Fixed Pitches with characters that have been designed for printing proportionally spaced can give pretty horrible results. Character Pitch PS is also practically essential where you are using different sizes of text. In particular, we wouldn't recommend using any of the Fixed Character Pitches with anything larger than 14pt as the characters will almost certainly overlap each other.

The four Fixed pitches are generally used either to give the styling effect described above or to match the Character Pitch to the design pitch of a printwheel.

Setting the Character Pitch

How you set the Character Pitch depends on whether you are using it as a styling effect or as an overall setting. If you want it as styling effect, then you need to insert a 'Pitch' code at each point in the document where you want to go over to using the different Character Pitch. Where you want a particular Character Pitch overall, you can set this through Pitch codes but it is best to set this in the Layout as described in Section 7.4.

Pitch codes generally take the form (+Pitch*n*) where *n* is the pitch you want for the following text, though there is also a (-PItch) code which puts the pitch back to that set in the Layout. These codes can be inserted either from the f4 Size menu or by using quick keystroking (see Section 6.3).

The steps used are given opposite.

Character Pitch and the screen display

The Character Pitch you set can't be shown directly on the screen because this can only show characters at one fixed spacing.

This has two important results. Firstly, it means that characters that appear to be aligned on the screen won't necessarily be aligned when the document is printed – particularly where you have selected proportionally spaced text (Character Pitch PS). If you want particular pieces of text to be aligned, you need to use tabs to align these because you can be certain that you'll get the alignment you want (unless you try to fit too much text between your tab positions). Setting tabs is described in Chapter 8.

Secondly, the Character Pitch you select affects the number of characters you can fit on each line of the document. For example, you can get almost twice as many characters on a line at Character Pitch 17 as you can at Character Pitch 10. If you have set Character Pitch PS, the number of characters you can fit on each line depends on how many thin characters and how many wide characters you've used.

The Ruler line, however, doesn't change with the result that the lines of text on the screen can either look as if they are stopping short of the right margin (where you have used more widely spaced characters) or they can appear to break far into the right margin (where you have used more closely spaced characters). Where you use Character Pitch PS, the lengths of the lines on the screen can vary quite a lot depending on what you have written.

However, this is purely a screen effect and there's no need to worry about it. The text will be correctly laid out when the document is printed.

Using the Size menu:

1. Position the cursor where you want to change Pitch.

2. Press ⌷ to display the Size menu.

3. Either type the Character Pitch you require directly on the top line of this menu (followed by D *if you want Double-width characters) and press* ⌷ENTER⌷*; or tick the spacing and the width you require from among the options shown in the rest of this section of the menu.*

4. Press ⌷ENTER⌷ *again.*

```
┌─────────────────────────────┐
│ Character pitch    PS        │
│   10   12   15   17  √PS     │
│ √ Normal width               │
│   Double width               │
├─────────────────────────────┤
│ Point size              72   │
├─────────────────────────────┤
│ Line spacing           1     │
│  0   ½ √1  1½   2   2½  3     │
├─────────────────────────────┤
│ CR extra spacing       0     │
│ √ 0    ½   1    1½            │
├─────────────────────────────┤
│ Line pitch          Auto     │
│ √Auto  5   6   7½   8         │
└─────────────────────────────┘
```

Using quick keystroking:

1. Position the cursor where you want to change Pitch.

2. Press ⊞ and type P. *Then type Character Pitch you require (followed by* D *if you want Double-width characters) and press* ⌷ENTER⌷.

Where you want to go back to using the Pitch set in the Layout:

1. Position the cursor where you want to go back to this Character Pitch.

2. Press ⊟ followed by PI.

7.3 Setting the spacing from line to line

The spacing from one line to the next down the page has three components: the Line Pitch, the Line Spacing, and, if the line ends in a ↵, the CR Extra Spacing.

The Line Pitch

The Line Pitch sets the fundamental spacing for lines of text down the page.

There are five possible settings for the Line Pitch: 5, 6, 7½, 8 and Auto. The first four settings each set a fixed spacing for the lines: 5mm apart, 6 lines per inch (ie. lines ⅙" apart), 7½ lines per inch and 8 lines per inch, respectively. The 'Auto' option can be thought of as the Line Pitch equivalent of Character Pitch PS. It sets the Line Pitch used for any line to approximately 20% larger than the largest Point Size selected on the line (the spacing recommended by typesetting experts). For example, if a line contains 20pt text, the Auto setting will make the Line Pitch 20% larger than this ie. 24pt which is ⅓" or 3 lines per inch.

This is some
12pt text printed
at Line Pitch 6

This is some
12pt text printed
at Line Pitch 8

This is some
12pt text printed
at Line Pitch Auto

9308

The 'fixed' Line Pitches allow you to set a specific spacing for your lines and they also allow you to match the Line Pitch set in your document to the Line Pitch your printer works in. But if you are using different sizes of text, we would strongly recommend setting Line Pitch Auto because it guarantees that your text will be suitably spaced, whatever Point Sizes you choose to use. We don't guarantee good results if you set a spacing that's smaller than the characters you are trying to print! Indeed, setting Line Pitch Auto may be the only way that you can ensure that there's sufficient space for tall characters at the top of a page.

Note: If you use Line Pitch Auto with 10pt text (the nominal size of fonts that are only available in one size), the Line Pitch this sets is 12pt or ⅙" – otherwise known as the 6 lines per inch that you have probably always used for text of that size.

Line Spacing

The Line Spacing setting is just like the Line Spacing setting on a typewriter: it sets the number of lines of the current Line Pitch (see above) that the paper is advanced between printing one line and printing the next.

LocoScript offers a range of possible Line Spacings – 0, ½, 1, 1½, 2, 2½ and 3. There is nothing to stop you setting any of these but as on a typewriter, the main choice will be between Line Spacing 1 which gives you a single-spaced document with text printed on every line, and Line Spacing 2 which gives you a double-spaced document with text printed on every line. Line Spacing 0 and Line Spacing ½ allow you to produce special effects, for example by printing one line on top of another (see the example on page 131).

Line Spacing 1
A Line Spacing of 1 gives you text on every line. This is the Line Spacing to use for finished documents.

Line Spacing 2
Use Line Spacing 2 for draft copies –

to give you room to mark changes.

The CR Extra Spacing

The CR Extra Spacing sets a number of *extra* lines of the current Line Pitch (over and above the current Line Spacing) for the paper to be advanced after a line that finishes in a carriage return.

The main purpose of the CR Extra Spacing is to give you a fixed amount of space between paragraphs. For example, a CR Extra Spacing of ½ gives you a half-line space between paragraphs. But you might also use it to give yourself more (or less) space around headings within your document.

CR Extra Spacing 0
This is text with a Line Spacing of 1 and a CR Extra Spacing of 0.
As you see, the paragraphs follow on without any break.

CR Extra Spacing ½
This is text with a Line Spacing of 1 and a CR Extra Spacing of ½.

This time you do see a break between the paragraphs.

9308

Setting the spacing

In general, we recommend setting any of these spacings in the Layout (see Section 7.4) rather than directly within the document – particularly the Line Pitch.

But you may also want to set a different spacing for individual lines or for a group of lines in order to produce special effects. Such changes are made by inserting (+LSpace*n*) Line Spacing codes, (+CR*n*) CR Extra codes and if necessary, (+LPitch*n*) Line Pitch codes on the line above the gap you want to affect. These codes can be inserted either using the f4 Size menu or by quick keystroking (see Section 6.3). The steps are given below.

Using the Size menu:

1. Position the cursor on the line above the gap you want to affect.
Anywhere on this line will do, but the best place is usually at the end of the line.

2. Press ⌑f4⌑ *to display the Size menu.*
The three settings that you might want to change are covered by the bottom three sections of this menu.

3. Move the cursor to the relevant section of the menu and either type the spacing you require followed by ⌑ENTER⌑ *on the top line of this section or tick the spacing you want from among the options given below.*

4. Press ⌑ENTER⌑ *again.*

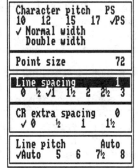

Using quick keystroking:

1. Position the cursor where you want to change the spacing.

2. Type the keystroking given in the table below.

	To set a specific value	*To return to the value set in the Layout*
Line Spacing:	⊞LS*n* ⌑ENTER⌑	⊟LS
CR Extra Spacing:	⊞CR*n* ⌑ENTER⌑	⊟CR
Line Pitch:	⊞LP*n* ⌑ENTER⌑	⊟LP

9308

7.4 Setting the underlying size, pitch and spacing

In the absence of any codes, the size, pitch and spacing used for your text are the ones recorded in the Layout.

Ideally, the size, pitch and spacing recorded in the Layout should be the ones that you want for the majority of the text in that section. There are two main advantages to this. Firstly, it means these are automatically selected for you at the start of the section that uses this Layout. Secondly, it means that if you change to a different size or spacing, you can return to the setting you want in the main simply by typing ⌷ followed by PT, PI, LS, CR or LP as appropriate.

The following steps may be used to set any of these aspects of a Layout already in the document – such as that used at the start of the document or for headers and footers. The steps used to set the size, pitch and spacing in a Stock Layout (see Chapter 13) or when you are preparing a new Layout code to insert (see Section 8.3) are much the same. The only difference is in the steps used to call up the Layout Editor, details of which are given in the appropriate section of this book.

The menu used within the Layout Editor is again the f4 Size menu.

To set the underlying size, pitch and spacing:

1. Edit the document and place the cursor in the part of the document that is controlled by the Layout you want to change.

2. Press ⌷f2⌷ *to display the Layout menu, select* Change layout *with the cursor and press* ⌷ENTER⌷ *to go into the Layout Editor.*

3. In the Layout Editor, press ⌷f4⌷ *to display the Size menu and make the required settings as described in the preceding sections (Sections 7.1 – 7.3).*

4. Press ⌷ENTER⌷ *to finish with the Size menu.*

5. Make any other changes you require to the Layout, then press ⌷EXIT⌋.

6. Save the document on disc to preserve the changes you've made.

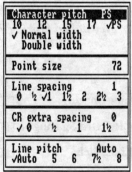

Using pitch and spacing in laying out an equation

Including an equation in a document, even one as simple as $y^2 = x_a^2 + x_b^2$, presents a bit of a problem because you can't normally have a superscript and a subscript at the same point on a line.

However with LocoScript, there's a straightforward solution. You just have to type the xs, ys and superscripts on one line and the subscripts (along with suitable spaces) on the next, and set the line spacing between them to 0 so that the second line is printed on top of the first – as follows. The only restriction is that you have to be using one of the 'Fixed' character pitches for the whole of the line containing the equation: the technique doesn't work if you are using proportionally-spaced characters (Character Pitch PS).

The first thing to insert is a Pitch code at the beginning of the equation (if not before) which selects a suitable Fixed Character Pitch. For example, if you opt for Pitch 12, you would type ⊞P12 ENTER .

Then you type the xs, ys and superscripts as follows:

y⊞SR2⊟SR=x⊞SR2⊟SR+x⊞SR2⊟SR

Finally on this line, you want the codes that tell the printer not to advance the paper between printing this line and the next – (+LSpace0) and (+CR0). Enter these by typing ⊞LS0 ENTER ⊞CR0 ENTER – then press RETURN to start the next line.

(⁺PItch12)y(⁺SupeR)2(⁻SupeR)=x(⁺SupeR)2(⁻SupeR)+x(⁺SupeR)2(⁻SupeR)(⁺LSpace0)(⁺CR0)↵

You now type the line for the subscripts as follows:

(four spaces)⊞SBa⊟SB*(two spaces)*⊞SBb⊟SB

Then, to follow this, you need the codes that tell LocoScript to go back to using its normal Character Pitch, Line Spacing and CR Extra Spacing – (-PItch), (-LSpace) and (-CR). Enter these by typing ⊟PI⊟LS ⊟CR – and finally press RETURN to move on to the next line.

....(⁺SuB)a(⁻SuB)..(⁺SuB)b(⁻SuB)(⁻PItch)(⁻LSpace)(⁻CR)↵

In all, this gives you:

(⁺PItch12)y(⁺SupeR)2(⁻SupeR)=x(⁺SupeR)2(⁻SupeR)+x(⁺SupeR)2(⁻SupeR)(⁺LSpace0)(⁺CR0)↵
....(⁺SuB)a(⁻SuB)..(⁺SuB)b(⁻SuB)(⁻PItch)(⁻LSpace)(⁻CR)↵

308

Margins, tabs and tables

In many cases, you will be quite happy to work with the default margins that LocoScript automatically gives you when you create a document: they are, after all, a very sensible 1" from either edge of a sheet of A4.

However, there is no need to keep these margins and in this chapter, we show you:

- *How to set the margins you want both for the whole document and for individual paragraphs*

- *How to set up any tabs you need in order to indent paragraphs or to set up tables of information.*

Both margins and tabs can be set up – and changed – at any time while you are editing the document.

The margins and tabs used at any point in a document are defined by the 'Layout' of that part of the document, so we start with an introduction to LocoScript's Layouts.

8.1 The key concept – Layout

Associated with every part of a document is a 'Layout' which tells LocoScript how the text should be laid out.

As described in the two previous chapters, this Layout defines the initial values for the Font, Point Size, Character Pitch, Line Pitch, Line Spacing and CR Extra Spacing used in the section of the text that has this Layout – and the ones that you return to using codes such as (-Font), (-PItch) and (-LSpace).

It also defines:

- the position of the left and right margins
- the position and the type of any tabs
- the scale of the markings on the Ruler line and the character that's recognised as the decimal point character

which are the aspects of the Layout that concern us in this chapter.

To start with, every document has two Layouts – one ready to be used for any Headers and Footers you set up (see Chapter 11), and the other ready to be used for the main text. But you can also introduce further Layouts into the main body of the document wherever you need a radical change of Layout – for example, a change of margin or a new set of tabs. Using additional Layouts is described in Section 8.3 where we look at how to include a table of information in your document.

Chapter 8: Margins & Tabs

8.2 Changing the 'main' Layout

In this section, we describe how to change the Layout that LocoScript gives you at the start of the document to give you the margins, tabs etc. that you want. If your document doesn't include any additional Layouts (as described in Section 8.3), these will be the margins and tabs used throughout the document.

Note: We strongly recommend showing codes (as described in Section 2.2) before starting work on a Layout so that any Layout codes in the document are clearly visible. Do this even if the document uses the same Layout throughout because you could find, for example, that you have a Layout code right at the beginning of your document. To get the results you require here, you will need to place the cursor after this Layout code (– or better, delete the Layout code though you will probably then have further settings to make within the Layout.)

8.2.1 Calling up the Layout Editor

The first step is to call up the Layout Editor to work on the Layout set at the start of the document. To do this:

1. If your document uses any additional Layouts, position the cursor between the start of the document and the first Layout code in the document.

If your document doesn't include any Layout codes, the position of the cursor doesn't matter.

2. Press ⌐f2⌐ *to display the Layout menu, move the cursor to* Change layout *and press* ⌐ENTER⌐.

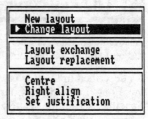

You are then put into the Layout Editor, with the Information lines showing the details of the Layout that's in force at the position of the cursor (which in this case should be the one set at the start of the document). The Ruler line shows the margins and tabs that are currently set in this Layout.

Details of the Layout   Ruler line for the Layout

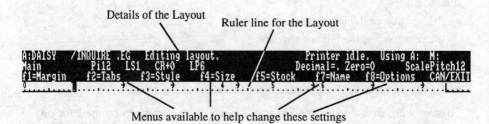

Menus available to help change these settings

The rest of the screen still shows your document – but you can't change any of the text while you are using the Layout Editor.

9308

8.2.2 Setting the margins

The steps used to change the position of either margin are very simple. You just:

1. Position the Ruler cursor at the new position you require for the margin (using the Cursor keys).

2. Press ⌐f1⌐ *to display the Margins menu, place the cursor on* Set Left Margin *or* Set Right Margin *as appropriate and press* ⌐ENTER⌐.

Alternatively, place the cursor at the margin you want to move (eg. by pressing the Space bar) and then use the ⊞ *and* ⊟ *keys to move this margin stepwise to its new position. Pressing* ⊞ *moves the margin one position to the right along the Ruler line; pressing* ⊟ *moves the margin one position to the left.*

The more difficult part of setting the margins is in deciding where you want the margins to be. If you simply want the margins to be a little wider or a little narrower than they currently are, it may be enough simply to move the margins a few places to the right or to the left as required. But if you want the margins a precise distance from the edge of the paper, you have to work out where on the Ruler line you need to place the margins to get the result you require. The key to this is the Scale Pitch that is being used – because the marks on the Ruler line count characters spaced at the Scale Pitch. For example, if the Scale Pitch is 12, each mark on the Ruler line represents one 12-pitch character ie. ½".

The zero position on the Ruler line corresponds to the left-hand edge of the page, so to convert the position you want for a margin into a position on the Ruler line, you need to measure the distance of the margin from the left-hand edge of the paper in inches and then multiply it by the Scale Pitch. For example, if you want to set the left-hand margin 1¼" from the side of the paper and the Scale Pitch is 12, you multiply 1¼ by 12 which gives 15: you therefore need to set the Left margin at character position 15 on the Ruler line. Similarly, if the position you wanted the right-hand margin turned out to be 6⅔" from the left-hand edge of the paper, you would multiply 6⅔ by 12 and set the Right margin at character position 80.

Changing the Scale Pitch

You will get the best impression of your document's layout on the screen if you set the Scale Pitch to match the (average) pitch of the text. You can change Scale Pitch for a particular Layout to a different Character Pitch in the f8 Options menu in the Layout Editor but before you do this, you should note that:

(i) All the Layouts in a document need to use the same Scale Pitch: otherwise you will find it difficult to align margins and tabs between the different Layouts.

(ii) After changing the Scale Pitch, you will need to re-adjust your margins and tabs: LocoScript does not automatically adjust these for you. A right-hand margin at character position 84, for instance, will leap from 7" from the left-hand edge to 8.4" if you change the Scale Pitch from 12 to 10!

(**Note:** Setting the Scale Pitch to PS is identical in effect to setting the Scale Pitch to 12.)

9308

8.2.3 Setting and clearing tabs

Tabs are markers that tell LocoScript where you want pieces of text directly under one another, for example in a table. They provide a very much better way of aligning text than typing spaces – particularly if you use proportionally spaced characters, because then what appears aligned on the screen won't necessarily be aligned when you come to print your document.

There are a number of different types of tab – Simple tabs, Right tabs, Centre tabs and Decimal tabs, each with their own way of aligning text.

For the most part, you will just want 'Simple' tabs. A Simple tab is the sort of tab you get on a typewriter – ie. one that sets the position of the first letter you type after pressing TAB. It is also the type of tab you need for such things as indenting the first line of a paragraph or indenting the whole of a paragraph.

(The other types of tab are mainly for use in tables and are therefore described in Section 8.3.2 which looks at setting up a Layout specifically for a table.)

LocoScript offers a range of possible actions from setting and clearing individual tabs to setting and clearing a whole group of tabs. The steps used in each case are given below.

Note: As with the margins, if you want tabs at particular positions across the page, you will need to work out the corresponding positions on the Ruler line by measuring these positions in inches from the left-hand side of the page and multiplying by the Scale Pitch. See Section 8.2.2 above.

To set a tab:

1. Position the Ruler cursor where you want to set the tab (using the Cursor keys).

2. Press f2 *to display the Tabs menu, place the cursor on the* Set Tab *option for the type of tab you require and press* ENTER *.*

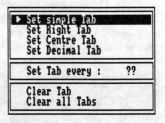

– or alternatively, press ⊞ *once to set a Simple tab at the current cursor position – or more than once to set one of the other types of tab (see Section 8.3.2). Pressing* ⊞ *cycles through the different types of tab in the order: Simple; Right; Centre; Decimal.*

For example, to set a Simple tab at character position 20, move the Ruler cursor to position 20 and press ⊞.

> **Note:** You can't set more than 15 tabs in the initial Layout of a document. If you need more than this, you will need to set up one of the 'alternative' Layouts described in Section 8.3.

To set a series of Simple tabs equally spaced along the Ruler line:

1. Position the cursor where you want the series of Simple tabs to start.
For example, if you want them to be spaced at equal intervals from the left-hand margin, position the cursor at the Left margin.

2. Press [f2] *to display the Tabs menu.*

3. Move the cursor to Set Tab every, *type the distance you want between the tabs (in characters of the current Scale Pitch) and press* [ENTER].
For example, to set tabs every 8 characters across the page, type 8 and press [ENTER].

4. If you want a tab at the cursor position as well, press [+] *to set this.*

To clear one tab:

1. Move the Ruler cursor to the tab you want to clear (eg. by pressing [TAB] *which moves the cursor directly to the next Tab position).*

2. Then press [f2] *to display the Tabs menu, move the cursor to* Clear Tab *and press* [ENTER].

– or alternatively, press [−] *to clear the tab under the cursor.*

To clear all the tabs on the current Ruler line:

• *Press* [f2] *to display the Tabs menu, select* Clear all Tabs *an ' press* [ENTER].

To move a tab:

1. Clear the tab at the current position (as described above).

2. Set a new tab at the new position (also as described above).

8.2.4 Returning to the document

When you are happy with the Layout, press [EXIT] to return to the document.

Your new margins and tabs should be clearly visible on the Ruler line but you will probably need to move the cursor down the document to see their effect on your text.

The part of the document up to the position of the cursor will have been re-laid to take account of the new margins and tabs (following LocoScript's standard rule that your document is correctly laid out up to your current working position: see Section 3.3), but everything beyond the cursor will still have its old Layout.

9308

8.3 Setting up additional Layouts eg. for tables

Documents that use the same set of margins and tabs throughout can be laid out perfectly well using just the Layout set at the start of the document and word-processing codes to introduce the changes of font etc. that are required.

But if your document needs different margins or different tabs anywhere in the document (for example, for tables or for paragraphs that you want to indent from both the left and the right margins), you need to introduce a couple of 'new' Layouts into the document – one where you want to go over to using the new margins and tabs, and another where you either go back to using the original set of margins and tabs or go on to use yet another set.

These additional Layouts take the form of 'Layout codes' holding the details of the Layout that you want to use, displayed on the screen as (LayouT).

Note: You may, of course, introduce additional Layouts into your documents for other reasons than simply changing the margins and tabs. Indeed, the easiest way to achieve consistency of style across a number of different documents is by using specific Layouts for such things as Headings and Notes, as we explain in Chapter 13. It is just that you *have* to use additional Layouts when you want to change the margins or the tabs: there are no Margin or Tab codes that you could use instead.

8.3.1 Introducing a new Layout

1. Place the cursor where you want to start using the new Layout.

2. Press ⌨︎f2 to display the Layout menu, check the cursor is on New layout *and press ⌐ENTER⌐.*

LocoScript then puts you into the Layout Editor so that you can set up the details of the new Layout. This starts as a copy of the Layout at this point – on the grounds that you probably only want to change one or two aspects of the Layout.

3. Make whatever changes you require to the details of the new Layout.
The steps used are exactly the same as those used to set any aspect of the main Layout. The only difference is that you can set up to 30 tabs in this Layout.

4. Use the f7 Name menu to set a name for the Layout.
This name can be up to 12 characters long and it will be shown on the Information lines while you are working in the part of the document controlled by this Layout. Not every character you can type can be used in this name – for example, you can't use symbols or Cyrillic characters – but you can use Greeks and some accented letters. (A full list of the characters you can use is given in Appendix III.)

5. Press ⌐EXIT⌐ to leave the Layout Editor. LocoScript then inserts a Layout code containing the details of the Layout you have set up, together with a ↵ because the margins and tabs of the Layout only come into force on the next line.

Important: Every time you change to using a different Layout, LocoScript starts afresh on all its special settings. The character size becomes the one set in the Layout, the Line Spacing becomes the one set in the Layout etc. etc. LocoScript also clears all the print styles like Bold, Italic and Underline – so if you want these to continue into the new Layout, you must follow the (LayouT) *code with the appropriate codes to 'turn on' the print styles you want.*

8.3.2 Example: Adding a table to the INQUIRE.EG document

Suppose you wanted to add the following table between the second and third paragraphs of the example document TABS.EG.

Description	Part No	Unit price	Number	
Wall Unit	WU321	@ £24.80	3	74.40
Mounting brackets	MB326	@ £6	4	24
Attachments	AT328A	@ £0.99	1 set	.99
Total				£99.39

1. Insert the Layout code that will restore the original Layout

(The reason for doing this first is that it is easy to set up at this point – thanks to the way LocoScript initially sets up the new Layout as a copy of the Layout that is currently in place.)

To set up this code, place the cursor at the start of the third paragraph, press ⌐f2⌐ to display the Layout menu, check that New layout is highlighted and press ⌐ENTER⌐.

When the Layout Editor is displayed, simply press ⌐EXIT⌐ to insert a Layout code containing a copy of the current Layout. (If you can't see this code, call up the f8 Options menu and tick the Codes option.)

```
→ For example, if you were to choose the Swedish style of finish, the
total cost would come to just £99.39 ⊣ made up as follows:↵
↵
(LayouT)↵
```

2. Set up the Layout required for the table

Move the cursor to the blank line above the code you have just inserted. Then press ⌐f2⌐ followed by ⌐ENTER⌐ to call up the Layout Editor to set the tabs needed for the table that is to be inserted.

Setting the tabs

The columns of this table need to be lined up in different ways. The first two columns want the left-hand end of each entry to be aligned. The third column wants the right-hand ends of the entries to be aligned. The fourth column wants the entries to be centred. In the last column, it's the decimal points that are to be aligned.

9308

LocoScript has a different type of tab for each of these cases.

- To align the left-hand ends, use a Simple tab →
- To line up the right-hand ends, use a Right tab ←
- To centre the entries over each other, use a Centre tab ↔
- To line up the decimal points, use a Decimal tab •

The Layout for the example table might therefore need a Simple tab at position 30, a Right tab at position 50, a Centre tab at position 60 and a Decimal tab at position 75. (You don't need a Simple tab for the first column because this column starts at the left margin and so will automatically be aligned along its left-hand edge.)

Start calling up the Tabs menu and taking Clear all tabs to clear away the current tabs from this Layout. Then insert the new tabs as follows:

- Move the Ruler cursor to position 30, and press ⊞ once.
- Move the Ruler cursor to position 50, and press ⊞ twice.
- Move the Ruler cursor to position 60, and press ⊞ three times.
- Move the Ruler cursor to position 75, and press ⊞ four times.

Remember how pressing ⊞ cycles through the different types of tab. You simply need to keep pressing ⊞ until the appropriate tab symbol is shown.

Setting the Layout name

As well as setting these tabs, you need to give the new Layout a name such as Table so that you can readily see from the Information lines when you are working in the area that is controlled this Layout.

`Name:     Main`   To set this name, press ⟨f7⟩ to display the Name menu, press ⟨-⟩ to clear away the current name (copied from the original Layout along with the other details), type the new name and press ⟨ENTER⟩.

Finally press ⟨EXIT⟩ to return to the document. Again LocoScript inserts a (LayouT) code and a ↵

3. Typing in the table

Once you have inserted the Layout code, you just need to type the entries in this table as follows:

Description⟨TAB⟩Part No⟨TAB⟩Unit price⟨TAB⟩Number⟨RETURN⟩
Wall Unit⟨TAB⟩WU321⟨TAB⟩@ £24.80⟨TAB⟩3⟨TAB⟩74.40⟨RETURN⟩ etc.

In other words, type each entry quite normally, then move on to the next column by pressing ⟨TAB⟩ and type the next entry. You don't need to do anything difficult like typing the right number of spaces as you might well have to do on a typewriter!

As you type Unit price (and other entries in the column controlled by the Right Tab), you should see each new character type pushing the previous ones to the left. LocoScript shuffles the characters in this way to ensure that all the entries end in the same place.

As you type Number (and other entries in the column controlled by the Centre Tab), you should see a similar but different action. To get the required centring, every other character you type shuffles the previous ones to the left.

As you type the final column of numbers (74.40, 24 etc.), the characters are again shuffled to the left – but only until you type the decimal point. Any characters you type after this character are positioned normally. This is how LocoScript ensures that the decimal points in the entries are aligned.

Note: Layouts are normally set up for decimal numbers like 35.20 where the character to align in a column of decimal numbers is full stop. If you want to align decimal numbers written in the Continental style (for example, 35,20), call up the Layout Editor as described in the next section, press ⬚ to display the Options menu and tick the option that offers comma as the decimal marker.

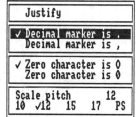

8.3.3 Changing the Layout defined by a Layout code

The steps used to change one of these additional Layouts are just like those used to change the 'main' Layout (see Section 8.2). The only difference is that once you have inserted Layout codes into your document, the position of the cursor is vital because this selects the Layout that you work on.

You therefore need to place the cursor in the part of the document that uses the Layout you want to change; then press ⬚ and take the Change layout option.

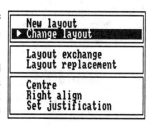

When you have made the changes you want, press ⬚ to return to the document. There will then usually be a slight pause as LocoScript updates the Layout code in the document and then relays the document up to the cursor.

8.3.3 Using the same Layout elsewhere in the document

Once you have set up a new Layout, you can readily use the same Layout again either elsewhere in the same document or in another document by copying the Layout code to a Block and then pasting this Block wherever it is required – exactly as if it were text (see Section 3.4).

For example, suppose you wanted to insert a similar table between the first and second paragraphs of the example document. You would save yourself the trouble of setting up all those tabs again by copying the (LayouT) code that sets these tabs to a Block and then pasting this Block in between the first and second paragraphs.

Note: As well as inserting a copy of the (LayouT) code that sets the details of the Layout, you will also need to insert a copy of the code that restores the original Layout so that the following text is laid out correctly once again.

8.4 Displaying the different Layouts

You can always get a rough idea of the different margin and tab positions used in a document by looking at the way the text is laid out on the screen. LocoScript gives as faithful a representation as possible on the screen.

However, there are also ways of seeing the margins and tabs you are using are in more detail.

Firstly, you can use the Ruler line. This always displays the margins and tabs at the cursor. So you can see what margins and tabs are in force where you are working simply by looking at the Ruler line.

The alternative is to tick the Rulers option in the f8 Options menu. When this option is ticked, LocoScript displays an extra Ruler line below each Layout code. These extra Ruler lines let you see the pattern of margins and tabs anywhere in the document – not just at the place you are working.

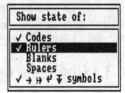

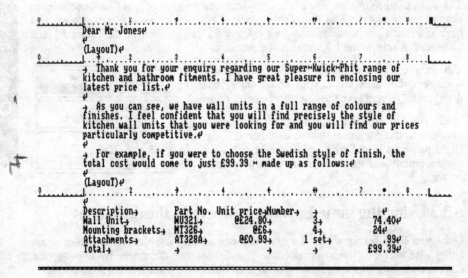

Note: These extra Ruler lines are for display only. You can't edit them.

Chapter 9

Indenting, centring and justifying

Text is normally laid out so that each line starts at the Left margin and finishes either at or just short of the Right margin, depending on the length of the words being used. This gives your text a straight left edge but a ragged right edge.

This chapter looks how you can vary this simple pattern by:

- *indenting lines and paragraphs*
- *positioning headings and other single lines centrally or over to the right*
- *justifying text – that is, giving it a straight right-hand edge as well as a straight left-hand edge*

The examples used here are taken from the TABS.EG document on the LocoScript 3 Examples disc, so if you want to try out any of the techniques we describe, open this document for editing.

9.1 Indenting lines and paragraphs

There are three effects that you can produce through indenting – ie. through moving the lefthand edge of a line or paragraph away from the left margin of your page:

- paragraphs with the first line indented
- paragraphs in which all the lines are indented from the left margin
- 'labelled' paragraphs – for example, paragraphs numbered 1), 2), 3)

9.1.1 Indenting the first line

This is the simplest way of indenting a paragraph.

The main thing you need is a 'Simple tab' on the Ruler line marking the place where you want the first lines of your paragraphs to start. The steps used to set this in the Layout are given in Section 8.2.

Note: The tab on the Ruler line must be a Simple tab for this to work correctly.

Once the required tab position has been set, you just need to start each paragraph by pressing the [TAB] key to insert a tab (shown on the screen as →). The cursor immediately moves to the first tab position marked on the Ruler line to show that the text you type next will be inserted at this indented position. If this doesn't give the indent you require, simply press [TAB] again.

[TAB] *key*

(If the text of the paragraph has already been entered in the document, just position the cursor at the start of the paragraph and press `TAB` to insert a tab. Initially this tab is shown above the current line (because it is being inserted at the start of a line) but when you press `RELAY`, the paragraph will be relaid with all the characters on the first line shifted to the right.)

```
0.........|....:|....?....?....?.........4.........5.........6.........7.........8....|....
         Advantages of a Word Processor⏎
         ⏎
       → There are lots of other jobs that you will want your word-processor to
       help you with. If you are a Secretary of a club, then you will want your
       word-processor to help you circulate details of forthcoming events or
       copies of the club newsletter to members. Or if you are preparing a report
       on something, then you will probably have one or more tables to prepare. Or
```

9.1.2 Indenting the whole paragraph

Once again, the main thing you need is a tab on the Ruler line marking the place you want the lines of your paragraph to start. This tab will normally be a Simple tab but it can, in fact, be any type of tab. Set this as described in Section 8.2.

Once the tab position has been set, you just need to start the paragraph with an 'Indent tab' which you type by holding down `ALT` as you press `TAB`. This type of tab is shown on the screen as ↦.

To see the effect of Indent tabs have, move the cursor to the beginning of the second paragraph in the example TABS.EG document, hold down `ALT` and press `TAB`. Immediately, an ↦ is inserted above the rest of the paragraph.

Press `PAGE` to force LocoScript to relay the document down to the bottom of the page and you will see that the effect of this Indent tab has been to move the beginning of every line of this paragraph (but only this paragraph) to the first tab position set on the Ruler line.

```
       you might have some sales literature to prepare, which you want to lay out
       and style really nicely. ⏎
       ⏎
     ↦   With LocoScript 3, there's essentially endless scope for revising and
         styling your text - so much so that you might get so carried away with
         producing the perfect document that you never actually get around to
         printing it! ⏎
       ⏎
       Moreover, because you can save your work on disc any time you like:⏎
```

The overall rule is that whichever tab position an Indent tab 'points to' is used as the left-hand margin for the rest of the paragraph. This means that you can pick out any of your current set of tab positions as the temporary left-hand margin. The last tab you type to take the start of the paragraph to your chosen indent position must be an Indent tab but the rest can be either Indent tabs or normal tabs.

9308

9.1.3 'Labelled' paragraphs

This looks the most complex type of indenting but it is actually no more complicated than indenting the whole paragraph. Again, the main thing you need is a tab on the Ruler line where you want the text of the paragraphs to start (see Section 8.2).

Once you have the tab position set, all you need to do is to insert an Indent tab between the 'label' and the main part of the paragraph.

For example, to lay out any of the numbered paragraphs of the example TABS.EG document in this way, move the cursor to the beginning of the text that follows the 'label' – eg. the 1), delete the space that is currently separating the label from the text, and press ⌷ALT⌷ ⌷TAB⌷. Press ⌷RELAY⌷ and you will see that the rest of the paragraph is then indented to this tab position.

```
Moreover, because you can save your work on disc any time you like:↵
↵
1)↦ You can start and stop work on a document at will; you don't have to
    finish somewhere that is easy to carry on from – like the bottom of a
    page – as on a typewriter.↵
↵
```

Once again, you are using the tab position the Indent tab points to as the left-hand margin for the rest of the paragraph.

9.2 Positioning single lines

Lines are normally positioned so that they start at the left side of your page. By inserting suitable codes, you can also:

– centre a line between the margins

– right align a line, ie. put the right-hand end of the line on the right margin (instead of the left-hand end on the left margin)

– combine a section over to the left, a section in the middle and a section over to the right on the same line.

Note: Once you have told LocoScript to centre or to align some text or, for that matter, to indent a paragraph, it remembers this – whatever changes you make to the line. This is by no means true of all the word-processors you might meet.

9.2.1 Centring a line

To centre a line:

1. Position the cursor at the start of the line.

2. Then either: type ⌷⊞⌷CE

or: Press ⌷f2⌷ *to display the Layout menu, move the cursor to the* Centre *option and press* ⌷ENTER⌷.

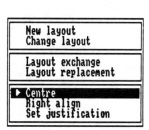

This inserts a (CEntre) code at the beginning of the line (which you can see if you tick the Codes option in the f8 menu) and the whole line is instantly moved right until it is neatly positioned midway between the margins.

For example, to centre the first line of the TABS.EG document, move the cursor to the start of this heading – ie. to the A of Advantages of a Word Processor. Press [f2] to bring the Layout menu onto the screen, move the cursor to Centre and press [ENTER].

```
0·········|····?···?···?···?█·········4·········5·········6·········7·········8···L····
                           Advantages of a Word Processor↵
     ↵
     →    There are lots of other jobs that you will want your word-processor to
     help you with. If you are a Secretary of a club, then you will want your
     word-processor to help you circulate details of forthcoming events or
     copies of the club newsletter to members. Or if you are preparing a report
```

Note: Each (CEntre) *code only affects the line it is on. If you want to centre a whole paragraph, you will need to split this paragraph into individual lines (each ending with a carriage return) and insert a* (CEntre) *code at the beginning of each line.*

9.2.2 Moving a line over to the right

Moving a line over to the right is very like centring it. To move a line to the right:

1. Position the cursor at the start of the line.

2. Then either: type [⊞]RA

or: Press [f2] *to display the Layout menu, move the cursor to the* Right align *option and press* [ENTER].

This inserts an (RAlign) code at the beginning of the line and the whole line is instantly moved right so that the right-hand end of the line is at the Right margin.

For example, to right align the name Fred Smith at the end of TABS.EG, move the cursor to the F of Fred, press [f2] to display the Layout menu, move the cursor to Right align and press [ENTER]. The name then jumps to the right-hand side of the screen. Notice how the h of Smith now touches the right margin.

Note: (RAlign) *codes, like* (CEntre) *codes, only affect the line they are on. If you want to right align a whole paragraph, you will need to split this paragraph into individual lines (each ending with a carriage return) and insert a* (RAlign) *code at the beginning of each line.*

9308

9.2.3 Positioning different parts of the same line

As well as centring and right aligning whole lines, you can centre and right align sections of a line, giving you effects like:

Author   Title   Cost

All you have to do is insert a (CEntre) code immediately before the section of the line you want in the middle of the page and an (RAlign) code immediately before the section you want over to the right – ie.

Author(CEntre)   Title(RAlign)   Cost

You can similarly split lines into a section over to the left and a section over to the right – or a section over to the left and a centred section. What won't give sensible results is telling LocoScript to move a section of a line over to the right and then telling it to centre part of that section because this is meaningless.

9.3 Justifying text

When text is justified, the spaces between the words are automatically expanded so that the text has a straight right-hand edge as well as a straight left-hand edge. This instantly makes the text look very professional – not least because it is impossible to do on a typewriter.

Justified text

Justified text has both a straight right-hand edge and a straight left-hand edge. The majority of the text in this user guide is justified.

Unjustified text

Unjustified text is text with a ragged right-hand edge. At the moment, all the text in the example document has a ragged right-hand edge.

The initial state of the text (justified or unjustified) is set in the Layout controlling that text. You can then use additional Justification codes to make local changes to the justification.

To set the justification in a Layout:

1. Position the cursor in the part of the document that is controlled by the Layout you want to change.

2. Press [F2] *to display the Layout menu, move the cursor to* Change layout *and press* [ENTER].

3. In the Layout Editor, press [f8] *to display the Options menu and either tick or clear the tick beside* Justify *as required.*

4. Press [ENTER] *to finish with the Options menu, followed by* [EXIT] *to leave the Layout Editor.*

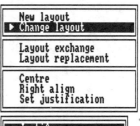

9308

To make local changes to the justification:

1. Position the cursor where you want to change the justification.

2. Either: type ⊞J to turn justification on, or ⊟J to turn it off.

Or: Press ⌐f2⌐ to display the Layout menu, move the cursor to the Justification option at the bottom of the menu and press ⌐ENTER⌐.

This option is shown as Set justification if the text is currently unjustified or Clear justification if it is justified.

The codes inserted are (+Just) where justification is turned on or (-Just) where justification is turned off.

For example, to justify the first couple of paragraphs of TABS.EG, place the cursor at the start of the first paragraph, press ⌐f2⌐ to display the Layout menu, move the cursor to Set justification and press ⌐ENTER⌐. Now move the cursor to the beginning of the third paragraph (as you do this, you will see LocoScript justifying each line to give you a nice straight edge), then press ⌐f2⌐, move the cursor to the Justification option which is now shown as Clear justification and press ⌐ENTER⌐. If you now press ⌐PAGE⌐ to force LocoScript to re-lay the text down to the bottom of the page, you will see that the remainder of the text is still unjustified.

Chapter 10

Line Breaks & Page Breaks

LocoScript's standard way of laying out text is to put as many whole words as possible on each line and to put as many lines as possible on each page while avoiding 'widows and orphans' (that is, the first or last line cut off from the rest of the paragraph). LocoScript also arranges that you start each page with text by treating any blank lines as at the start of the page as 'spare' lines hanging off the bottom of the previous page.

While this approach is fine in general, there will be times when line breaks and page breaks don't appear in the best place for your text – or you need to leave space at the top of a page, for example for a picture. In this chapter, we show you:

- *How to allow a line to break within a word rather than just between words*

- *How to stop lines from breaking somewhere you don't want*

- *How to tell LocoScript to keep a group of lines together on the same page*

- *How to tell LocoScript to start a new page at a particular point in your text*

10.1 Controlling Line Breaks

LocoScript normally fits as many words as it can on each line before moving onto the next, breaking the line at the last possible space or hyphen.

This gives good results most of the time but:

- Lines can be uneven in length (or words unevenly spaced), particularly where you are using long words or lists of options like French/German/Spanish which are effectively just long words.

- You can have someone's initials on one line and their surname on another, or even the initials split across the break between two lines.

- The line can break somewhere that doesn't look good – for example, at the hyphen in a short word like add-on.

It's possible to remedy most of these problems by putting in extra hyphens and spaces. For example, you can fill a gap at the end of one line by putting a hyphen at a suitable point in the first word on the next line. But the problem with this simple solution is that the moment you make even a small change to the paragraph, these extra characters will probably be in the wrong places and you will have to rub them out again.

LocoScript has some very much better solutions.

10.1.1 'Soft' hyphens and spaces

LocoScript's Soft hyphens and spaces solve the problem of short lines or lines that are too widely spaced – without giving you any extra hyphens or spaces to get rid of later when other changes are made.

Soft hyphens and spaces are word-processing codes which can be used to mark places within a word where the line can break. They only become visible as hyphens or spaces when LocoScript breaks the line at the Soft character. The rest of the time, you can only see they are there when codes are displayed (see Section 2.2): then soft hyphens are displayed as (-), while soft spaces are displayed as (⌴).

The way to insert these Soft characters is described below. The choice of which character to insert is simply a matter of whether you will want a hyphen to appear at the line break. If you do, insert a Soft hyphen; if you don't, insert a Soft space.

To insert a Soft hyphen:

Position the cursor, press [⊡] and then type a hyphen.

To insert a Soft space:

Position the cursor, press [⊡] and then type a space.

For example:

The example SPELL.TXT document has a large gap at the end of the fourth line because there isn't enough room for the word encyclopaedia. The paragraph would look very much better with encyclo- at the end of the fourth line and paedia at the beginning of the fifth. To arrange this, place the cursor after the o, press [⊡], type a hyphen – and then press [RELAY] to see the effect this has on the paragraph.

Before: that most tedious of jobs - checking it over and over for
spelling mistakes and typing errors. And that assumes that   —— Excessive gap
you know, in any case, how to spell words like
encyclopaedia! Well, with LocoScript 3, you don't have to do

After: that most tedious of jobs - checking it over and over for
spelling mistakes and typing errors. And that assumes that
you know, in any case, how to spell words like encyclopaedia! Well, with LocoScript 3, you don't have to do this

Similarly, the fifth line of the second paragraph is short because there isn't enough room for French/German/Spanish at the end of this line. The paragraph would look better with French/ on the end of one line and German/Spanish at the beginning of the next line. To arrange this, place the cursor after the first slash, then press [⊡] and type a space. Once again, press [RELAY] to see the effect of this change.

To see that these characters really do disappear when they are not needed, move the Text cursor to the beginning of the word 'words' in the first paragraph and type longer; then press ⟨RELAY⟩. When the paragraph is re-laid, there is no longer any need to split the word encyclopaedia and, sure enough, the hyphen disappears.

But if you use the Options menu (⟨f8⟩) to display word-processing codes, you will see that the hyphen is still there – shown now as (-). The Soft space you inserted is now shown as (⌴). If the text is changed in the future, LocoScript could use the Soft characters again: you won't need to insert these characters again.

10.1.2 'Hard' hyphens and spaces

LocoScript's Hard hyphens and spaces solve the problem of line breaks in the middle of someone's initials or at a hyphen you don't want any break at.

To ensure that someone's name isn't split over two lines, you need to replace the spaces in the name by Hard spaces. Similarly, you can stop a line breaking at a particular hyphen by replacing the hyphen by a Hard hyphen. LocoScript will never break the line at the Hard character.

The steps used to insert Hard hyphens and spaces are just like those used to insert Soft hyphens and spaces except that you press ⟨⊞⟩ instead of ⟨⊟⟩ – ie:

To insert a Hard hyphen:

Position the cursor, press ⟨⊞⟩ and then type a hyphen.

To irsert a Hard space:

Position the cursor, press ⟨⊞⟩ and then type a space.

For example:

If you look at the second paragraph of SPELL.TXT, you will see the name A B Smith is split after the B.

```
be a waste of effort for LocoSpell to pick out the B in A B
Smith as a spelling mistake!↵
```

To re-unite Mr Smith's initials with his surname, you obviously need to delete the space after the B of his initials and replace it by a Hard space by pressing ⟨⊞⟩ followed by the Space Bar.

But unfortunately, just putting a Hard space between the B and the Smith doesn't fully solve the problem – because now the line break is after the A.

```
be a waste of effort for LocoSpell to pick out the B in A
B Smith as a spelling mistake!↵
```

To solve this, you also have to replace the space between the A and the B by a Hard space.

9308

10.2 Controlling Page Breaks

The simplest way of deciding where the page breaks should be in a document is by putting as many lines on each page as will fit. But this could give you:

- one line of a paragraph on a different page from the rest of the paragraph – the so-called widows and orphans that professional typesetters will go to great lengths to avoid (Note: LocoScript documents are usually set up to prevent these appearing)
- page breaks in the middle of paragraphs – when you might well prefer page breaks to be between paragraphs
- part of a table (for example) on one page and the rest on the next, when it is much better to have a complete table on one page

In addition, the way LocoScript ensures that each page starts with text means you can't simply leave space for a picture at the top of a page.

To help you achieve the results you want, LocoScript lets you:

- *Mark lines that you want kept together on the same page – see Section 10.2.1 below*

- *Put in your own page breaks (after which blank lines aren't 'swallowed') – see Section 10.2.2*

- *Set overall Page Break rules to prevent breaks in the middle of paragraphs or widows and orphans if you don't want these – see Section 10.2.3*

10.2.1 Keeping lines together

If it is important that a section of your text – for example, a table – isn't split across a page break, you can ensure that this doesn't happen by marking this section with some special word-processing codes known as Keep codes. These codes can be used to keep any group of lines together, whether these are within a paragraph, span a couple of paragraphs or cover a number of paragraphs. *(Note: If you simply don't want paragraphs to be broken at the bottom of a page, the way to prevent this is not by using Keep codes but by setting this as an overall feature of your document as described in Section 10.2.3. You can also use this feature to prevent people's names and addresses being split across page breaks, provided these are written as a continuous block without any extra space between the lines.)*

Each Keep code tells LocoScript to keep a certain number of lines together, either starting with the line containing the code or finishing with the line containing the code. Codes that keep lines together starting with this line are shown as (+Keep*n*), while those that keep lines together finishing with this line are shown as (-Keep*n*) – where *n* is the number of lines. So if, for example, you wanted to keep the following 11 lines of SPELL.TXT together, you would insert either a (+Keep11) code on the first line of the group or a (-Keep11) code on the last line of the group.

*11 lines
to be kept
together*

```
 ↵
 There are a number of different checks you can do. You can
 check the whole document, or just a section of the document
 'forward' or you can check the spelling of a single word.↵
 ↵
 All these options are available through the Spell menu,
 which you bring onto the screen by pressing [f7] (As always,
 you can see that this is the key to press by looking at the
 Information lines at the top of the screen.) If you aren't
 ---------------------------------------
 using LocoSpell, then the menu just displays the single
 option to 'Count words'. How to use this feature is
 explained in Part III of the Installation book.↵
```

```
 ↵
 ..........................................
 (*Keep11)There are a number of different checks you can do. You can
 check the whole document, or just a section of the document
 'forward' or you can check the spelling of a single word.↵
 ↵
```

Keep code

Once again, LocoScript gives you a choice of ways of putting these codes into a document – through the Page menu or by keystroking. The steps are given below. In either case, the page break instantly changes to take account of the code you have inserted.

(i) Using the Page menu:

1. Position the cursor on either the first line or the last line of the group you want to keep together.

2. Press [f5] to display the Page menu.

3. If the cursor is on the first line of the group, place the Menu cursor on ?? lines below; *if it is on the last, place the Menu cursor on* ?? lines above.

4. Type the number of lines you want to keep together and press [ENTER].

```
┌─────────────────────────────┐
│  Find page         ????     │
├─────────────────────────────┤
│  End page here              │
│  Last line of page          │
├─────────────────────────────┤
│ Keep current line with:     │
│ ▶ ?? lines above            │
│   ?? lines below            │
└─────────────────────────────┘
```

(ii) Using keystrokes:

1. Position the cursor on either the first line or the last line of the group you want to keep together.

2. If the cursor is on the first line of the group, press [⊞]; *if it is on the last line of the group, press* [⊡].

3. Type K *followed by the number of lines you want to keep together and press* [ENTER].

Note: It's a good idea to put Keep codes on both the first and the last lines of any section you expect to add to. Providing you don't more than double the number of lines in the section, these codes will ensure that the whole section is kept on one page – without you having to change the codes.

10.2.2 Putting in your own page breaks

Wherever you want to move on to a new page in your document (for example to leave a gap for a picture at the bottom of a page), you need to insert:

- *Either an 'End page here' (or 'Form Feed') character marking the precise place in the document you want the new page to start*

- *Or a 'Last Line' code making the following line the first line of a new page.*

You also want to insert one or other of these special codes where you wish to reserve space for a picture at the top of a page. Blank lines following either an End page here character or a Last Line code are not 'swallowed' and so can be used to leave the space you need for the picture.

The crucial difference between these two ways of inserting a page break is that the End page here character finishes any paragraph in which it is inserted – stopping the wrapping of text from line to line and leaving the last line unjustified – whereas the Last Line code doesn't change either the wrapping of the line it is on or its justification. So if you want to move over to a new page in the middle of a paragraph, the way to do this is with a Last Line code, not an End page here character.

Once again, LocoScript gives you two possible ways of inserting these special codes – through the Page menu or by keystroking.

Note: End page here characters and Last Line codes override Keep codes, so there's no need to remove Keep codes that conflict with them.

Inserting an End of page character (or Form Feed)

1. Position the cursor at the precise point in your document where you want the new page to start.

2. Then either: type [ALT] [RETURN]

or: press [f5] *to display the Page menu, move the cursor to* End page here *and press* [ENTER].

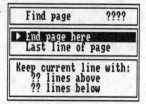

LocoScript then inserts its End of page character ↓, followed immediately by an End-of-page line to show that the text following the ↓ character will be placed on the next page. Like ↵, ↓ is only ever displayed on the screen: it is never printed.

For example, to make the second paragraph of the SPELL.TXT document start a new page, place the cursor at the start of this paragraph and type [ALT] [RETURN].

```
be a waste of effort for LocoSpell to pick out the B in
A B Smith as a spelling mistake!↓
- - - - - - - - - - - - - - - - - - - - - - - - - - - -
There are a number of different checks you can do. You can
```

Note: The ↧ character also finishes the preceding paragraph in the same way that a ↵ does, so there's no need to have both a ↵ and a ↧ at the end of a paragraph. Indeed, if the ↵ follows the ↧ you will probably want to delete the ↵ because otherwise you will get a blank line at the top of the following page. Blank lines following a ↧ are not treated as spare lines to be 'swallowed'.

Inserting a Last Line code

1. Position the cursor somewhere on the line you want as the last line on the current page.

2. Then either: type ⊞ LL

or: press ⑤ *to display the Page menu, move the cursor to* Last line of page *and press* ENTER .

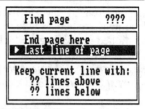

LocoScript then inserts a (LastLine) code, telling LocoScript that this must be the last line on the page. It also puts the End-of-page line immediately below the line you have marked as the last line of the page, showing that the following line is being placed at the top of the next page.

Suppose, for example, that you wanted to end the second page of SPELL.TXT after the last line of the third paragraph. You could do this by placing the Text cursor somewhere on the last line of the third paragraph, pressing ⊞ and typing LL. That would give you a (LastLine) code on this line. Alternatively, you could move the Text cursor to the very end of the paragraph, hold down ALT and press RETURN to put in a Form Feed character.

Note: It is a good idea to finish preparing your text before you insert any Last Line codes because subsequent changes you make to the text could change, for example, the size of the gap left below the line you've marked as the last line.

10.2.3 Setting the overall page break rules

As well as letting you pick out specific places where you do or don't want there to be a page break, LocoScript also lets you specify for the whole of the document whether you want it to:

* *only allow page breaks between paragraphs;*

* *allow breaks within paragraphs but prevent widows and orphans; or*

* *put the maximum number of lines on every page by allowing any page break*

(Widows and Orphans are the names used to describe single lines separated by a page break from the rest of the paragraph – either at the bottom of the page or at the top of the next page.)

Unless you tell it otherwise (for example, by setting this in your Template – see Chapter 14), LocoScript will lay out your document assuming that it is OK to split a paragraph between one page and another but Widows and Orphans are not allowed – ie. if the paragraph is divided, then at least two lines of the paragraph must appear both at the bottom of one page and at the top of the next. (You may have noticed pages finishing a line or two early as a result.)

These overall page break rules are set as part of the 'Document Set-up'. This is a special area of the document that records all the general features about the document – such as which paper it is to be printed on, how the text is to be positioned on the page, which fonts are to be used, what header and footer text is to be used etc. etc. *(There is a more detailed introduction to the Document Set-up at the beginning of the next part of this book, much of which is concerned with setting different aspects of the Document Set-up.)*

To set the overall page break rule you require:

1. Edit the document in which you want to set this rule (if it is not already displayed on the screen).

2. Press ⬚ to display the Actions menu, check that Document setup *is selected and then press ⬚ to go into Document Set-up.*

The screen immediately changes to show LocoScript's Document Set-up screen.

3. Once you are in Document Set-up, press ⬚ to display the Page menu, move the cursor to Page break control *and press ⬚.*

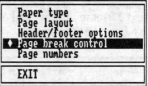

The menu that appears shows the three page break rules that are offered, with a tick beside the one that is currently used.

4. Tick (for example by using ⬚) the rule that you want LocoScript to apply. Then press ⬚ to return to the Page menu.

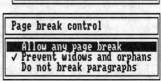

If you don't care where paragraphs are split, then you want the first option (Allow any page break); if you don't mind paragraphs being split but you don't want any Widows and Orphans, select the second option (Prevent widows and orphans); if you don't want any paragraphs to be split, select the third option (Do not break paragraphs).

The tick next to the option that was previously selected is automatically cleared.

5. Press ⬚ followed by ⬚ to leave the Page menu and then press ⬚ followed by ⬚ again to leave Document Set-up and return to the document.

6. Save your selection by saving the document on disc.

Part III

Advanced facilities

This part of the LocoScript 3 User Guide describes some of the more sophisticated features of LocoScript 3, through which you can really fine-tune the preparation of your documents.

Many of these features are concerned with your documents' 'Document Set-up'. This is the part of the document which records overall details of the document such as:

- *The printer that it is intended to be printed on and the fonts on that printer which you intend to use*

- *The type of paper that you intend to print the document on*

- *The Headers and Footers that are to be used and where these are to be positioned on the page*

- *The number of the first page*

- *The overall page break rule that is applied*

It also records a set of 'Layout patterns' known as the ***Stock Layouts*** which can be used to set standard Layouts for such things as Headings, Notes and Quotations wherever these appear in a document.

This part of the User Guide describes how to set all these different aspects of a document (with the exception of the overall page break rule which is covered in Chapter 10 at the end of Part II). It also describes:

- *How to make new documents really easy to prepare – by setting up Templates for each type of document you produce*

- *How to make it easy to type phrases you use frequently – by setting up glossaries of these standard phrases; and*

- *How to make use of text prepared outside LocoScript in your documents and, equally, how to make text from LocoScript available to other programs*

Note: The steps used to call up a document's Document Set-up and to leave it again are given overleaf.

To call up a document's Document Set-up

1. Edit the document.

2. Press ⌐f1⌐ *to display the Actions menu, check* Document setup *is highlighted and press* [ENTER].

LocoScript then displays its Document Set-up screen, the main part of which is used to set up any Header and Footer text that is required (see Chapter 11). The screen also offers a range of menus for setting different aspects of the document's Document Set-up.

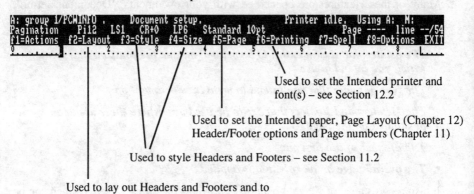

```
A: group 1/PCWINFO .    Document setup.              Printer idle. Using A: M:
Pagination    Pi12    LS1    CR+0    LP6    Standard 10pt         Page ----  line --/54
f1=Actions  f2=Layout  f3=Style  f4=Size  f5=Page  f6=Printing  f7=Spell  f8=Options  EXIT
```

Used to set the Intended printer and font(s) – see Section 12.2

Used to set the Intended paper, Page Layout (Chapter 12) Header/Footer options and Page numbers (Chapter 11)

Used to style Headers and Footers – see Section 11.2

Used to lay out Headers and Footers and to set up Stock Layouts – see Chapter 13

To leave Document Set-up

1. Press [EXIT].
LocoScript then displays a short menu.

2. Take whichever option suits you better and press [ENTER].
Both of the options offered put the settings you have made into force and return you to the document. The only difference is whether you return to the beginning of the document or to the place you were working before you called up the Document Set-up.

Note: Changes that you make to the Document Set-up only become permanent when you save the document to disc. If you abandon the edit, the changes you have made to the Document Set-up won't be saved either.

Chapter 11

Headers, Footers and Page numbers

Headers and Footers – that is, special pieces of text at the top and bottom of every page – make documents very smart indeed. Most books have Headers and Footers and so do magazines, if for no other reason than they are the best way of putting in page numbers. They can also be used to produce the effect of company headed notepaper on blank sheets of paper.

This chapter describes:

- *How to set up the Headers and Footers used for a document*

- *How to make these Headers and Footers give the effect of left and right pages in a book*

- *How to arrange that you have a different Header/Footer (or no Header/Footer at all) on the first or the last page of the document*

- *How to include a slot for the page number that LocoScript will fill in automatically for you*

- *How to set the page numbers of a document – and in particular, how to give a series of documents consecutive page numbers.*

9308

11.1 Where do Headers and Footers go?

To allow you to set up Headers and Footers in any document, every document has:
- – an area at the top of each page reserved for a Header – the Header Zone;
- – an area at the bottom of the page reserved for a Footer – the Footer Zone; and
- – an area between that is used for your document – known as the Page Body.

These zones exist even when the document doesn't use any Headers or Footers:. Indeed, unless you have set something else in your Template, each document that is created will automatically have 3 lines reserved for a Header and 4 lines reserved for a Footer – which, on A4 paper, leaves you with 54 lines on each page for your text. These allow you to add one- or perhaps two-line Headers and Footers to your documents without having to change the size of these zones. (How to set these Zone sizes is described in Section 12.4.)

(**Note:** The lines referred to here are not actual lines of text but a way of measuring depths on the page. Each line is ⅙", so the depth of the Header zone here is ⅜" = ½".)

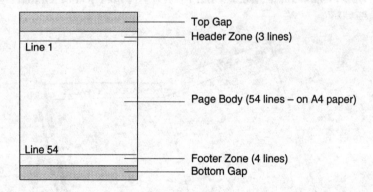

As you can see from the above diagram, your page isn't simply divided into a Header Zone, a Footer Zone and a Page Body. There is also something called the Top Gap at the top of the page and a Bottom Gap at the bottom of the page.

These Gaps mark areas of the paper on which it is either impossible to print (because of the way the paper is handled in the printer) or that you simply want to avoid printing on (eg. the area close to the row of perforations between sheets of continuous stationery or on the backing paper between different labels).

The size of these Gaps are part of the description of the paper itself – the 'Paper Type' – and are described in more detail in Chapter 12.

11.2 Setting up Header and Footer text

The text used for the Headers and Footers in a document is recorded – along with all the other details about the Headers and Footers – as part of the document's Document Set-up (see the Introduction to this part of the book).

The text itself is prepared on the main part of the Document Set-up screen. This is divided into four sections because LocoScript allows you to set up two sets of Header and Footer text. If you want the same Header and Footer on every page, you only need one set of Header/Footer text; but if you want artwork for the left and right pages in a book or to have something special on the first or the last page, you will need two sets.

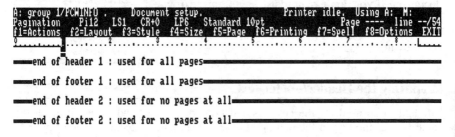

The legend in the 'End-of-page'-type line beneath each of the four sections tells you how the text set up in that section is currently set up to be used. For example, the legend under the first section shown here shows that text in this first section will be used as the header throughout, while that under the third section shows that any text that you set up in this section won't be used on any pages (unless you change how the sets of Header/Footer text will be used – as described in Section 11.3).

Before any Header/Footer text has been set up, each section is shown as a single blank line but this doesn't mean that you can only have single-line Headers and Footers. The sections automatically expand to accommodate any extra lines you require.

But, at the same time, it is important not to 'overflow' the Header or the Footer Zone. If you set up more text than these Zones allow for, this can push a few lines of text from each page over onto a separate page. You must either reduce the size of your Header/Footer text – or increase the size of the Zones as described in Section 12.4 *Remember that the Zone sizes are given in 6-pitch lines, not lines of text.*

The other thing to remember is that the text will be printed starting at the top of the appropriate zone. This means that the Footer text will be printed immediately below the main text of the document. To leave a space between the document text and the Footer, you will need to start your Footer text with one (or more) blank lines.

Detailed steps are given overleaf.

9308

Calling up the Header and Footer text display

To set up the Header and Footer text (or to see what Header and Footer text is currently set up), you need to go into Document Set-up – ie. you need to:

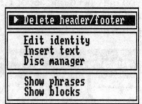

1. Edit the document.

2. Press ⌷fl⌷*, check the cursor is on* Document setup *and press* ⌷ENTER⌷*.*

When the Document Set-up screen is displayed, you see the Header/Footer text is currently set up for the document. If you don't want to use any of this text, you can remove it by calling up the fl Actions menu, checking that Delete header/footer is highlighted and pressing ⌷ENTER⌷.

Preparing the Header/Footer text

The text to be used for the Headers and Footers is typed and styled in much the same way as the text in the main part of the document – except you don't have to worry about turning off any special styles you use at the end of any Header or Footer. Each Header or Footer is treated like a separate document and styles turned on for the Headers and Footers and those turned on in the document itself are totally independent. You don't even need to put in a carriage return at the end of any Header or Footer text.

The other important difference is that you only have one Layout to work with, though you can of course set this Layout up in any way you want: you can't insert any additional Layout codes. The steps used to set up this Layout are just like those used to set up the 'main' Layout in the document (see Section 8.2). You just press ⌷f2⌷ to display the Layout menu, check that Change layout is highlighted, press ⌷ENTER⌷ and make whatever changes you need.

Note: The way to move the cursor from one section of the screen to another is by using the Cursor keys, not by pressing ⌷RETURN⌷. If you press ⌷RETURN⌷, all that will happen is that you add extra lines to the Header/Footer text you have been working on.

Returning to the document

• *Press* ⌷EXIT⌷*, select the option from the Exit menu that you prefer, and press* ⌷ENTER⌷ *to return to the main part of the document.*

11.3 Header/Footer options

When you prepare a chapter of a book, you want to use different Header and Footer text on even-numbered pages to that used on odd-numbered pages, in order to make even-numbered pages look like left-hand pages and odd-numbered pages look like right-hand pages. Similarly, when you prepare a business letter, you may well want a different header and footer on the first page to that used on continuation pages – or you may want no header on the first page at all.

So that you can produce the effects you want, LocoScript allows you to set up two sets of Header and Footer text and to specify how you would like these different pieces of text to be applied. The following sections describe the settings you need to make in order to produce the various different effects you may require.

11.3.1 Setting how the Header/Footer text is used

How the Header and Footer text is used is recorded as the Header/Footer options within the document's Document Set-up. So to change this, you need to set these Header/Footer options as follows:

1. If you are not already within Document Set-up, edit the document, then press ⌐f1⌐*, check that* Document setup *is highlighted and press* ⌐ENTER⌐*.*

2. Press ⌐f5⌐ *to display the Document Set-up Page menu.*

3. Move the cursor to Header/footer options *and press* ⌐ENTER⌐*.*
LocoScript then immediately puts up a 'follow-on' menu of options – all to do with the different ways in which the Headers and Footers can be applied.

4. Tick (eg. using the ⌐⊞⌐ *key) the options you require within the Header/Footer options menu, then press* ⌐ENTER⌐ *to return to the main Page menu.*
There are three sections to this menu – each of which you need to consider if you are going to get the results you require. The most important setting to get right is the one in the top section of the menu because this sets the general rules for how the Headers and Footers are applied.

Which options to tick in order to get the effect you want is explained in the following sections.

5. Press ⌐EXIT⌐ *followed by* ⌐ENTER⌐ *to leave the Page menu and return to Document Set-up.*

9308

11.3.2 Setting for Left- and Right-hand pages

If you want to produce left- and right-hand pages, the crucial option to tick is odd pages in the first section of the Header/Footer Options menu. Ticking this option means that the first pair of Header and Footer texts are used for odd-numbered (right-hand) pages.

This automatically means that the second pair of Header and Footer texts are used for even-numbered (left-hand) pages.

Which options to tick in the other parts of the menu isn't affected by opting for 'odd pages'. It is simply a matter of how you want the first and last page of the document to be handled and what you want to happen if the document is one page long. Advice on handling the first and last pages is given in Section 11.3.3, while the options for one-page documents are explained in Section 11.3.4. (Of course, if you know you don't need to cater for a one-page document, then you can ignore the third part of the menu altogether. Which option is ticked won't make any difference.)

The other part of imitating left- and right-hand pages is positioning the individual pieces of Header and Footer text across the page, because you will probably want the two Headers and the two Footers to form matching pairs – one with the text over to the left and the other with the text over to the right. For example, you might use the following set of Header and Footer text for the example PCWINFO document.

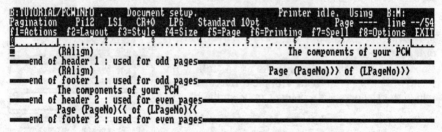

11.3.3 Special handling for first and last pages

There will be many occasions when you will want to treat the first and last pages of the document specially. For example, if you have a main heading on the first page, you probably won't want a Header there as well – even though you will want a Header on every other page. Similarly, if you use continues... at the bottom of each page, you won't want this at the bottom of the last page.

LocoScript has two features to help here:

– The option of using one of your two pairs of Header and Footer text specifically for either the first page or for the last page. (All the rest of the pages would then use the other set of Pagination text.)

– Independent selection of whether to have a Header and/or a Footer on the first and last pages, regardless of how Headers and Footers are used in the rest of the document. So if you don't want a Header on the first page, you needn't have one.

930

Suppose for example you wanted:

- 1st page: No Header; Special footer
- Middle pages: Header and Footer
- Last page: Header; No Footer

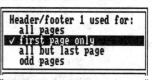

Analysing these requirements, you see that you want the same Header text everywhere (except for the first page where you have no Header) but you want two different Footers – one for the first page and the other for all the rest of the pages (except the last).

To get this, you first need to tick `first page only` in the top section of the Header/Footer Options menu (eg. by using the ⊞ key). Header/footer 1 used on only the first page means that Header/footer 2 are used for every page except the first.

```
Header/footer 1 used for:
   all pages
 ✓ first page only
   all but last page
   odd pages
```

The other requirements are set by ticking options in the middle part of the menu. There are four options in this part of the menu, each of which is 'true' when it is set (ticked) and 'false' when it is clear (no tick).

```
   First page header enabled
 ✓ First page footer enabled
 ✓ Last page header enabled
   Last page footer enabled
```

So, for example, when `First page Footer enabled` is ticked, LocoScript will put the relevant Footer at the bottom of the first page but when this option is clear, no Footer will be printed at the bottom of this page. What we want here is:

- No Header on the first page – ie. `First page Header enabled` clear
- A Footer on the first page – ie `First page Footer enabled` ticked
- A Header on the last page – ie. `Last page Header enabled` ticked
- No Footer on the last page – ie. `Last page Footer enabled` clear

Tick the options you want using ⊞ or clear existing ticks using ⊟.

11.3.4 The special case of One-page documents

'One-page' documents need special handling because the beginning and the end of the document are on the same page, rather than on separate pages. You will almost certainly want the first page's Header at the top of this page – but whether you should have the Footer from the first page or the one from the last page at the bottom of the page, depends on the details of your document.

So LocoScript lets you specify which of these you want through the last section of the Header/Footer Options menu. If you have a special Footer for the first page that, for example, lists all the Directors of the company, you will probably want this as the Footer on one-page documents as well – in which case you need to tick `Use footer for first page` (for example, by using ⊞). But if you have the Footer `continues...` on all pages except the last, you will probably want to tick `Use footer for last page` instead.

```
For one page document
 ✓ Use footer for first page
   Use footer for last page
```

11.4 Putting in page numbers

Something that you will often want to include in either your Header or your Footer is the current page number – so that each page you print has its page number on it. You might also want to include the total number of pages – so that you can give your pages labels like Page 3 of 5.

The page number itself is inserted by LocoScript when you print the document. What you do is mark the place you want the page number to be inserted by putting in a special code, immediately followed by a number of special markers, marking out the space on the page you want the page number to occupy. *Without the special markers reserving space, no page number can be printed.*

Note: Headers and Footers are the usual places to put page numbers but you can equally well put them into the main part of your document – by using the same keystroking that we describe here.

11.4.1 Just the current page number

Where you want LocoScript to insert the current page number, you need to insert:

* *a* (PageNo) *code (typed by pressing* ⊞ *followed by* PN, *or selected from the corresponding Set menu), followed by*

* *one* <, > *or* = *for each digit of the largest page number you might print here (Use* < *if the number is to be positioned to the left within the space these characters reserve for it;* > *if it is to be positioned to the right; or* = *if it is to be centred.)*

IMPORTANT: There mustn't be any spaces or codes between the (PageNo) code and the characters reserving space for the page number or between the characters themselves. Otherwise the characters will be treated as normal characters and won't reserve any space. Indeed, if you find that these characters are printed instead of a page number, the chances are that there is a space between the code and the characters.

11.4.2 Including the Total number of pages

The steps used to mark a place you want LocoScript to insert the total number of pages in the document (or a series of documents) are just like those used to mark a place you want it to insert the current page number. The only difference is in the code used. In this case, you need to insert:

* *an* (LPageNo) *code (typed by pressing* ⊞ *followed by* LPN, *or selected from the corresponding Set menu), followed by*

* *one* <, > *or* = *for each digit of the largest number you might print here*

Again, these won't have the desired effect unless the characters reserving the space for the page number immediately follow the (LPageNo) code.

Note: When LocoScript processes a (LPageNo) code, it normally inserts the number of the last page in the document – because for a single document, this is also the total number of pages. However, where the document is one of a series, the number you require will be the total number of pages across the whole set of documents. So LocoScript lets you set a specific 'Total Pages number' which LocoScript will then insert instead of the number of the last page (see Section 11.5).

Example: Adding Page n of m to the end of each Header

Suppose you wanted Page n of m at the right-hand end of each Header in a particular document (where n represents the current page number and m the total number of pages) and that you needed to allow space for numbers up to 50 (ie. two digits).

To achieve this, edit the document, then press ⌷, check that Document setup is highlighted and press ⌷ENTER⌷ to go into its Document Set-up.

Once you are in Document Set-up, place the cursor at the end of any existing Header text, and type the following sequence of characters and codes:

1. ⌷⊞⌷ RA to insert the (RAlign) code needed to place the page number grouping at the right-hand end of the line

2. Type Page followed by a space

3. ⌷⊞⌷ PN to insert the (PageNo) code

4. >> to reserve space for the current page number, placed to the right in the space reserved for it

5. Type a space, then of followed by another space

6. ⌷⊞⌷ LPN to insert the (LPageNo) code

7. >> to reserve space for the total number of pages, also placed to the right in the space reserved for it

– giving you the following addition to the Header text:

(RAlign)   Page (PageNo)>> of (LPageNo)>>

The code that tells LocoScript to insert the current page number

The characters that mark out the space reserved for the page number

The characters that mark out the space reserved for the total pages

The code that tells LocoScript to insert the total number of pages

---

LocoScript 3 User Guide

9308

11.5 Setting page numbers

Documents normally start of Page 1. This is just what you want except where you have a series of documents which together make one long document. Then you will want the page numbers in the separate documents to follow on from each other. Moreover, if you include the total number of pages in your numbering scheme (see Section 11.4.2), you will want this to insert the total number of pages across all the documents.

The number of the first page in a document is recorded in its Document Set-up, alongside a Total Pages number (if this is needed). One option is therefore to set either of these numbers directly in Document Set-up – but they can be set in other ways as well. In particular, you can use LocoScript to set up the First Page numbers of a series of documents for you – and the Total Pages number as well, if you want.

The following sections describe the different ways in which these numbers can be set.

11.5.1 Setting the page numbers of an individual document

There are two ways of setting the page numbers of an individual document:

(i) By setting these numbers directly within its Document Set-up while you are editing the document; or

(ii) By setting the numbers within the menu of information that's shown when you 'inspect' the document.

To set the numbers directly within Document Set-up:

1. Edit the document whose numbers you wish to change. Then press ⎡F1⎤*, check that* Document setup *is highlighted and press* ⎡ENTER⎤ *to go into Document Set-up.*

2. Once in Document Set-up, press ⎡F5⎤ *to display the Page menu, select* Page numbers *and press* ⎡ENTER⎤.
The following menu is then displayed. If the Total Pages number is shown as ????, no specific Total Pages number has been set – ie. LocoScript would respond to any (LPageNo) code by inserting the number of the last page in the document: see Section 11.4.2.

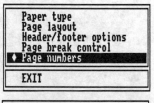

3. To set either number, place the cursor on the appropriate line of the menu, type the number you now require and press ⎡ENTER⎤.

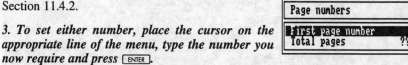

Note: If the Total Pages number has been set in the past, you can 'un-set' it again by placing the cursor on this line of the menu and pressing ⎡-⎤. The entry then becomes ???? again.

4. Press ⎡ENTER⎤ *again to return to the Page menu, then press* ⎡EXIT⎤ *followed by* ⎡ENTER⎤ *to leave the Page menu and return to the Document Set-up.*

5. Preserve the new page numbers by saving the edited document on disc.

To set the numbers via the Inspect menu (see Section 5.7):

1. Display the Disc Manager Screen.

2. Place the cursor on the document whose numbers you wish to change, press `f5` *to display the Document menu, check that* Inspect document *is highlighted and press* `ENTER`. The bottom part of this menu shows the current settings for the First and Total Pages number. If the Total Pages number is shown as ????, no specific Total Pages number has been set.

```
▶ Inspect document
  Set first pages
  Set total pages

Name:     SECTION .TXT
Group:       group 0
Drive:    A

LocoScript 3 document
■

First page               1
Last page                1
Total pages           ????
```

3. To set either number, move the cursor to the relevant line of the information that is displayed, type the new value you require and press `ENTER`.

Note: If the Total Pages number has been set in the past, you can 'un-set' it again by placing the cursor on this line of the menu and pressing `□`. The entry then becomes ???? again.

4. Press `ENTER` *again to leave the Inspect Document menu and save the new page numbers on disc.*

11.5.2 Setting page numbers across a series of documents

If you want to set the page numbers across a series of documents, there's no need to set the page numbers in each document by hand. Instead you can use LocoScript to arrange that the page numbers are consecutive across the different documents and that they all contain the same Total Pages number (if you want to use this).

The key to this operation is a counter which LocoScript uses to work out both the First Page number of the next document and the Total number of pages. Immediately after LocoScript has been loaded, this counter is set to 1 but after you have made use of it, the counter starts again at its most recent value – so that, for example, you can set the page numbers for the documents you have on one disc; stop and change discs; and then carry on the sequence with documents you have stored on another disc.

The procedures used to set first the First Page numbers and then the Total Pages numbers across a number of documents are given below. You can if you wish, try out the steps on three of the documents on the LocoScript 3 Examples disc – SECTION.TXT, SECTION1.TXT and SECTION2.TXT. (These documents all have Footers containing suitable Page Number codes, so that you can check that you have carried out the procedure correctly by printing these documents out.)

Note: It's not worth carrying out these procedures until you have finished preparing the various component documents – because if you change something that makes the page numbers change, you will have to reset the numbers all over again (or at least some of them)!

9308

Setting the First Page numbers

The procedure used to set the first page numbers is carried out from the Disc Manager Screen as follows:

1. 'Inspect' the first document of the sequence you are about to set to check that it has the correct First Page number. If necessary, set this number by hand.

The steps used to do this are given in on the previous page.

2. With the File cursor on this first document, press ⬜ *to call up the Document menu, move the cursor to* Set first pages *and press* ⬜.

3. The menu that is displayed shows the current setting of the page numbers and the counter and offers a choice of actions, Set counter = first page *and* Set first page = counter.

For the first document in the sequence, you will normally want to pick Set counter = first page *which sets the counter to the First Page number in the document. So check this option is selected and press* ⬜.

4. When a message appears telling you to pick out a document, move the File cursor to the next document in the sequence and press ⬜.

5. The menu that is then displayed just offers to Set first page = counter, *so just press* ⬜ *to accept this option.*

The counter has automatically been set to one more than the last page of the previous document.

6. Repeat Steps 4 and 5 until you have picked out all the documents in the sequence or at least all that you currently have access to.

7. When the message asking you to pick another document appears, press ⬜.

You are then returned to the Disc Manager Screen. If there are further documents to set on another disc, swap discs, then repeat these steps from Step 2 – only this time take Set first page = counter at Step 3.

If you pick out the wrong document:

If you accidentally pick out the wrong document at any stage in this process – don't panic. You don't have to start all over again. Instead, just press ⬜ *(which takes you back to the Disc Manager Screen), pick out the **correct** document with the File cursor, then press* ⬜ *and select* Set first pages *as if you were starting afresh. LocoScript then displays the version of the menu with two 'Command' options at the bottom of the menu. The option to select this time is* Set first page = counter – *because the counter will be showing the right value. You can then carry on setting the page numbers as if nothing had happened.*

Setting the Total Pages number

A similar procedure is used to set the Total Pages number in each of the documents – so that you can use the Page *n* of *m* numbering scheme in these documents. The steps are given below.

The only special feature to note about this procedure is that it is important to carry it out immediately after you set the First Page number of the last document in the sequence – so that you know that the counter will be set to the right value.

Again, the procedure is carried out from the Disc Manager Screen.

1. Pick out one of the documents in the sequence with the File cursor, press [f5] *to call up the Document menu, move the cursor to* Set total pages *and press* [ENTER].

The order in which you pick out the documents doesn't matter in this case but you will probably find it easier to remember which documents to pick out if you pick them out in their standard order.

2. When the menu is displayed, press [ENTER] *to take the option to* Set total pages = counter.

3. When the message appears telling you to pick out a document, move the File cursor to the next document to be set and press [ENTER]. *Then when the menu appears, press* [ENTER] *to set its Total Pages number to the counter.*

4. Repeat Step 3 until you have picked out all the documents in the sequence or at least all that you currently have access to.

5. When the message asking you to pick out a document now appears, press [CAN].

You are then returned to the Disc Manager Screen. The Total Pages numbers of the documents you have picked out have all been set to the same value.

If you have further documents to set on another disc, simply swap discs and then repeat these steps.

Note: Once again, if you pick out the wrong document, simply press [CAN]. *When you are returned to the Disc Manager Screen, pick out the correct document with the File cursor, select* Set total pages *from the f5 menu – and carry on as if nothing had happened.*

9308

9308

Chapter 12

Printer and paper

LocoScript documents are set up by default for printing on A4 sheets of paper on your PCW's built-in printer. They are also laid out to use this paper in a specific way – in particular, leaving ½" for a Header and ⅔" for a Footer at the top and the bottom of each page.

This is all very reasonable if you only ever print on A4 paper on your PCW's built-in printer: A4 is, after all, the commonest type of stationery to be used. But you could be restricting yourself unnecessarily. LocoScript documents can be printed both on a wide range of printers (with the addition of the LocoScript 3 Printer Support Pack) and on a wide range of types and sizes of paper from large A3 sheets to small A5 sheets, 11" fanfold paper, various types of labels stationery – whatever your printer can handle. You can also set the area of the page that is set aside for Headers and Footers.

This chapter explains:

- *How to set up a document for printing on a particular printer*

  (Note: The special steps needed to use a printer other than your PCW's own printer are given in the External Printers Guide supplied in the LocoScript 3 Printer Support Pack.)

- *How to set up documents for printing on different types of paper – particularly the standard ones that LocoScript knows about (A4, A5 and 11" fanfold)*

- *How to set the amount of space that is set aside for Headers and Footers*

- *What to do when you want to print on a particular type of paper*

- *How to add further types of stationery to the list of types LocoScript knows about*

To start with, however, a brief introduction to the key features of the system which allows you to work with different printers and different types of paper. We recommend reading this introduction because it will help to make sense of the steps you need to take in order to get the results you require.

Note: *It is worth studying this chapter even if you only have one printer and you only use one type of paper because it explains how LocoScript works with your printer and your paper – which in turn will help you get the best from your printer and paper.*

12.1 The key features of the system

Using different printers and different types of paper is not just a matter of attaching the printer to your PCW and loading paper into it. Different printers may offer similar facilities but the instructions they respond to and the characters they print vary considerably even among printers that their manufacturers describe as 'compatible'.

As a result, LocoScript needs to know a great deal of information in order to use a particular printer and a particular type of paper correctly – what commands the printer responds to, which fonts it offers, what characters are available in those fonts, their widths (for proportional spacing), how the paper is fed into the printer etc. etc.

But rather than burden you with these details, LocoScript parcels up the different pieces of information and allows you to specify which printer etc. you want by picking these out by name from a menu. The key features of the system are as follows:

Printer files and Printer details

The information LocoScript needs to work with a particular printer and its fonts or printwheels are provided by various 'Printer files'. In general each printer is supported by a 'Printer Driver' with the name *printer-name*.PRI containing the commands used to 'drive' this particular printer and a number of 'Character Set' files (*printer-name*.# files), containing details of a font or of a printwheel 'family', though further files are needed to work with an external printer or with LocoScript 3's LX fonts.

These files need to be in group 0 on Drive M when you want to use the printer and its fonts, and they also need to be recorded in your Settings file (see below) – but in general, you can pretty much ignore them. You don't even need to copy the files to Drive M because they should be automatically copied from your Start-up discs as part of the process of loading LocoScript. All you have to do is pick out the names of the printer and fonts you want to use – or in the case of a daisy-wheel printer, pick out the printer, Character Set and Character Style you require where the Character Set and the Character Style together identify the printwheel that you require. The steps required are given in Section 12.2.

Paper Types

To handle a particular type of paper correctly, LocoScript needs to know:

- whether the paper comes in single sheets or as continuous stationery
- the length of each sheet
- the areas at the top and bottom of each sheet which either the printer cannot print on or you want to avoid printing on (known as the Top and Bottom Gaps)

Rather than expect you to remember these details, LocoScript records the information about different types of paper as separate, named Paper Types within your Settings file (see below). To start with, it just has information about A4 and A5 single sheet stationery and 11" continuous stationery, but you can add Paper Types for other types of paper you use (and remove ones for types of paper that you don't use) up to a total of 10 types.

However, this doesn't mean that you can only use the types of paper you have recorded in your Settings file or that you always have to use them with the Top and Bottom Gaps that have been defined. If you want to use a 'special' type of paper for a particular document – or to use one of the standard types in a slightly special way – you can set up and use a 'special' Paper Type for it.

The Settings file SETTINGS.STD

The Settings file is LocoScript's central source of information about the printers and types of paper that you use. For each printer you have on your system, it records the name by which this printer is known and the fonts it offers, together with such details as the type of paper you normally use in the printer and whether it has a sheet feeder. It also records the details of your standard Paper Types.

The Settings file is recorded on your Start-of-day disc and it is important to keep it up to date. Indeed if LocoScript notices that you haven't updated your Settings file since adding further printer files to your Start-up discs, it automatically updates its working version of the Settings file (copied from the one on your Start-of-day disc) and then offers to write the updated version to your Start-of-day disc!

You gain access to your Settings file by calling up the f6 Settings menu from the Disc Manager Screen. You can then see what printers and fonts have been installed, add new Paper Types, change the default settings on a printer... (Detailed steps are given either elsewhere in this chapter or in the External Printers Guide). If you make any changes, LocoScript will offer to save the updated Settings file to your Start-of-day disc when you leave the Settings menu. You should take this offer: otherwise your changes will have been forgotten the next time you load LocoScript.

'Current' and 'Intended'

When you print a document, there are two distinct sets of printer details to consider – the 'Intended' printer, paper and fonts and the 'Current' printer, paper and fonts.

The 'Intended' printer, paper and fonts are the ones recorded in the document and so are the ones for which the document has been set up. You will always get the best results from printing a document using the Intended printer set-up.

However, the crucial details are the 'Current' set because this tells you the printer set-up that LocoScript believes you to be using. This must describe the printer set-up you actually use – the correct printer, the correct paper and, on a daisy-wheel, the correct printwheel. If there's any mismatch between the 'Current' details and the actual details, you can get anything from gibberish to nothing printed at all!

As you may well use the same printer set-up for several documents in a row (or even for all your documents), LocoScript remembers the Current set-up from one printing to the next. But it also lets you know when the document you are about to print has been laid out for a different printer set-up in case you want to change over to using its Intended set-up. Switching over to the Intended set-up (which then becomes the Current set-up) will give the best results but you MUST make the corresponding changes to the printer itself (eg. load the Intended paper, fit the Intended printwheel) – otherwise you will just print rubbish again.

9308

12.2 Setting up a document for a particular printer

To get the best results, you need to set up each document for the printer on which you intend to print it – or more precisely, the printer on which you intend to print the finished version of this document – because this allows LocoScript:

(i)   to offer you the appropriate range of fonts or printwheels to choose from

(ii) to lay out proportionally-spaced text correctly (because it knows the correct character widths to use)

(iii) to prompt you to switch to the intended printer (and printwheel) before printing the document.

Printing a document on a printer other than the one for which it has been set up generally doesn't give as good results because LocoScript typically has to make some compromise in the choice of fonts that are used and/or in the way the characters are spaced. (The exceptions are documents that use LocoScript 3's LX fonts because these can be printed on any printer that supports the LX fonts.)

To set a document up for your printer, you just need to record the name of this printer in the document's Document Set-up. You also get the opportunity to set the fonts or the printwheel you intend to use at the same time. The steps are as follows.

1. Edit the document; then press [f1]*, check that* Document setup *is highlighted and press* [ENTER] *to go into its Document Set-up.*

2. Once in Document Set-up, press [f6] *to display the Printer Selection menu.*
This shows the printer and fonts (or printwheel) for which the document is currently set up. If the document has been set up for someone else's printer or for a printer or fonts you no longer have installed on your system, some or all of the entries in this menu will be marked ? to show that these aren't available on your current system.

3. Move the cursor to the Printer *line of this menu and press* [ENTER]*.*

4. When the list of printers is displayed, use [+] *to tick the name of the printer you intend to use and then press* [ENTER] *to return to the Printer Selection menu.*
Note: The form of this menu may now have changed depending on the printer you've selected. If this printer allows you to use a selection of fonts in your documents, the upper part of this menu should show slots for four fonts. If you have selected a daisy-wheel printer (or some other printer that only allows you one font per document), the upper part of the menu will have slots for a Character Style and a Character Set.

5. If any of the fonts or the Character Set/Style shown is marked ? – or isn't what you want to use, change the current selection as described in Section 6.5.

6. When the details are set as you require, press [EXIT] *followed by* [ENTER] *to leave the Printer Selection menu and return to the Document Set-up.*

• *Save the document on disc to save the printer selection that you have made.*

Note: The steps needed to work with a printer other than your PCW's built-in printer are given in the External Printers Guide in the LocoScript 3 Printer Support Pack.

12.3 Setting up a document for a particular type of paper

Just as you get the best results by setting up a document for the printer on which you intend to print it on (see Section 12.3), you also get the best results by setting it up for the paper you intend to use. Doing this allows LocoScript to divide the document correctly into pages for you: it also allows LocoScript to prompt you to load this paper when you print the document (see Section 12.5).

LocoScript is able to set up documents for printing on any type of paper that your printer is capable of printing on. You just need to record the details of this paper in the document's Document Set-up. The steps are given below.

Note: Some printers such as the inkjet printer supplied with some models of the PcW9512+ are what are known as 'Page Printers'. This restricts the printer to handling individual sheets of paper: moreover, in some cases, you are restricted to using just A4 paper.

1. Edit the document; then press ⌐Fl⌐, *check that* Document setup *is highlighted and press* ⌐ENTER⌐ *to go into its Document Set-up.*

2. Once in Document Set-up, press ⌐f5⌐ *to display the Page menu, check the cursor is on* Paper type *and press* ⌐ENTER⌐.

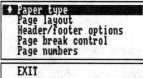

3. When the Paper Type menu is displayed, use ⌐⊞⌐ *to tick the name of the paper you wish to use.*

If your paper isn't described by any of the Paper Types listed in the menu (or you want to use a special version of a standard Paper Type, or you simply want to check the details that are being set), follow the instructions given in the box overleaf.

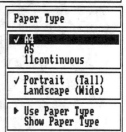

4. If you have selected a single sheet type of stationery, tick whether this paper is to be used 'Portrait' or 'Landscape'.

Note: Portrait means the paper is used lengthways in the conventional way. Landscape means it is used widthways. Only select Landscape if your paper can be passed widthways through the printer or if you have a laser printer or a Deskjet that can print in either orientation.

5. Check that Use Paper Type *is selected (has the* ▶ *next to it) and press* ⌐ENTER⌐. You are then returned to the Page menu.

6. Press ⌐EXIT⌐ *then* ⌐ENTER⌐ *to leave the Page menu and return to the Document Set-up.*

• *Save the document on disc to save the paper selection that you have made.*

(PTO)

IMPORTANT: After setting up a document for a different type of paper, there are two other things you may need to adjust:

(i) The Header and Footer Zones (ie. the Page Layout). Indeed if the paper you pick is too short to accommodate the current Header and Footer Zones, LocoScript will automatically display a message giving you the option of either altering the Page Layout, altering the Intended paper or cancelling (in which case you simply go back to the Intended paper that was selected before). See Section 12.4.

(ii) The positions of the margins, in particular the right-hand margin, because these stay in their old positions relative to the left-hand edge of the paper. See Section 8.2.

• *To print the document on the paper that it is set up for, simply be careful to pick the option to Change to intended paper if LocoScript offers you this – and to load this paper into your printer.* (For further information, see Section 12.5 below.)

If your paper isn't described by a standard Paper Type:

If your paper isn't described by any of the Paper Types listed when you get to Step 3 of the above procedure, tick the type of paper that is nearest to the paper you intend to use, then move the cursor to Show Paper Type at the bottom of the menu, press [ENTER]. LocoScript then displays a menu showing the details of the Paper Type you ticked.

```
 Paper Type
 ✓ A4
   A5
   11continuous
 ✓ Portrait  (Tall)
   Landscape (Wide)
   Use Paper Type
 ▶ Show Paper Type
```

Change the details shown to the equivalent details for the paper you wish to use. (The individual settings are explained in Section 12.6.) We also recommend that you set a special name for the paper at the top of the menu. The moment you start changing the details within the menu, LocoScript automatically adds a ? to this name to show that the Paper Type is not one of the standard Paper Types recorded in your Settings file – but a Paper Type with the name A4 ? or A5 ? is unlikely to remind you which type of paper you actually wish to use.

When all details have been set, press [ENTER] to return to the main Paper Types menu. This should now show your 'Special' Paper Type (still marked ?) at the bottom of the list of Paper Types and ticked to show that it is the current selection. Simply continue from Step 4 of the above procedure.

Notes: (i) If you subsequently tick one of the other Paper Types, all the details of this Special Paper Type will be instantly lost and can only be restored by setting them up again as described here.

(ii) Now is a good time to carry out the steps given in Section 12.6.1 if you would like the Paper Type you have just set up to be added to your list of Standard Paper Types, because the New Paper Type menu will be primed with the details you have just set.

12.4 Dividing up the page

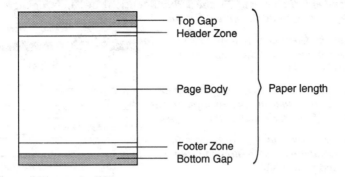

Each page of a LocoScript document is divided into the five areas shown here.

The overall length of the page and the size of the Top and Bottom Gaps are aspects of the type of paper that is used and so are fixed by your choice of Intended paper (see Section 12.3). In particular, the Top and Bottom Gaps are often imposed on you by the way the paper is handled by the printer (see Section 12.6.1). For example, single sheet stationery used on the PCW8256/8512/9256/PcW10 matrix printer or the PCW9512 daisy-wheel printer must have a Top Gap of at least 6 lines and a Bottom Gap of at least 3 lines because the printer cannot print on either the top 1" or bottom ½" of each sheet.

How the area between the Top Gap and the Bottom Gap is used is defined by the document's *Page Layout*, which is recorded in the Document Set-up. This specifies the number of standard 6-pitch lines immediately below the Top Gap that are set aside for a Header (the Header Zone) and the equivalent number of lines above the Bottom Gap that are set aside for a Footer (the Footer Zone). The area that is left between – the Page Body – is what is used for the main body of the text. The steps used to set the Page Layout are given overleaf.

Note: The size of Header and Footer Zone you have is entirely up to you. But you do need to ensure that they are large enough to accommodate any Header and Footer text that you will be using and that you leave enough space for at least one line of the main text. Moreover these Header and Footer Zones are expressed in terms of 6-pitch lines (ie. lines spaced ⅙" apart) – not lines of text. So in deciding how big you need to make them, you don't just need to think about the number of lines of text (including any blank lines) you have in your Header and Footer text but also the Line Pitch and the Line Spacing that you use. If you are using Line Pitch Auto, you need to think about the Point Size that you are using for this text. For example, if your Header or Footer uses 10pt text and Line Spacing 1, then each line of the text does correspond to one of these 6-pitch lines, but if you use 20pt text or Line Spacing 2, each line of the text corresponds to two 6-pitch lines.

To set the Page Layout:

1. Edit the document; then press ⬚fı⬚, *check that* Document setup *is highlighted and press* ⬚ENTER⬚ *to go into its Document Set-up.*

2. Once you are in Document Set-up, press ⬚f5⬚ *to display the Page menu, check the cursor is on* Page layout *and press* ⬚ENTER⬚.

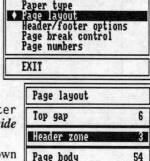

Paper type
♦ Page layout
Header/footer options
Page break control
Page numbers

EXIT

3. To set the Header Zone, check that the cursor is on Header zone, *type the number of 6-pitch lines you want set aside for the Header and press* ⬚ENTER⬚.

To set the Footer Zone, move the cursor to Footer zone, *type the number of 6-pitch lines you want set aside for the Footer and press* ⬚ENTER⬚.

As you set these values, the size of the Page Body shown in the menu automatically changes so that you can see how many lines you are leaving for the main text. If the Header and Footer Zones you are setting are too large for the paper, this number will be shown as ??: if you leave the menu without changing these sizes, you will be forced to change either the Page Layout or the Paper type until the Zones do fit.

Page layout	
Top gap	6
Header zone	3
Page body	54
Footer zone	4
✓ Fixed footer zone Floating footer zone	
Bottom gap	3
Paper length	70

4. Tick (eg. using ⬚⊞⬚*)* Fixed footer zone *or* Floating footer zone *depending on where you want the Footer to appear on the page (see below).*

5. Press ⬚ENTER⬚ *to return to the Page menu. Then press* ⬚EXIT⬚ *followed by* ⬚ENTER⬚ *to leave the Page menu and return to the Document Set-up.*

• *Save the document on disc to save the Page Layout you have set.*

The position of the Footer Zone

Footers can either be printed at the same place on every page of a document or they can be printed immediately below the last line of the main text on each page, as you may prefer if you want to use the Footers to put continues... on most pages but ends on the last page.

You specify which of these you want by ticking Fixed footer zone or Floating footer zone in the Page Layout menu. If you want the Footer to be in the same position on every page, tick Fixed footer zone. But if you want the Footer to 'float up' under the last line of the main text on each page, you need to tick Floating footer zone.

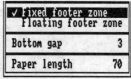

✓ Fixed footer zone
Floating footer zone

Bottom gap   3
Paper length   70

12.5 Printing on a particular type of paper

When you print a document, you will probably want to print it on the paper for which it has been set up but you might equally well want to print it on some other type of stationery. It is, after all, very reasonable to use 11" continuous stationery for draft versions of reports which will ultimately be printed on A4 sheets and so have been set up for printing on A4.

LocoScript lets you print on any type of paper you want. The crucial factor is the Current Paper Type because this must describe the paper that is actually used in the printer. You can set the Current Paper Type directly (this is described in Section 12.5.2), but you will rarely need to do this. If your document has been set up for the type of paper you want to use, LocoScript will set the Current Paper Type for you: you just have to print the document.

The following sections explain what to do when you want to print on the Intended paper and what to do when you want to print on some other type of paper.

12.5.1 Printing on the Intended paper

To print on the paper for which the document has been set up:

1. Select the document for printing and specify the number of copies etc. you want in the normal way. (For details, see Chapter 4.)

2. If a message appears saying that 'Paper types differ', take the option to Change to paper intended for document *(ie. move the cursor to this option and press* [ENTER] *).*

Then load the printer with the Intended paper.

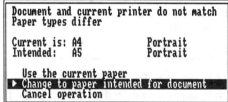

3. If an 'About to print' message appears, then before you take the option to Proceed, *check that the paper loaded in the printer matches the paper specified in the 'About to print' message (and that the other print details match).*

Then press [ENTER] *to proceed.*

This is a very useful feature of LocoScript. If you think about it, it means you never need to worry about which paper you should be loading into the printer for the document you want to print. If the document is set up for something other than the paper you have been using, LocoScript puts up an Alert message reminding you which paper the document is set up for and giving you the option of changing over to this paper. All you need to do is feed the right paper into the printer!

Note: The paper used for this document is now the Current paper ie. the paper that LocoScript expects you to use in the printer, until you change it again (eg. by 'Changing to intended' when you print another document).

• *If the 'Paper types differ' message shows what seems to be the same type of paper as Current and Intended, what you have here is two different specifications for the same paper. At least one of Paper Types will be marked ? to show that its details aren't as recorded in the Settings file. The difference could have arisen because you have updated the Paper Type details in the Settings file but you have not updated the Intended Paper Type recorded in the document: this isn't automatically updated for you. To print the document as Intended, you still need to take the* Change to intended *option, but you may prefer to Cancel the operation and update the Paper details recorded in the document's Document Set-up before printing again.*

12.5.2 Printing on some other type of paper

If you want to print a document on something other than the Intended paper, you need to ensure that this paper is selected as the Current paper **before** you start to print the document. LocoScript can't select it for you.

If you have just been printing on the type of paper you want to use, there's nothing to do – because this is already selected as the Current paper. But if you have been printing on some other type of paper, you first need to go into Printer Control State and set the Current paper as described below.

To set the Current paper

1. Press the PTR *key to go into Printer Control State.*

2. Press f3 *to display the Paper menu.*

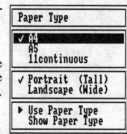

This should look familiar because it has exactly the same design as the Paper Type menu that is used to set the Intended paper within Document Set-up (see Section 12.3). Moreover it works in the same way.

3. Use ⊞ *to tick the name of the paper you wish to use.*

If your paper isn't described by any of the Paper Types listed in the menu (or you want to use a special version of a standard Paper Type, or you simply want to check the details that are being set), take the option to Show Paper Type and set up the details of the paper you want to use as described on page 178.

4. If you have selected a single sheet type of stationery, tick whether this paper is to be used 'Portrait' or 'Landscape'.

Note: Portrait means the paper is used lengthways in the conventional way. Landscape means that it is used widthways. Only select Landscape if your paper can be passed widthways through the printer or you will be printing on a laser printer that can print in either orientation on the page.

5. Check that Use Paper Type *is selected (has the* ▶ *next to it) and press* ENTER .

6. Load the printer with this paper.

7. Press EXIT *to leave Printer Control State.*

To print on the Current paper

1. Select the document for printing and specify the number of copies etc. you want in the normal way. (For details, see Chapter 4.)

2. When the message appears telling you that 'Paper types differ', take the option to Use the current paper *(ie. check the cursor is on this option and press* ENTER *).*

```
Document and current printer do not match
Paper types differ

Current is: 11continuous    Continuous
Intended:    A4              Portrait

▶ Use the current paper
  Change to paper intended for document
  Cancel operation
```

3. If an 'About to print' message appears, then before you take the option to Proceed, *check that the paper loaded in the printer matches the paper specified in the 'About to print' message (and that the other print details match).*

Then press ENTER *to proceed.*

Note: The document is printed with the same line and page breaks and the same Header and Footer Zones that it would have on the Intended paper. Only the length of the paper and the Top and Bottom Gaps change to those for the Current paper.

Obviously, there's no problem if the area between the Top and Bottom Gaps on the Current paper is at least as long and as wide as that on the Intended paper – because then the printer can easily fit each page onto a separate sheet of paper. But if this page area is shorter, LocoScript will use two (or more) sheets of paper for every page of the document, while if the page is narrower, you may lose some of the text off the right-hand side of the paper.

It is up to you to ensure that the paper you use has a large enough page area to take the text you want to print.

12.6 Changing the range of standard Paper Types

The supplied Paper Types cover the commonest types of stationery, but they may not cover all the sorts of paper you use. In particular, the supplied Paper Types don't include any Labels stationery, so before you can use any labels you will have to set up a Paper Type for those. (You can have up to 10 different Paper Types in all.)

You might also want to change some of the supplied Paper Types eg. to reduce the size of the Top and Bottom Gaps on A4 and A5 stationery if your printer is able to print nearer to the top or the bottom of the page than the standard definitions allow. Or you might want to remove the Paper Types we supply for 11" continuous or A5 paper if you aren't able to use these types of stationery in your printer.

The standard Paper Types are stored in your Settings file. The following sections describe how to set up Paper Types for further types of paper, change Paper Types that have already been recorded and throw away ones you don't require.

12.6.1 Adding a new Paper Type

Adding a new Paper Type is simply a matter of recording the relevant details about this paper in your Settings file, together with a name by which to pick out these details when you want them.

The steps to use to set up these details are given below. A good time to carry out these steps is immediately after you have set the details of this paper in a document or as the Current paper in Printer Control State (if you have found yourself having to do this), because then you will find the menu that you use here already primed with details of your paper – saving you the effort of setting up this information twice!

Note: If the new Paper Type is similar to one of your existing Paper Types, it might be easier to set it up by modifying the existing Paper Type and then recording it as a new Paper Type as described in Section 12.6.2.

1. Finish work on whatever you are doing and display the Disc Manager Screen.

Note: You can't change any aspect of your Settings file while you have a document open for editing.

2. Press ⬚f6⬚ *to call up the Settings menu, check that the cursor is on* New Paper Type *and press* ⬚ENTER⬚.

A menu then appears, made up of LocoScript's standard display of Paper details (filled in with the details of the last Paper Type you worked with) together with the option to Create new Paper Type.

3. Set the details shown in the menu to give an accurate description of the paper you want to add.

The panel opposite explains what the different settings represent and what values you need to set.

4. Give the Paper Type a different name from that of any of your other Paper Types.

This name can be up to 12 characters long and you can use a wide range of characters in addition to A...Z and 0...9 in this name. (If you type a character that can't be used, your PCW will simply bleep.)

It is, of course, a good idea to choose a name that will help you to recognise which Paper Type you need to pick out when you want to use this paper.

5. Check that the details are set as you want and then press ⬚ENTER⬚ *to take the option to* Create new Paper Type. *You are then returned to the main Settings menu.*

6. Press ⬚EXIT⬚ *followed by* ⬚ENTER⬚ *to leave the Settings menu. When the message appears, offering to save the updated Settings file on disc, insert your Start-of-day disc in Drive A and press* ⬚ENTER⬚ *to accept this option.*

The Paper Type details

Paper Type name: The name used to identify the paper. This name can be up to 12 characters long and a wide range of characters can be used in addition to A...Z and 0...9. The characters that can be used in this name are listed in Appendix III.

Single sheet/Continuous: The type of stationery.

In general, if the paper is provided as separate sheets, Single sheet should be ticked, but if it comes as a continuous roll or 'fanfold', Continuous should be ticked instead. However, on the PCW matrix printer, what matters is whether the paper is 'tractor fed' or 'friction fed', because the definitions of Continuous and Single sheet allow for the different speeds at which the paper is fed through the printer in these two cases. If the tractor feed is used, Continuous should be ticked but if the tractor feed isn't used, Single sheet should be ticked even where the paper is continuous.

Height: The length of a sheet of the paper – or on labels stationery, the distance between the top of one label and the top of the next label – expressed as a number of 6-pitch lines.

To find out the value to set, measure the length of a sample sheet in inches, multiply by 6 and round to the nearest whole number.

Width (Single sheet stationery only): The width of a sheet of the paper, also expressed as a number of standard 6-pitch lines.

Note: The purpose of recording this width is to tell LocoScript the 'length' of the paper when this paper is used 'Landscape' rather than 'Portrait'.

Left Offset (Continuous stationery only): The distance the printhead's start position needs to be moved to the right of its normal position in order for the text to be printed in the correct position across the page – expressed in tenths of an inch.

Finding the correct Left Offset to set is usually a matter of trial and error.

Top Gap: The gap at the top of the page below which the usable area of the page starts – expressed as a number of 6-pitch lines.

This gap is forced on single sheet stationery by the way in which the paper is loaded into your printer. For example, both the PCW matrix printer and the PCW9512 daisy-wheel printer feed the first 1" of each page through when the paper is loaded, which means that you have to have a Top Gap of at least 6 lines for single sheet paper on these printers. But on the bubblejet supplied with some models of PcW9512+, the Top Gap only needs to be 2 lines deep.

With continuous stationery, the printer doesn't place any restrictions on where you can print. So instead the Top Gap is typically used in conjunction with the Bottom Gap to avoid printing on the line of perforations between the sheets or on the backing paper between labels.

With headed stationery, you can use the Top Gap to avoid printing on your pre-printed heading. *(contd.)*

308

Bottom Gap: The corresponding gap at the bottom of the page – also expressed as a number of 6-pitch lines.

Again, this gap is forced on single sheet stationery by the way in which the paper is handled in the printer. In particular, you want a Bottom Gap of at least 3 lines with the PCW matrix and daisy-wheel printers to avoid printing in the last ½" of each page where the paper is not held firmly enough for the text to be straight!

Ignore paper sensor: Specifies whether 'Paper out' signals from the printer's built-in paper sensor are needed in handling this paper.

These signals are useful when you are using continuous stationery because they prevent you printing off the end of the roll, but they aren't needed for single sheet stationery (because LocoScript automatically calculates when it is at the bottom of each page). Indeed, they get in the way of using single sheet stationery because the end of the paper is signalled before you have printed the last few lines of the page.

This option needs to be ticked when the signals are to be ignored but cleared when the signals are required.

Example: Setting up a Paper Type for 1½" labels

To set up a Paper Type for the 1½" labels shown here, first finish the work you are currently doing on any document and return to the Disc Manager Screen.

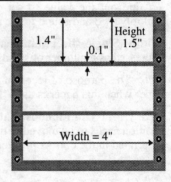

Now press ⌐f6¬ to bring the Settings menu onto the screen, check that the cursor is on New Paper Type and press ⌐ENTER¬. LocoScript then displays its Paper Type menu (showing the details of the last Paper Type you worked with). You just have to work down the menu, changing the details shown to those for the 1½" labels.

Starting at the top:

The Paper Type name: With the cursor on the Paper line of the menu, press ⌐−¬ to clear away the name that's currently shown and type a suitable name for the labels – for example 1½" Labels.

Continuous or Single Sheet: The labels are provided on a continuous roll, so move the cursor to Continuous stationery and press ⌐+¬ to tick this option.

If Single sheet was selected before, you will see the menu change. The previous version had a Width entry – but the new menu doesn't because it describes Continuous stationery. Continuous stationery can only be used one way round and so its width is irrelevant. Instead, LocoScript inserts the option to set the Left Offset.

The Height: The distance between the top of one label and the top of the next on our example labels is 1½" so the Height to set is 1½ x 6 = 9 lines. So move the cursor to Height, type 9 and press ⌐ENTER¬.

The Left Offset: Finding out the Left Offset to set will take trial and error because it depends on precisely where you have chosen to put the paper holders on your printer's tractor feed unit. There is nothing that you can measure until you try printing out with some initial Left Offset – say, ½" – and then see how you need to adjust this to get the text in the position you want.

½" is 5 tenths of an inch, so to set this initial value, move the cursor to Left Offset, type 5 and press [ENTER].

The Top and Bottom Gaps: Because you are working with continuous stationery, you have a completely free choice as to how large you make these Gaps. You could make both Gaps 0 in order to give you as many lines as possible on each page. However, you would then run the risk of printing on the backing paper between the labels. We suggest setting both Gaps to 1 line to prevent this from happening. So move the cursor to each of these lines in turn, type 1 and press [ENTER].

The Paper Sensor: A warning when the paper is about to run out is very useful in this case, so use [−] to clear any tick beside Ignore paper sensor.

With all these details set, press [ENTER] to take the Create new Paper Type option at the bottom of the menu. This returns you to the main Settings menu.

Press [EXIT] followed by [ENTER] to leave this menu. LocoScript then displays its message offering to save the new Settings file on your Start-of-day disc. If you want to have this Paper Type available the next time you use LocoScript, insert your Start-of-day disc in Drive A and press [ENTER]. You are then returned to the Disc Manager Screen.

12.6.2 Changing an existing Paper Type

To change any of your existing Paper Types:

1. Finish whatever you have been doing and display the Disc Manager Screen.
You cannot change your Settings while you are still working on a document.

2. Press [f6] to display the Settings menu.

3. Move the cursor to Paper Types *and press* [ENTER].
LocoScript then displays a list of Paper Types currently on your system.

4. Place the cursor on the Paper Type that you want to change and press [ENTER].
LocoScript then displays the current details of the Paper Type you have picked out.

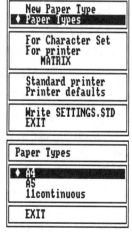

(contd.)

5. Make the changes you require to these details.
The different settings are explained on pages 185–186.

6. To replace the existing Paper Type by the new details, check that Set new details **is selected (marked with the ▶) and press** [ENTER].

To record the details as a separate Paper Type, check that you have set a new name at the top of the menu, then select Create new Paper Type **and press** [ENTER].

You are then returned to the list of Paper types.

7. Press [EXIT] **followed by** [ENTER] **to leave the list of Paper Types and then press** [EXIT] **followed by** [ENTER] **again to leave the Settings menu. When the message appears, offering to save the updated Settings file on disc, insert your Start-of-day disc in Drive A and press** [ENTER] **to accept this option.**

```
Paper: A4

✓ Single sheet
  Continuous stationery

Height          70
Width           50

Top gap          6
Bottom gap       3

✓ Ignore paper sensor

▶ Set new details
  Create new Paper Type
  Remove Paper Type
```

Note: If you don't save the updated Settings file on your Start-of-day disc, you will go back to the old definition of the Paper Type the next time you load LocoScript.

IMPORTANT: To update the details in the documents that have this paper as their Intended paper, you will need to re-select this paper within their Document Set-up (as described in Section 12.3). These details are not automatically updated.

12.6.3 Getting rid of a Paper Type

The procedure used to remove a Paper Type is similar to that used to change an existing Paper Type. The steps are as follows:

1. Finish whatever you have been doing and display the Disc Manager Screen.
You cannot change your Settings while you are still working on a document.

2. Press [f6] **to display the Settings menu.**

3. Move the cursor to Paper Types **and press** [ENTER].
LocoScript then displays a list of Paper Types currently on your system.

4. Place the cursor on the Paper Type that you want to remove and press [ENTER].
LocoScript then displays the details of the Paper type you have picked out.

5. Move the cursor to Remove Paper Type **at the bottom of the menu and press** [ENTER]. **You are then returned to the list of Paper types.**

7. Press [EXIT] **followed by** [ENTER] **to leave the list of Paper Types and then press** [EXIT] **followed by** [ENTER] **again to leave the Settings menu. When the message appears, offering to save the updated Settings file on disc, insert your Start-of-day disc in Drive A and press** [ENTER] **to accept this option.**
If you don't save the updated Settings file on your Start-of-day disc, this Paper Type will be back again the next time you load LocoScript.

93

Chapter 13

Stock Layouts

Every LocoScript 3 document has 10 Layout definitions recorded within its Document Set-up. These Layout definitions are known as its Stock Layouts and their purpose is to make it easy for you to style particular types of text consistently both within a document and across a number of documents.

The idea is that you set up each Stock Layout to record the details of the Font, Point Size, Line Spacing, Margins, Tabs etc. that you need for a particular type of text within your document. For example, you might set up one Stock Layout for your main text, another for headings within the text, and a third for notes or for quotations from books.

Once you have set up the details you require for these different types of text as Stock Layouts, you can set the styling you need for these different types of text within your document simply by inserting a Layout code that contains a copy of the relevant Stock Layout. There's even a quick keystroking that you can use.

The 10 Stock Layouts are usually referred to as Stock Layouts 0...9, but they can also be given descriptive names to help you remember what each Stock Layout is meant to be used for.

The following sections describe:

- *how to record the Layouts you require as Stock Layouts*

- *how to pull in a copy of the relevant Stock Layout where you need it, and*

- *how to update the Layouts already used in the document when you decide to change how you style a particular type of text*

> *IMPORTANT: The main role of these Stock Layouts is as patterns for additional Layouts but Stock Layouts 0 and 1 each have an extra role to play. Stock Layout 0 sets the Layout used for any Header and Footer text in the document, while Stock Layout 1 sets the Layout used for the main text right at the beginning of the document.*
>
> *These Layouts are taken directly from these Stock Layouts with the result that:*
>
> - *Any change that you make to Stock Layout 1 instantly changes the Layout used at the beginning of the document. Equally, any change you make to the Layout at the beginning of the document instantly changes Stock Layout 1.*
>
> - *Any change that you make to Stock Layout 0 instantly changes the Layout used for the Headers and Footers. Equally, any change you make to the Layout used for the Headers and Footers instantly changes Stock Layout 0.*
>
> *It is important to remember the special features of these two Stock Layouts when you are deciding what Stock Layouts to set up.*

0402

13.1 Setting up (and changing) Stock Layouts

Each document has 10 Stock Layouts set up within it from the moment it is created. But to be any use to you, these Stock Layouts have to record the Font, Point Size, Margins etc. that you want for the different types of text you use in your document.

The Stock Layouts are held in the document's Document Set-up, so to set them up, you need to go into Document Set-up. The steps are given below.

These steps are also the ones to use if you decide later that you want to change any of the Stock Layouts you have set up. But it's important to remember that any Layouts that you have created from these Stock Layouts won't be updated automatically when you change the Stock Layouts: instead there's a special procedure to follow, which is explained in Section 13.3.

Note: (i) It is worth setting up Stock Layouts in any document but it is particularly worth while setting them up in your Templates (see Chapter 14). Setting up your Stock Layouts in Templates makes it easy to use consistent styles across a number of different documents because these Stock Layouts are automatically copied to each new document that is created from that Template.

(ii) Before you embark on setting up your Stock Layouts, it is worth thinking about what Stock Layouts you need and what styling you want them to select. In particular, it is important to decide how you want to set Stock Layouts 0 and 1 in view of their extra roles (see the bottom of the previous page).

To set up (or change) the Stock Layouts:

1. Edit the document in which you want to set the Stock Layouts. Then press `f1`*, check that* Document setup *is highlighted and press* `ENTER` *to enter its Document Set-up.*

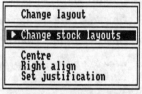

2. Once you are in Document Set-up, press `f2` *to display the Layout menu, move the cursor to* Change stock layouts *and press* `ENTER`.
LocoScript then displays a list of the 10 Stock Layouts, together with their current names.

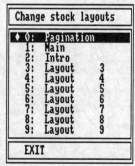

3. Move the cursor to a Stock Layout that you wish to set up or change and press `ENTER`.
This puts you into the Layout Editor, working on the Stock Layout that you have picked out.

4. Make the settings needed to give the Stock Layout the features you require.
The steps to use are the same as those used to make these settings within any other Layout (see Chapters 6 – 9). But note that the maximum number of Tabs you can set is 15 (compared with 30 in other Layouts).

9308

5. Press ⟨f7⟩ **to display the Name menu and set a descriptive name for the Layout.**

6. When you have made the settings you want, press ⟨EXIT⟩**. You are then returned to the list of Stock Layouts.**

7. Repeat Steps 3 – 6 for any other Stock Layouts you wish to set up or change.
Note: If you have set similar details in another Stock Layout, you can copy these to your current Stock Layout by pressing ⟨f5⟩ and selecting the Stock Layout you want to copy from the menu that is shown. But note that *all* the details of this Layout are then copied to your current Layout (including the name): you will need to set whatever is different about the current Layout *after* you have made the copy.

8. When all the details of the Stock Layout have been set, press ⟨EXIT⟩ **followed by** ⟨ENTER⟩ **to leave the list of Stock Layouts and return to the Document Set-up.**

IMPORTANT: Remember to save the document on disc after setting or changing the Stock Layouts. If you abandon the edit, the Stock Layouts you have set up will also be lost.

13.2 Using Stock Layouts

Stock Layouts act as patterns for Layout codes used in the document. So once you have the different Layouts you require set up as Stock Layouts, you can put these to use in your text by inserting Layout codes that copy their details from the Stock Layouts.

There are two ways in which you can create a Layout code that contains details copied from a Stock Layout. You can either:

- *Use the standard New Layout route to create the Layout code, but arrange to copy its details from a Stock Layout; or*

- *Use a special quick keystroking*

In general, it's best to use the quick keystroking if you want an exact copy of the Stock Layout, but if you want to vary any of the details, it is best to use the New Layout route.

As usual with Layouts, you will generally need to insert two Layout codes – one where you want to go over to using the new Layout and another where you wish either to change again or to go back to using the previous Layout. If you are using Stock Layouts throughout, you will be able to use quick keystroking to insert both these codes.

Important: Layouts set up by copying a Stock Layout can be changed in exactly the same way as other Layouts. But the important thing to remember is that the changes only affect the details stored in the Layout code that applies to the part of the document you are working on: in particular, they don't affect the Stock Layout you copied when you were creating the new Layout. (This is a major difference between LocoScript 3 and the earlier LocoScript '1' where changing a Layout was tied in with changing all the other uses of the same Layout.)

402

*It's also important to remember that the details held in the Layout code are a copy of the details set for the Stock Layout **when you put the Layout code into the document**. If, later, you change the Stock Layout, you don't automatically change the copies of the Layout in the document. (The procedure used to 'update' Layouts throughout a document is described in Section 13.3.)*

13.2.1 Using 'New Layout' to insert a Stock Layout

Using the New Layout option to insert a copy of a Stock Layout is just like using this option to insert any other Layout code – except that, instead of setting the margins, etc. individually, you tell LocoScript to set up a Layout with the same settings as the Stock Layout.

The steps are therefore as follows:

1. Place the cursor where you want to introduce the new Layout into the document.

2. Press ⬚ *to display the Layout menu, check the cursor is on* New layout *and press* ⬚ .

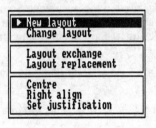 

3. Once you are in the Layout Editor, press ⬚ *to display the Stock menu, move the cursor to the Stock Layout you want to copy and press* ⬚ .
All the details of the new Layout are then instantly set to those of Stock Layout you have selected.

4. Make any changes you want to the Layout that has been copied from the Stock Layout.

5. Press ⬚ *to leave the Layout Editor. LocoScript then inserts a Layout code containing the details of the Layout you have set up, together with a* ↵.

As before, the new line is inserted so that you start using this Layout immediately. You can rub out the extra ↵ *if you don't need it.*

13.2.2 Using keystrokes to insert a Stock Layout

When the Layout you want is simply a copy of one of the Stock Layouts, you don't have to use the Layout menu to insert the relevant (LayouT) code. Instead you can use a sequence of keystrokes (or the corresponding Set menu) to change between using one Layout and another – in very much the same way that you use keystrokes to turn on and turn off changes of style like bold or italic (see Chapter 6).

The only special information you need to know is the number of the Stock Layout you want to insert.

The steps used are as follows:

1. Place the cursor where you want to introduce the new Layout into the document.

2. Press ⊞*, type* LT *followed by the number of the Stock Layout, and press* [ENTER]. LocoScript then inserts a Layout code containing a copy of this Stock Layout but no carriage return: if a carriage return is needed (because remember, Layouts don't take full effect until the next line), you need to type it yourself.

Note: This quick keystroking plus the fact that the original Layout is taken from Stock Layout 1 give you an easy way of returning to the original Layout anywhere in your document: you just have to type ⊞ LT1[ENTER] *(followed by a* ↵ *if required). But do remember that you will need to 'update' these Layout codes if you change the Layout at the start of the document in any way: these codes aren't updated for you.*

Example: Applying an Intro style to the first paragraph of INQUIRE.EG

The example document INQUIRE.EG has an 'Intro' style defined as Stock Layout 2.

To apply this style to the first paragraph of this document, edit INQUIRE.EG and position the cursor at the end of the line that immediately precedes this paragraph (so that there's just a ↵ between the Layout code and the text it is to affect).

Cursor here →
```
Dear Mr Jones↵
▓
Thank you for your enquiry regarding our Super⁻Kwick⁻Phit range of kitchen
and bathroom fitments. I have great pleasure in enclosing our latest price
list.↵
↵
```

Now press ⊞, type LT2 and press [ENTER]. LT because you want to insert a (LayouT) code; 2 because this is the number of the Intro Layout; and [ENTER] because you have typed a number (see Section 6.3).

That's put not only the first paragraph into the Intro style but the following paragraphs as well, which actually need to be in the original Layout (ie. the Layout used at the start of the document). To restore the original Layout for these following paragraphs, move the cursor to the end of the last line of the first paragraph, press ⊞ and type LT1[ENTER] to insert a copy of the current Stock Layout 1. *(Remember, the Layout used at the start of the document is taken directly from Stock Layout 1.)*

9402

13.3 Updating a document's Layouts

There are several reasons why you might want to update the Layouts in a document:

- *You may simply have changed your mind about the styling you want for one particular type of text and want to change this throughout the document.*

- *You might need to replace the Layouts you have used for the planning stage of a document by Layouts suitable for the finished text.*

- *You may want to 'clean up' a document by giving it a more consistent set of Layouts.*

(Using a consistent set of Layouts throughout a document is not just more aesthetically pleasing: there is a practical advantage as well. With the same Layout used for similar jobs throughout, it becomes more straightforward to move text around the document or between documents that use the same range of Stock Layouts – because you don't have to make sure that the text includes a Layout code in order to ensure that is laid out correctly in its new location.)

LocoScript has two procedures for updating the Layout codes in a document from its Stock Layouts called Layout Exchange and Layout Replacement.

- *Layout Exchange is the type of updating to use to get a more consistent set of Layouts throughout.*

- *Layout Replacement is the type of updating to use after you change the definitions of any of your Stock Layouts.*

Note: The way to replace the Layouts you have used at the planning stage by the Layouts needed for the finished text, is to insert the initial text into a new document that has the 'finished text' Layouts as its Stock Layouts and then use Layout Replacement to update all the Layout codes.

13.3.1 Layout Exchange

Layout Exchange works forward through the document, picking out each Layout code in turn and asking you whether you want to leave the Layout as it is, replace it by a copy of a Stock Layout or change it in some other way.

Use this to give yourself a more consistent set of Layouts. The steps are as follows:

1. Position the cursor higher up the document than the first Layout code that you want to update.

2. Press [f2] *to display the Layout menu, move the cursor to* Layout exchange *and press* [ENTER].

---

3. When LocoScript displays a message like this, showing that it has found a Layout code, pick the option you want with the cursor and press ⌐ENTER⌐.

The options are as follows:

Replace by stock layout: LocoScript displays a list of the Stock Layouts, from which you pick the one you want by placing the cursor on it and pressing ⌐ENTER⌐.

Leave layout as it is: LocoScript simply searches for the next code.

Change layout: LocoScript then displays the Layout Editor so that you can make whatever changes you want. When you have finished, press ⌐EXIT⌐ to leave the Layout Editor and continue.

Abandon layout exchange: You simply return to the document.

4. Continue in this way until the last Layout code you want to update has been processed or you have reached the end of the document.

13.3.2 Layout Replacement

In Layout Replacement, you tell LocoScript to replace all Layouts created from particular Stock Layouts with fresh copies of these Stock Layouts.

Use this to update Layout codes after you have changed your Stock Layouts. The steps are as follows:

1. Position the cursor higher up the document than the first Layout code that you want to update.

2. Press ⌐f2⌐ *to display the Layout menu, move the cursor to* Layout replacement *and press* ⌐ENTER⌐.

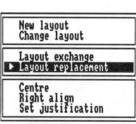

3. When LocoScript displays a list of the Stock Layouts, use the ⌐+⌐ *key to tick the Stock Layouts you want to update and press* ⌐ENTER⌐.

(If you pick out by accident or change your mind, clear the tick by pressing either ⌐-⌐ or the Space Bar in the usual way.)

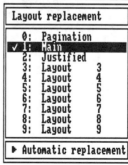

LocoScript then searches through the document for Layout codes with the same name as the Stock Layouts you picked out. Whenever it finds one, it automatically replaces this with a fresh copy of the relevant Stock Layout.

Note: Updating in this way involves a lot of reformatting and so takes a little time.

Templates

As you can imagine, a document is very much easier to prepare if it is set up from the start with the following already in place:

– the Stock Layouts you require

– the fonts you want to use

– the Page Layout you want

– the Header and Footer options you need

...

LocoScript's system of Templates allows you to have exactly that. You just need to set up a Template document with the characteristics you want in documents of a particular type and store it where LocoScript can find it when it creates a new document of this type. LocoScript will then use the Template as the pattern for the new document, with the result that the new document is created with the features you specified already in place. All you need to do is to type the text you want in this particular document (and add any additional styling you require).

Moreover, all the documents created from the same Template are automatically set up in the same way. This makes it very easy to lay out similar documents in a similar fashion: you just have to create them from the same Template. And if you put a little effort into designing your Template – for example, using a special style of text for the address – you will get very professional-looking results in all your documents without any extra effort.

You can have as many Templates as you like, up to a maximum of one in each group on every disc (though you are unlikely to need as many as that). This chapter explains how to go about setting up a suitable range of Templates – where to store them and how to give them the characteristics you need.

This chapter:

• *Explains LocoScript's Template system, then*

• *Takes you through the steps involved in setting up a Template – from deciding where you want to create a Template, to setting it up with the details you need.*

14.1 The Template System

Templates are simply LocoScript documents with the special name TEMPLATE.STD.

When you create a new document, LocoScript looks to see if there's a Template for it to use. It searches for this:

• First in the group in which the new document is being created.

• Then in the corresponding group on Drive M.

• Then in the first group (group 0) on the disc on which you are working.

• Finally in group 0 (or the SYSTEM group) on Drive M.

If it finds a TEMPLATE.STD document in any of these places, LocoScript creates the new document by making a copy of this Template. This automatically gives the new document the same features as the Template that has been used. If no TEMPLATE.STD document is found, the new document is created instead from a simple model for a document that is held within LocoScript itself.

In order to have your documents set up the way you want, you simply need to set up a document called TEMPLATE.STD with the characteristics you want for each different type of document you produce and store it where it will be found when you create a document of this type.

The hardest part of this is sorting out how to organise your discs.

• *The simplest approach to take is to have a TEMPLATE.STD document in every group, defining the characteristics of new documents created in that group.*

The order in which LocoScript searches for a Template to use guarantees that each new document will then be created from the TEMPLATE.STD document stored in the same group.

• *Another option is to use the same group on every disc for a particular type of document and store the Template for these documents in the corresponding group on your Start-of-day disc.*

For example, you could decide to always store memos in group 3 and put your Memo Template in group 3 of your Start-of-day disc.

This Template will then be copied to the corresponding group on Drive M as a part of loading LocoScript, where it will be picked up at the second stage of the search for a Template (see above). There's then no need to have a Template in this group on any other disc (except where you use the group to store a different type of document).

As there are eight groups on each disc, you can have eight different types of document defined in this way – for example, letters on A4 paper; letters on A5 paper; memos; reports; articles for magazines; meeting agendas; labels; and acknowledgements.

- *Another possibility is to use a separate disc for each type of document and store the Template for this type of document in the first group (group 0) of this disc* where it will be picked up at the third stage of the search for a Template – provided you don't have any Templates from your Start-of-day disc on Drive M (found first).

- *If there's a type of document you want to prepare unless something specific is required, you should store the Template for this is group 0 (or the SYSTEM group) on your Start-of-day disc.*

This Template will then be copied to group 0 on Drive M when you load LocoScript, from where it can be picked up at the fourth stage of the Template search (if not before).

14.2 Creating a Template

Stage 1: Deciding where to store the Template

As we explained in the previous section, where you need to store a Template depends on how you intend to use the Template and how you organise your discs.

- *If the Template is to be used solely for documents created within one particular group on one particular disc, store it in this group.*

- *If the Template is to be used to create the same type of document in one particular group on every disc, store it in that group on your Start-of-day disc (from where it will be copied to the corresponding group on Drive M).*

- *If the Template is to be used to create the same type of document across the whole of a disc, store it in the first group (group 0) on that disc.*

- *If you want to the Template to be used in the absence of any more specific Template, store it in group 0 (or the SYSTEM group) of your Start-of-day disc (from where it will be copied to group 0 on Drive M). Indeed, setting this last Template up first will make setting up the others easier!*

Stage 2: Working out what you will need to set in the Template

Creating a Template is an area in which sitting down and planning precisely what you want to do definitely pays off. Get the Template right in every detail and you won't have to do any time-consuming adjusting of such things as Stock Layouts or Header and Footer Zones within the documents themselves. Instead, you will be able to concentrate on your text.

There are a lot of things to decide: what printer and paper to use; which fonts to use; how large a Header and Footer Zone you want; what page break rules to apply; what Headers and Footers you want (if any) and how they are to be applied; what margins etc. you want, both for the main text and for any Headers and Footers (set by Stock Layouts 0 and 1); what other Stock Layouts you will want; whether there's any standard text it would be helpful to have in the Template – in short, just about everything that we have covered in Parts II and III of this book.

Chapter 14: Templates

But these are only the decisions that you make, one way or another, for every single document you work on. LocoScript's Templates mean that you think about these things once for each type of document you want to produce, because after that you know that every document created from the Template is set up correctly.

To help you prepare the Template for a particular type of document, it's useful to prepare a checklist of the features you need to set – for example, through a Question and Answer session such as that shown below.

	A5 Letters	**Labels**
Which printer should the documents be set up for	The PCW dot-matrix printer	The PCW dot-matrix printer
Which fonts do you want to use	LX Roman & LX Sanserif	LX Sanserif
What paper do you want to use	A5 single sheet	3" labels (18 lines long)
How large a Header and Footer Zone do you want	3 lines each (As you won't be able to print on the top 6 lines or the bottom three lines, that leaves 50–6–3–3–3=35 lines for text on each page	None
What rules do you want to set about page breaks	No split paragraphs	Don't care
How are the Headers and Footers to be applied	First page – Special Header and Special Footer; Other pages – Header only	Irrelevant
Are any Headers and Footers the same for all documents	The First Page Header and Footer will be the same (Company details)	Irrelevant
What margins etc. do you want set in Stock Layout 1	Margins at 10 and 60, a simple tab at character position 15, LX Roman 12pt, character pitch PS, line spacing 1, CR Extra Spacing ½, line pitch Auto, justified	Margins at 5 and 50, no tabs, LX Sans Serif 12pt, character pitch PS, line spacing 1, CR Extra Spacing 0, line pitch Auto, unjustified (ragged)
What layout you want for the Header and Footer	Same as Stock Layout 1	Irrelevant
What are other Stock Layouts do you want to set	Layout 2– as Layout 1 but CR Extra Spacing 0; Layout 3 – as Layout 1 but with simple tab at character position 30	Irrelevant
What standard text do you want in the template	The company's address, the words Ref:, Your ref: and Dear, and the Yours sincerely	None

Stage 3: Creating the Template

Template documents are just perfectly standard LocoScript documents with the special name TEMPLATE.STD. So to create the Template, you simply need to:

1. Display the Disc Manager Screen and move the cursor to the group in which you want to store the Template.

2. Type C to create a new document, give this document the name TEMPLATE.STD *and press* [ENTER]*.*

Alternatively, if you have a document already set up that has many of the features that you want to put into the Template, make a copy of this called TEMPLATE.STD in the appropriate group (as described in Section 5.4) and then open it for editing. Working from an existing document in this way could save you a lot of effort.

Stage 4: Setting the details of the Document Set-up

The first area of the Template to set is its Document Set-up, ie:
- the printer and the fonts (see Section 12.2)
- the Intended paper (see Section 12.3)
- the Header and Footer zones (see Section 12.4)
- the Stock Layouts (see Section 13.1)
- the Header and Footer text and the way this text is to be applied (see Sections 11.2 & 11.3)
- and the Page Break rules (see Section 10.2.3)

To set these:

1. Press [f1] *to display the Actions menu, check that* Document setup *is highlighted and then press* [ENTER] *to go into the Template's Document Set-up.*

2. Use the steps described elsewhere in this book to check, and if necessary set, each of the above aspects of the Document Set-up.

These can be set in any order but it is a good idea to set the Paper Type before you set the Header and Footer Zones. (The page length and gaps quoted in the Page Layout menu are taken from the current Paper Type – so by setting the Paper Type first, you ensure that you see the right numbers in the Page Layout menu.) It is also a good idea to get the Layout used for the Header and Footer text (Stock Layout 0) sorted out before you type any Header and Footer text.

3. When you have set these, press [EXIT] *followed by* [ENTER] *to leave the Document Set-up and return to the main part of the Template.*

9402

Stage 5: Setting up any standard text

The other thing to set within the Template is any text that you will want in every document that uses this Template. For example, if you are creating a Template for business letters, you might want to include the Company address, 'Your Ref', 'Our Ref' and the final 'Yours sincerely' in your Template – together with any special styling these require.

Type this text and style it exactly as you would in any other document – or if you are working from a document that already contains this text, simply delete everything from the document until you are left with just the standard text you require.

Stage 6: Saving the template

Once you've set everything up, all that's left to do is to save this Template – exactly as you would any other document.

To do this, press [EXIT], *check that* Finish edit *is highlighted and press* [ENTER] *to save the Template on disc.*

Phrases

It's quite likely that you have a number of standard pieces of text that you use over and over again in your documents – everything from 'Yours sincerely' to names of colleagues and details of standard payment terms. You may also use particular combinations of word-processing codes at a number of points in your documents.

You can save yourself a great deal of effort in preparing your documents by making these standard pieces of text and combinations of codes into Phrases. Once a piece of text has been stored as a Phrase, inserting it into a document is simply a matter of pressing two keys.

15.1 About Phrases

Phrases are short pieces of text or groups of codes, held in memory as you work. You can have up to 26 different Phrases available at any one time – each associated with a different letter of the alphabet.

In many respects, Phrases are very similar to the Blocks used for Cut and Paste editing (see Section 3.4). Text is copied into both Phrases and Blocks in essentially the same way and, once stored, the text can be 'pasted' in anywhere you like by pressing the [PASTE] key followed by a character key. In both cases, the character key pressed is the name of the Block or Phrase to be inserted. With Blocks, this is one of the numbers 0 . . . 9: with Phrases, it is one of the letters A . . . Z.

But there are also differences between Blocks and Phrases. In particular, Blocks are forgotten the moment you switch off or reset your PCW but your current set of Phrases can be carried over from one session to the next by saving them in a file on disc which you can then re-load.

Indeed, you can set up a number of such Phrases files and switch between different sets of Phrases by loading different files. You can even arrange that one set of Phrases that is loaded automatically as part of the process of loading LocoScript – by saving the Phrases in a file called PHRASES.STD in group 0 on your Start-of-day disc. (LocoScript 3 is in fact supplied with such a file, giving you Phrases such as Paid by Access, Cash with order and Yours sincerely ready set up.)

The other important difference is that you can only store a limited amount of text – about 1000 characters – in any set of Phrases. Each Phrase is meant to be just a few words or a few codes, whereas you typically store one or more paragraphs in a Block.

The following sections describe:

- *How to see what Phrases are currently available*
- *How to set up pieces of text or groups of codes as Phrases and save them for future use*
- *How to insert Phrases into a document*
- *How to switch between different sets of Phrases that you have stored*

Note: You are not advised to store Layout codes as Phrases because these tend to fill up the space you have available for Phrases.

15.2 Seeing what Phrases are currently available

If you want to know what Phrases are currently available, you can find this out by taking the Show phrases option from the f1 Actions menu either while you are editing a document or from the Disc Manager Screen.

The steps are as follows:

1. Press [f1] *to display the Actions menu.*

2. Move the cursor to Show phrases *and press* [ENTER].
LocoScript then displays a list of the Phrases that have been stored, like that shown here – giving either the whole phrase or the first few words of this phrase.

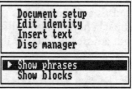

Initially, only the first 12 Phrases are displayed, but the list automatically scrolls as you cursor through it. Alternatively, if you want to see a particular Phrase, type the name of the Phrase. LocoScript will then move the cursor directly to this Phrase, adjusting the section of the list that's displayed as necessary. For example, you can readily display Phrase Z by typing Z.

Note: The list only shows the Phrases that are currently being used. If a Phrase isn't shown, then nothing is stored in that Phrase, but if an apparently empty Phrase is shown, it is just being used to store word-processing codes.

3. When you have finished looking at the Phrases shown, press [ENTER].

15.3 Setting up Phrases

The basic steps used to set up a piece of text or a group of codes as a Phrase are very simple. You just need to copy an example of the phrase you require as if you were copying it to a Block except that when the message appears asking you to type a letter or a number, you type the letter that you want to associate with the Phrase.

However, if this were all you did:

(a) You would probably land up with a hotchpotch of Phrases as you typically start with a number of Phrases already in place.

(b) You would only have these Phrases until you switch off or reset your machine.

To get the most effective use from your Phrases, you need to:

1. To clear out any Phrases from your current set that you don't need

2. Add the new Phrases you want

3. Last, but not least, save the set of Phrases you have created on disc for use on future occasions

15.3.1 Clearing out Phrases you don't need

There are two ways of removing a Phrase from your current set. One is to copy nothing to this Phrase – ie. to go through all the steps of copying something to this Phrase, except that you don't move the cursor between the two times that you press [COPY]. The other is to clear it from the 'Show Phrases' display (see Section 15.2 above) as follows:

1. While editing a document or at the Disc Manager Screen, press [f1] to display the Actions menu, move the cursor to Show phrases *and press [ENTER].*

2. Move the cursor to each Phrase you wish to remove in turn and press [–].

For example, if you don't want to keep Phrase Z, type Z to move the cursor to this Phrase and then press [–].

Pressing [–] clears the text next to the Phrase name – in the same way that it clears Find & Exchange text, for example (see Section 3.5).

3. When you have cleared out the Phrases you don't want, press [ENTER] to finish with the menu.

Note: These Phrases have only been removed from your 'working' set of Phrases. If these Phrases are stored in a Phrases file on disc, they will be restored the next time you load the Phrases – unless you save a new version of this file (as described in Section 15.3.3).

15.3.2 Adding new Phrases

To add phrases to your current set, you have to be working on a document that contains samples of the phrases that you want to add to your set. (If necessary, type these phrases in temporarily and get rid of them when you have finished copying them into Phrases.)

Then to convert any of these samples into a Phrase:

1. Place the cursor at the beginning of the chosen phrase and press [COPY].

2. Move the cursor to the end of the phrase and press [COPY] *or* [CUT] *as appropriate.*

3. Type a letter as the name of the Phrase you want to store the phrase in.

Choosing the letter to type at this point is probably the hardest part of the operation. To help you remember which Phrase you want, the letter needs to be appropriate to the phrase you are saving – for example the first letter of the phrase. But, at the same time, you must remember which letters you have already used. You don't want to choose a letter that is already being used for another Phrase (unless you no longer want this Phrase).

The new phrase has now been added to your current set of Phrases – but only *until you switch off or reset your machine.* To make the phrase a permanent member of the set of Phrases, you have to save the whole set – as described in Section 13.3.3 below.

Note: You can have up to 26 Phrases (Phrase A...Phrase Z) but their total length is limited to about 1000 characters. When you use up all the available space, you will see a message on the screen telling you that you have over-run your phrase store.

When this message appears, you will lose some of the phrase you were setting up. It is a simple enough task to set up the phrase again, but first you must make some space by getting rid of some phrases you no longer want to use.

15.3.3 Saving the Phrases on disc

If you want to have the Phrases you've set up available the next time you load LocoScript (for example), you need to save them on disc. The steps to use are given on the following page.

Note: If you want the current set of Phrases to generally be available when you use LocoScript, you need to store them in group 0 (or the 'SYSTEM' group) of your Start-of-day disc from where they will be automatically loaded as part of the process of loading LocoScript. If you will only want to call on this set of Phrases occasionally, we suggest storing them alongside the documents with which you might want to use them.

1. Display the Disc Manager Screen.

Note: You can do this from within a document but you may then have to save your Phrases temporarily on Drive M and copy the file to the correct disc later, because you can't remove the disc containing the document you are working on.

2. Insert the disc on which you want to save the Phrases and press [f7].

3. Move the cursor to the group in which you want to store the Phrases, press [f1] to display the Actions menu, select Save phrases **and press [ENTER].**

LocoScript then displays a Confirmation menu, showing where you have chosen to store the Phrases file and suggesting PHRASES.STD as the filename.

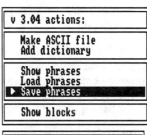

Change this name if you want – unless you want these Phrases to be loaded automatically in which case the filename has to be PHRASES.STD.

Note: It's a good idea to keep **PHRASES** as the first part of this name in any case – to make it easier for you to remember what is stored in this file.

4. Press [ENTER].

When you store the Phrases in a new file, LocoScript simply creates the new file and then returns you to whatever you were doing before. But when you choose to replace an existing file, LocoScript first puts up an Alert message to warn you that you are about to overwrite an existing file. You confirm that this is what you want to do by pressing [ENTER].

15.4 Using Phrases

Whenever you want to use one of your current set of Phrases in a document, you simply have to:

1. Position the cursor where you want the Phrase to be inserted.

2. Press [PASTE] and then type the letter that's the name of the Phrase you want.

The text stored in the Phrase you name is then inserted into the document at the cursor position. Of course, if you specify a Phrase that's empty, nothing will be inserted.

For example, to insert Phrase H, position the Text cursor where you want this phrase to be inserted, press [PASTE] and then type H.

It is obviously important to know which Phrase holds the text you want. If you (or the person who set up the Phrases) chose the letters well, you should be able to remember pretty much what is stored in each Phrase. However, you can always check by 'looking up' the Phrase in the Show Phrases menu (see Section 15.2).

Chapter 15: Phrases

15.5 Using different sets of Phrases

LocoScript automatically loads the Phrases stored in the PHRASES.STD file in group 0 (or 'SYSTEM' group) of your Start-of-day disc as part of the process of loading the LocoScript 3 software. You don't have to do anything.

To use any other set of Phrases that you have stored on disc, you will need to switch over to this different set as follows:

1. Display the Disc Manager Screen.
Note: If you are currently working on a document, you will need to finish work on this first – unless the Phrases are stored on the same disc as this document or you have a second disc drive you can use.

```
v 3.04 actions:

Make ASCII file
Add dictionary

Show phrases
▶ Load phrases
Save phrases

Show blocks
```

2. Insert the disc on which the Phrases are saved and press ⌐F7⌐ *.*

3. Move the cursor to the file containing the Phrases, press ⌐f1⌐ *to display the Actions menu, move the cursor to* Load phrases *and press* ⌐ENTER⌐ *.*

LocoScript then displays a Confirmation menu, showing the file you have picked out.

```
Load phrases

Name:     PHRASES .STD
Group:      group 0
Drive:    B
```

4. Check that the details shown are correct, then press ⌐ENTER⌐ *.*

LocoScript then 'forgets' the previous set of Phrases and replaces them by your chosen set of Phrases – as you can readily confirm by showing the current set of Phrases (see Section 15.2 above).

9308

Chapter 16

Exchanging text with other programs

LocoScript doesn't restrict you to working with text that has been prepared using LocoScript. You can, if you wish, 'import' text from other word processors into your LocoScript documents. You can also 'export' text that you have prepared in LocoScript for use by other programs.

In each case, the text is transferred in the form of an 'ASCII' or 'Simple text' file. Such a file just contains the characters of the text that is being transferred, together with any tabs, carriage returns and form feeds (page breaks) that have been put into this text.

The advantage of using this form of file to transfer the text is that it is 'understood' by almost any program. The disadvantage is that it only transfers the text: it doesn't transfer any of the styling that has been put into this text, so any stylin~ *that is required has to be set up again.

The other thing to note is that the standard ASCII encoding doesn't cover more exotic characters like the Greek and Cyrillic letters. As a result, when you open up the text in LocoScript or in the program you export your LocoScript text to, you may find that these characters have been replaced throughout by some other character.

However, it is usually fairly easy to make whatever corrections are needed for example, by using Find & Exchange to replace the wrong character with the correct one throughout.

The following sections describe:

- *How to 'import' text into LocoScript from another word processor (for instance)*

- *How to 'export' text from LocoScript for use in other programs*

Note: If you want to export a document for use on a PC, it might be best to use *LocoScript* Professional to export the text (if you have this). *LocoScript* Professional is able to export text in a range of common document formats including those of WordStar and WordPerfect documents. (For further information, contact our Sales Department.)

16.1 'Importing' text into LocoScript

Using text that has been prepared by another program is a three-stage operation.

1. Put the text into the form of an ASCII or Simple text file

Unfortunately, we can't tell you how to do this because it depends on the program that was used to create the text. But assuming it is possible to set up such a file from within your program (and it usually is), you should find the steps to take in the program's own user guide.

2. Store this file on a disc that you can use in your PCW

If you created the text on your PCW, the file should automatically be stored on the right kind of disc. But if it was created on a different computer, you will have to find a way of making a copy of the ASCII file on a PCW disc. You may need the help of an 'expert' here – your dealer, perhaps.

3. Insert this file into a LocoScript document

1. If the LocoScript document into which you want to insert the text is stored on a different disc to the ASCII file, display the Disc Manager, insert the disc containing the ASCII file, press [f7]. *If your PCW only has one drive or only one that can read both discs, copy the ASCII file to Drive M.*

2. Either edit the LocoScript document into which you want to put this text or create a new document for this text.

3. Position the cursor where the text is to be inserted, then press [f1] *to display the Actions menu, move the cursor to* Insert text *and press* [ENTER].

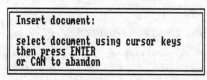

4. When the message appears asking you to pick out the file to be inserted, move the File cursor to the ASCII file and press [ENTER].

5. Check the details in the details in the Confirmation menu that is shown and then press [ENTER] *again.*

You now return to the document and LocoScript inserts the document. This will probably take a little while. After the file has been inserted, you can go through putting in word-processor codes to lay it out nicely, exactly as if you had just typed the text in the normal way.

(**Note:** These are basically just the same steps that are used to insert one LocoScript document into another – see Section 2.4)

16.2 'Exporting' text from LocoScript – Making an ASCII file

LocoScript documents contain a number of special codes that specify how the text appears on the screen and how it is printed. These codes are special to LocoScript and can't be used by other programs. A number of the codes used to represent characters are also special to LocoScript. So before you can use a LocoScript document in another program, you have to make 'an ASCII file'.

There are two types of ASCII file you can make.

One is called a 'Simple text file'. This simply records the characters you typed and where you pressed TAB and RETURN. A Simple text file is the type of ASCII file you need to make when you simply want to pass information between LocoScript and another program.

The other type of ASCII file is a 'Page image file'. The special feature of this type of file is that it preserves the spacing, line breaks, page breaks, etc. you have in the LocoScript document by putting in extra spaces, extra carriage returns and extra Form Feeds (End-of-page characters). This is the type of ASCII file to make when you want to 'paste' your LocoScript document into a document prepared on another word processor.

ASCII files are made from the Disc Manager Screen. The steps are as follows:

1. Finish whatever you are working on and display the Disc Manager Screen.

2. Insert the disc containing the document you want to export and press ⟨f7⟩*.*

3. Place the File cursor on this document, press ⟨f1⟩ *to display the Actions menu, check that* Make ASCII file *is highlighted and press* ⟨ENTER⟩*.*

4. When the message appears, move the cursor to group 0 (the first group) on the disc on which you want to store the ASCII file and press ⟨ENTER⟩*.*
Storing this file in the first group on this disc makes it easier for other programs to access the file.

If the disc you require isn't in the drive at the moment, move the cursor to one of the groups on Drive M – for temporary storage.

5. Check the details in the Confirmation menu that is then displayed and, if necessary, set a different name for the ASCII file.
Note: You must pick a different name for the ASCII file if you will be storing it in the same group as the original LocoScript document. The ASCII file cannot replace the LocoScript document it is being made from.

```
v 3.04 actions:

▶ Make ASCII file
  Add dictionary

  Show phrases
  Load phrases
  Save phrases

  Show blocks
```

```
Make ASCII file

New Name:  DISCINFO.
Group:        group 0
Drive:     B

Old Name:  DISCINFO.
Group:        group 1
Drive:     B

▶ Simple text file
  Page image file
```

9402

6. To create a Simple text file:

Simply check that Simple text file *is selected at the bottom of the menu (ie. has* ▶ *beside it) and then press* [ENTER].

To create a Page image file:

Move the cursor to Page image file *and press* [ENTER].

LocoScript then creates the ASCII version and stores it in the file you specified. Before you use this file, move it to one of the discs you use with your other program – for example, by using LocoScript's f3 Copy or Move options (see Section 5.4). Your LocoScript discs are best used only for LocoScript documents.

Important: Not all of LocoScript's characters have standard codes which are recognised by every program you may use the file with. As a result, when you open the ASCII file in another program, you may find that some of the characters have been replaced by different characters. This can usually be corrected simply by exchanging the wrong character for the correct one throughout, you may be able to avoid it happening in the first place by running the ASCII file through a special conversion program before using it in your program. You may need a 'tame expert' to put together such a program for you.

9309

Part IV

Troubleshooting

This part of the LocoScript 3 User Guide looks at what to do and what might have gone wrong when your system doesn't work in the way you expect. To structure this part of the guide, we've divided the likely problems into the followingareas:

- *Trouble with the machine as a whole*
- *Trouble during Start-up or while resetting your PCW*
- *Trouble using the keyboard*
- *Trouble with discs*
- *Trouble when you edit or create a document*
- *Trouble while working on a document*
- *Trouble selecting fonts*
- *Trouble when trying to print a document*
- *Trouble while printing a document*
- *Document printed incorrectly*
- *Quality of result not as expected*

> If you need any further help, either write to our Customer Support Department at the address given at the front of this book – or 'phone the LocoScript Support Line on a week day on 0891 515717 between 10am and 12 noon or between 2pm and 4pm. Please note that, at the time of writing, calls are charged at 49p per minute at these times.

Trouble with the machine as a whole

The screen doesn't come up bright after you switch on

Check that the mains socket you are using is working by plugging in and switching on a lamp that you know is working. Check that the PCW's mains plug is wired correctly and that the fuse hasn't blown. If neither of these actions show you where the problem is, consult your dealer.

The screen goes blank or your machine seems 'dead'

Remove the disc(s) from the drive(s). Then try resetting your machine by holding down [SHIFT] and [EXTRA] and pressing [EXIT]. If this doesn't bring your PCW back to life, switch off, wait a few seconds and then switch on again. Reload LocoScript and then repeat what you were doing when the problem happened. The chances are that it won't happen again but if it does, consult your dealer or write, giving full details, to Locomotive Software (see the Introduction to this User Guide).

Trouble during Start-up or while resetting your PCW

The PCW just bleeps or the screen flashes

The disc in Drive A either:

– doesn't have the LocoScript software on it; or

– has been damaged; or

– isn't suitable for your computer

Check that you inserted your LocoScript 3 Start-of-day disc and then press the Space Bar to try again. If it bleeps again, try loading an earlier version of LocoScript (if you have a suitable Start-of-day disc) or CP/M. If this loads OK, your Start-of-day disc has become damaged and you simply need to prepare a new Start-of-day disc; but if this fails too, you need to consult your dealer.

Software is loaded from the disc but you don't see the LocoScript 3 Copyright screen or the Disc Manager Screen

You have inserted a disc with the wrong software on it. Check that you inserted your *LocoScript 3 Start-of-day disc* and then try again.

Message about Settings when you load

If you see the following message when you load, it either means that LocoScript failed to find a Settings file on your Start-of-day disc or that the one it found hasn't been updated since you last installed any printers.

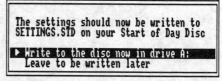

All you need to do when you see this message is check that you have your current Start-of-day disc in Drive A and then press [ENTER] to take the option to write the updated Settings file to this disc. (If you load from more than one Drive A disc, your Start-of-day disc is the first of these discs that you insert.)

If you continue to get this message when you load LocoScript, you must be saving the new Settings file to the wrong Start-of-day disc eg. one for a different version of LocoScript. LocoScript can warn you if the disc you offer it to write on isn't a Start-of-day disc but it can't spot if you insert the wrong Start-of-day disc.

Incompatible version

If an 'Incompatible version' message appears, the most likely explanation is that you have used out-of-date instructions to add LocoSpell or LocoMail to your Start-of-day disc.

Create a new Start-of-day disc – by following the instructions given in the most recent copy of the Installation book you have.

Trouble using the keyboard

LocoScript doesn't respond to anything you type

Your keyboard may be faulty. Unplug the keyboard from the Monitor unit and then plug it in again. If LocoScript doesn't respond after this, reload LocoScript. If it still fails to respond, consult your dealer.

Your PCW bleeps as you press a key

The key you pressed isn't one of the ones LocoScript was expecting – so it bleeped to tell you that it couldn't process your keystroke.

The likely reasons for this are:

- – you have pressed [RETURN] when you should have pressed [ENTER] or vice versa (you tell LocoScript to go ahead in menus by pressing [ENTER] – not [RETURN])
- – you are forgetting that LocoScript is currently in Printer Control State – for example, because you have just loaded a piece of paper into the printer
- – you are forgetting that you still have a menu or an Alert message on the screen

Think again about the key you should be pressing.

Your PCW bleeps when you try to cursor around a menu

You are currently working with Num Lock set. Hold down [ALT] and press [RELAY] to clear this.

Typing produces all the wrong characters

If these characters are Greek letters, Cyrillic letters or Symbols, then your keyboard is currently working in one of its alternative Supershifts. Hold down [ALT] and press [f1] to go back to typing the standard range of 'Latin' script characters.

If what you are getting is Capital letters rather than small letters, you are currently working with Caps Lock set. Hold down [ALT] and press [ENTER] to clear this.

Using the Textual Movement Keys just produces numbers

You are currently working with Num Lock set. Hold down [ALT] and press [RELAY] to clear this.

308

Trouble with discs

You can't insert your disc in the drive

Press the Eject button on the drive to release any disc already in the drive. If this doesn't solve the problem, check that there isn't anything else in the drive – for example, a piece of cardboard. (If your machine is new, you may have forgotten to take the pieces of cardboard packing out of the disc drives.)

Check that you were trying to insert the disc the right way round.

If you still can't insert the disc, consult your dealer – whatever you do, don't force the disc into the drive. You will only succeed in damaging the drive.

You can't release the disc from the drive

Consult your dealer. Don't try poking anything into the drive to release the disc.

A message appears telling you that the disc is unformatted

The disc either:

– is completely blank; or

– isn't suitable for your computer

Either insert a different disc or use the `Format disc` option in the Disc menu to mark the disc out correctly.

Note: If there's a chance that the disc contains data that you want, don't format it. Formatting a disc destroys any data that is currently stored on it.

A message appears saying that the disc is 'Write-protected'

You are trying to copy to or format a disc which has its Write-protect hole open. Check that you inserted the disc you intended and then either:

– close the Write-protect hole and select `Disc write enabled: continue`; or

– select `Cancel operation` if you realise that you will destroy information you didn't mean to lose if you continue.

A message appears reporting a 'Disc Error'

Your disc may have been damaged.

To start with, select the `Retry` option and press `ENTER`: this may well clear the problem. However, if the message simply reappears, select `Cancel operation` and press `ENTER`. This returns you to the Disc Manager Screen.

Try copying the disc. If coying is successful, simply abandon using the original disc (though you might try reformatting it), but if this fails too, rescue what files you can from the damaged disc by using the File menu to copy these one by one to a different disc. Then abandon using the disc.

Trouble when you edit or create a document

A message appears telling you that what you have picked out is 'Not a LocoScript document'

You are trying to edit a file that is not a LocoScript document. It could, for example, be one of your Phrases files or an ASCII version of a document.

To work on text that you have stored as an ASCII document (eg. created using another program), you need to create a new LocoScript document and then 'insert' ASCII file into your new document. (For further information, see Chapter 16).

A message appears telling you that the 'Disc is write-protected'

The disc holding the document you selected to edit is write-protected – so LocoScript won't be able to save the new version you create back on the same disc.

Unless you particularly want the disc to remain unchanged, you can release the disc, close its write-protect hole, return it to the drive and select Disc write enabled: continue. But if you have only opened the document for editing so that you can look at it or copy a section of it into a Block, you might prefer to select the option to Send result to Drive M:.

A message appears on the screen telling you that the document may not fit

There isn't enough space on the disc you're working on to save a new version of the document you have picked out for editing. (For safety, LocoScript always saves the new version before erasing the old version.)

If you are expecting to make the new version much smaller than the old one, you might opt to Continue anyway but if you have only opened the document for editing so that you can look at it or copy a section of it into a Block, you might prefer to simply select Send result to Drive M:.

A message appears telling you that the 'Directory is full'

You have so many files on the disc that you have filled up the space reserved for filenames. (This allows for up to 64 names on each side of a 180k disc or up to 256 names on a 720k disc). You can't store any more documents on this disc – but you can edit the documents on the disc without any problems.

The PCW bleeps as you set the name of a document

You are trying to use characters that are outside the set that can be used in filenames. The PCW bleeps in response to each invalid character to tell you that it hasn't been able to use the character you typed.

A full list of the characters that can be used are given in Appendix III.

Trouble while working on a document

Text is poorly laid out on the screen

The poor layout you are seeing is purely a screen effect. The problem is that the screen lays out text on a regular grid and so shows a fixed number of characters between the margins marked on your Ruler line. However, LocoScript wants to show you the text that fits between the margins when the document is printed, and when the characters are spaced according to their width by setting Character Pitch PS (as we recommend), you actually get a very different number of characters between your margins – depending on the fonts and point sizes you have chosen to use.

Where the characters are larger (wider), you get fewer characters between the margins and so the lines of text on the screen appear to stop short of the margin. (In justified text, the text still goes to the margin but the spaces between the words appear very wide.) Where you have specified smaller, narrower characters, you can get more characters between the margins and so the lines of text on the screen break into the right-hand margin. Depending on the font and the point size you have used, the text may appear to go a very long way into the right-hand margin.

As we said above, this is purely a screen effect. The text will be correctly laid out when the document is printed.

A message appears telling you that the 'Disc is full'

There is either no longer room on the disc to store your new version of the document or no longer room on Drive M for the temporary files LocoScript has created while editing your document.

Look at the message to see which drive has run out of space; then select Run disc manager. You can then move files off the affected disc onto another disc or erase them – until you have made enough room. If you run out of space on Drive M, another option is to use the Show blocks option in the f1 Actions menu and the [−] key to remove Blocks that you no longer need. The steps are similar to the ones used to clear Phrases (see Section 15.3).

When you believe you have done enough, press [EXIT]. If you haven't made enough room, the message will appear again, giving you another chance to sort the problem out – but if all is well, you can just continue editing.

Note: It is possible that when you try to erase a printer file on Drive M, you just see an Alert message telling you the file is 'in use'. If you need to free the space occupied by this printer file, you must 'close' the file as follows. First finish any printing you are currently doing. Then press [PTR] to go into Printer Control State; press [f5] to display the Printer menu, select Remove Current Set and press [ENTER]. Press [EXIT] to leave Printer Control State and you will now be able to erase the printer file.

If you later want to print a document, you must first restore all the relevant printer files to Drive M. (Alternatively, you could re-load LocoScript.)

93(

A message appears telling you that there is a 'Data error' or a 'Missing address mark'

The document you are editing has been damaged.

The first thing to try when this message first appears is taking the disc out of the drive, re-inserting it carefully and then taking the `Retry` option – because this may well make the problem go away.

If the message just returns, which option you take depends on how much editing you have done:

- If you have made a lot of changes up to the point you are currently working, select the `Ignore` option. You will then see another message warning you that you are working with a damaged document. Save this document and recover the previous version from Limbo.

- If you haven't made any changes up to this point, select `Cancel operation`. This returns you to the Disc Manager Screen – as if you hadn't started editing the document.

If you don't have a back-up copy of this document on another disc, you should now try using the `Copy file` option in the File menu to copy the original document to another disc. However, this may fail.

Re-edit the original document and the new version (if you saved this) and copy undamaged sections of these documents into Blocks. Paste these sections into a new document. Use this technique to 'rescue' as much of the damaged document as you can.

A message appears telling you that the 'Editor data buffer is full'

The page you are working on is either excessively large or excessively complicated. Simplify it, for example by reducing the number of tabs you are using.

'Set tabs every' doesn't set tabs all the way to the right-hand margin

The maximum number of tabs has been set in this Layout (15 in a Stock Layout; 30 in a Layout code).

Note: If the problem is in a Stock Layout, you could always add the remaining tabs you need where you actually use this Layout in the document.

The Phrases you set up last time have been forgotten

To keep Phrases from one session to the next, you don't just need to copy the text to particular Phrases, you also need to save the set of Phrases on disc in a Phrases file. The steps to use are given in Section 15.3.

Trouble selecting fonts

Note: *If you are having problems selecting the fonts you have just added to your Start-up discs, it is a good idea to start by updating your Settings file as follows. This may well solve the problem for you.*

1 *From the Disc Manager Screen, press* `f6` *to display the Settings menu.*

2 *If you wish to check that the fonts you want to use are recorded in the Settings file, select the* For Character Set *line of the menu and press* `ENTER`. *You will then see a list of the fonts that will be recorded for the printer named at the bottom of the menu. (Press* `CAN` *when you have finished at this list.)*

If you have more than one printer, you can see which fonts will be available on another printer by selecting For printer, *pressing* `ENTER`, *ticking the other printer in the menu that's displayed and pressing* `ENTER` *– then selecting* For Character Set *as before.*

3 *Press* `EXIT` *followed by* `ENTER` *to select the EXIT option in this menu.*

4 *If the message offering to write SETTINGS.STD to disc appears (see above), make sure that you have your Start-of-day disc in Drive A (ie. the first of the discs used in this drive when you load LocoScript) and then press* `ENTER` *to accept this option.*

The Printer Selection menu within the document doesn't mention fonts and/or is full of ?s

You need to set up the menu for the printer you will be using. Simply move the cursor to the Printer line of the menu, press `ENTER` and then use the `⊞` key to tick your printer in the list that is displayed. When you've ticked this printer, press `ENTER` to return to the Printer Selection menu. This will now be set up for the printer you have selected and should now include a short list of fonts (assuming the printer that you have selected lets you use different fonts).

• *If the printer needs to be re-selected in existing documents:*

The chances are that, when you were upgrading to LocoScript 3, you opted to 'add' this printer as if it was a new printer rather than 're-install' it. As a result, LocoScript now knows the printer under a different name.

You could simply select the printer afresh under its new name but you would have to do this in every document that is set up for this printer. It would be better in the long run to run the Installation program again and update your printers, this time being certain to 'Re-install' your printer under its old name. (Alternatively, if you understand the relationship between printer names and printer filenames in LocoScript, you could rename this printer's .PRI file and associated .#xx files to give the printer its old name and then update your Settings file as described above.)

The font you want isn't included in the list of fonts numbered 0...3

If there's an empty slot in this list of fonts (shown as a line of dashes), simply tick this font number and press ⌐ENTER⌐. When you 'continue' from the Alert message that appears, LocoScript displays a list of the fonts available on your printer from which you can pick the font you want.

If there isn't an empty slot in the list, you will need to change the Font table in the Document Set-up as described in Section 6.5.

The font you want is missing from the list of fonts available offered within the document – or is marked with a question mark

The font you want isn't recorded in your Settings file. Check first to make sure that the correct printer is selected as the Intended printer (see Section 12.2); then return to the Disc Manager Screen to sort this problem out. (See below.)

The font you want is missing from the Settings menu

If a font is missing from the Settings menu, the first thing to check is that you aren't trying to record too many fonts. The most you can record for any printer is 15 fonts. If you already have 15 fonts installed, press ⌐CAN⌐ twice to leave the Settings menu and then follow the steps given in either the External Printers Guide or any of the LocoFont booklets to remove one or more of the existing entries. The missing font should be automatically added to the list once you have made room for it.

The other possibility is that the Character Set (.#*xx*) file supporting this font has not been copied to group 0 on Drive M, which in turn means either that this file is missing from your Start-of-day disc (in which case you will probably need to install the printer again) or that there wasn't room for this file on Drive M (in which case you should consider increasing the memory of your PCW).

The font you want is marked ? in the Settings menu

When a font is marked ?, it generally means that there's no .#*xx* file for this font on Drive M – which in turn means either that this file isn't on your Start-of-day disc or that there wasn't room for this file on Drive M (in which case, you should consider increasing the memory of your PCW). If the font is an LX font, this file isn't in fact needed either for editing or for printing, but with other fonts, you should correct the problem and then re-load LocoScript.

But if you have installed several fonts, particularly ones available at a number of sizes, there's a small chance that the Settings file itself may have reached its maximum size of 16k. Any font you add after that is marked ? to show LocoScript doesn't have room to record anything other than its name in the Settings file. To record this font fully, you will have to make room for it by following the steps given in either the External Printers Guide or one of the LocoFont booklets to remove one or more of your existing fonts – either from this printer or from another printer.

> Note: Group 0 will probably be called SYSTEM if your Start-of-day disc was originally created from an Amstrad Master disc.

LocoScript 3 User Guide **221**

406

Trouble when trying to print a document

Note: If you are using an 'External' printer, you should also consult the Troubleshooting section of the External Printers Guide.

There is no 'Save and Print' option in the Exit menu

There is no printer currently connected to your PCW – or the printer is already busy. Save the document, press [PTR] and then use the Document menu to see if the printer is printing anything.

If this menu gives details of a document, then LocoScript is in the middle of printing this document: perhaps you haven't fed in enough paper to finish that last document you asked LocoScript to print.

If the menu doesn't give details of a document, switch your PCW off and check that the printer is connected properly. Then reload LocoScript and look at the Information lines on the Disc Manager Screen. If these show the P=Print document and D=Direct printing options, then all is well and your printer is now correctly attached. If not, your printer may well be faulty – so consult your dealer.

You press P or D and you see a message telling you that the printer is absent

There is no printer currently connected to your PCW. Switch your PCW off and check that the printer is connected properly. Then reload LocoScript.

Look at the Information lines on the Disc Manager Screen. If these show the P=Print document and D=Direct printing options, then all is now well and your printer is now correctly attached. If not, your printer may well be faulty – consult your dealer.

A message appears telling you that what you have picked out is 'Not a LocoScript 3 document'

You are trying to print a file that is not a LocoScript 3 document. It could, for example, be a document you created under an earlier version of LocoScript and have not yet converted to LocoScript 3 or it could be an ASCII version of a document.

If it's an old document, just edit it and then save the edited version to disc. If it's an ASCII file, you will first need to insert the text into a LocoScript document as described in Section 16.1.

A message appears telling you the Intended fonts aren't available

If LocoScript displays its 'Fonts are unavailable' message, it means that one or more of the fonts you've used in the document aren't available on the printer you are proposing to print on. The fonts concerned are marked ?.

If you are about to print on a different printer to the one for which the document has been set up, the fact that these fonts aren't available probably won't be any surprise. Just press ⌈ENTER⌋ to print with the font that LocoScript is proposing to use instead.

But if you are proposing to use the Intended printer, a ? beside a font you were expecting to use means that either the .#xx file or all the .@xx files for this font are missing from Drive M. In this case, we suggest that you take the Cancel option and check that the files needed to support these fonts are in group 0 on Drive M before starting to print the document again. (The files you need are listed in Section 4.1.)

The Current and Intended paper appear to be the same but LocoScript says they don't match

The two Paper Types may have the same name but the paper they define is different in some way. In particular, at least one of them will be marked ? to show that it sets different values to those set by the Paper Type recorded in your Settings.

The chances are that you have changed the details for this paper in your Settings file at some stage, but haven't updated the paper details recorded in the document. These details aren't updated automatically so that the layout of your document isn't changed 'behind your back'.

The printer doesn't start to print

First check that there is paper in the printer. If there isn't any paper in the printer, load a sheet of paper, check that your printer is ready to print and then press ⌈EXIT⌋: your document will probably print now.

If there was already paper in the printer, press ⌈PTR⌋ to put LocoScript into Printer Control State and then press ⌈⊞⌋ to 'clear waiting for paper and resume printing'.

If your document still doesn't print, press ⌈PTR⌋ again. This time use the f5 Printer menu to check which printer LocoScript is expecting to print on and, if necessary, change it. If it was set up for the printer you expected, check that this printer is 'on-line'. Press ⌈EXIT⌋ again.

If the document still doesn't print and the problem is with a printer other than your built-in printer, consult the Troubleshooting section of the External Printers Guide. Otherwise, consult your dealer.

The Printer Actions menu just has the one entry – Reset Printer

Your printer has been left in a strange state. Press ⌈ENTER⌋, so that LocoScript resets the printer.

Trouble while printing a document

The printer stops printing before the end of a page

Press ⌈PTR⌉ to put LocoScript into Printer Control State and see if the current printer state is No Paper. If it is, then the printer has detected the end of the paper you are feeding into the printer.

Don't load fresh paper yet. First use the f1 Actions menu to 'print to end of page'. When printing stops again, load fresh paper and then use the menu to 'Resume printing'.

This typically only happens when you are using continuous stationery.

The paper jams in the printer

Press ⌈PTR⌉ so that the printer stops printing as soon as possible. (Unfortunately, if the printer keeps a large store of characters to print, this may take a while!)

Clear out the damaged paper, reload with fresh paper and then use the f7 Document menu to restart printing the document (see Section 4.5).

Document printed incorrectly

The printer prints rubbish

You didn't set up the printer to match the printer set-up LocoScript told you it was about to print on. Depending on the type of printer you are using, you may have done anything from not fitting the correct printwheel to failing to switch the printer into the correct printer mode.

Press ⌈PTR⌉ to go into Printer Control State and check the details of the printer set-up LocoScript thought you were using (shown on the Information lines), set up your printer to match, then press ⌈EXIT⌉ to return to the Disc Manager and re-print the document.

Missing characters

If LocoScript prints a blank space instead of a character, this simply means that the required character isn't available in this font you are using. *Note:* Only LocoScript's LX fonts and Download fonts offer the full range of characters that LocoScript supports (with extra files in the case of the LX fonts).

If you are using LX fonts, the answer is to add Character Shape files (.@*xx* files) for the Symbol Set that contains the character you want to print (see Appendix VI).

The wrong font is used

In general, LocoScript will only use a different font if the one you've specified isn't available – and it will tell you that it is about to do this before it starts printing (see Chapter 6). The message you see also tells you which font LocoScript is proposing to substitute for the missing font.

On a laser printer, however, you may find that the wrong font is used when you opt to print Landscape rather than Portrait. In this case, the printer itself has substituted a different font because there isn't a Landscape version of the font you requested.

The wrong print style (bold, italic etc.)

In general, when text is printed in the wrong print style, it means that the printer you are using isn't capable of printing in this style.

If you are using the LX fonts, however, the wrong print style means there weren't any Character Shape files (.@xx files) offering the print style you asked for on Drive M, nor anything that LocoScript could generate the required print style from in the specified font and Point Size. For example, you asked to print in italic when the only suitable Character Shape file contained bold characters. Such problems can be solved by adding further Character Shape files to your selection on Drive M.

In either case, LocoScript will have used the nearest style that was available.

Do check that the styling you want is correctly specified in the document.

The wrong Point Size

While LocoScript 3 allows you to specify a range of different Point Sizes, text can only be printed at a particular Point Size if the font you are using is available at that size – or, in the case of the LX fonts, if LocoScript can generate this size from the Character Shape files you have for this font. If the required size isn't available, then the nearest size that's available in this font is used instead.

In general you should pick a different Point Size to use – one that is available – but if you are using LX fonts, you may be able to print your text at the size you want by buying further Character Shape files (see Appendix VI).

Note: It is generally only possible to print different sizes of text where you are using LX fonts or some of the 'scalable' or 'multi-size' fonts offered on LaserJets and on 'ESC/P2' printers. Other fonts can only be printed at one size (nominally 10pt).

Ends of lines missing

The probable explanation is that LocoScript has had to use a very much larger Point Size than you specified in the text. LocoScript will have done what it can to adjust for the different size of characters but it may not have succeeded in fitting all your text on the line. Either change the Point Size you've specified to one you do have or, if you are using LX fonts, add either the Character Shape file for the Point Size you want or one from which this size can be generated (see Appendix II).

Characters printed all over each other

You are trying to print these characters in a Character Pitch and/or a Line Pitch that is too small to accommodate them. If the characters overlay previous lines of the text, the Line Pitch is too fine (ie. its value is too big) or you need to use a larger Line Spacing; if the characters overlay each other, the Character Pitch is too fine (again, value too big).

We strongly recommend using Character Pitch PS and Line Pitch Auto throughout all your documents, because then you can be certain that every character of your text is correctly spaced both along the line and from line to line. In particular, if you use any of the fixed Character Pitches, characters larger than 14pt are almost certain to be printed over each other.

Characters cut off at the top (or a bottom) of a page

If the upper parts of LX font characters are cut off on the first line of a page, the chances are that you have set a Line Pitch that's too small to accommodate the full height of these characters. Setting Line Pitch Auto will cure this.

The other possibility is that you are printing on paper that's shorter than the Intended paper. The way the LX fonts are handled makes it quite possible for the top part of characters to appear at the bottom of one page and the rest to appear at the top of the next page. We suggest you always use the Intended paper when you print documents that include LX fonts.

Text not aligned as on the screen

When you set Character Pitch PS (as we recommend for the LX fonts in particular), the characters remain evenly spaced on the screen, because this is the only way in which they can be displayed. But when they are printed, the characters are 'proportionally-spaced' – that is, spaced according to the individual widths of the characters. As a result, it is almost inevitable that characters that appear to be aligned on the screen aren't aligned when the document is printed.

The way to get the alignment you require is to set tabs at the crucial positions on the Ruler line of your Layout. How you do this is explained in Section 8.2. You won't get anywhere trying to use spaces to align this text.

Lines too short or mis-positioned

This is also a result of LocoScript having to use the wrong Point Size – in this case, one very much smaller than that specified in the text. Unless the text is justified, each line of text will then fall short of the right-hand margin. One effect of this is that headings etc. that you asked to be centred or to be aligned with the right-hand edge of the text may seem in the wrong position: however, this is just an effect of the neighbouring lines being too short.

Quality of result not as expected

LX Font characters seem 'lumpy'

If it's the larger characters that seem 'lumpy', you could just be noticing the loss of resolution that comes from producing larger characters by 'multiplying up' the shapes supplied for printing text at smaller Point Sizes. The way to get properly-formed characters at larger sizes is to buy Character Shape files specifically for the sizes you require (see Appendix VI).

It is also worth noting that you will get very much smoother shapes on an inkjet printer (such as a bubblejet) or a laser printer because these work at a higher resolution (ie. use finer dots) than, say, a 9-pin dot matrix printer.

LX Font characters seem jagged

Because of the way text in the LX fonts is printed, the characters can have jagged edges if your printer doesn't align what it prints very well from one line to the next.

If the problem is with an External printer (ie. one which is used as an alternative to your PCW's built-in printer), you may be able to cure this by turning off bi-directional printing (if your printer is doing that). The alignment from line to line won't necessarily be perfect when you opt for uni-directional printing but it is typically very much better because every line is printed in the same direction. The steps to use are given in Troubleshooting section of the LocoScript 3 External Printers Guide.

Lines across the page

If you are getting white lines across your text, you should check that the switches on your printer select 8 data bits. You will lose parts of the characters if 7 data bits is selected.

White lines across the page could also mean that one or more of the pins on your printhead has become blocked, while if you are getting black lines across your text, it's possible that one of these pins is firing continuously. In either case, you need to consult either your dealer or a maintenance company.

Uneven blackness especially on larger characters

If you don't get an even level of blackness, check and if necessary replace the ribbon/toner you are using. If you get a poor result from a new ribbon, switch to a better quality ribbon. On the PCW matrix printer, for example, there is a marked difference between the quality of the black you get from a fabric ribbon and that from a 'multi-strike' carbon ribbon.

Letters or words not spaced as expected

Poor letter spacing usually means that you are using the wrong Character Pitch for the font you are using. In particular, characters can seem very poorly spaced if you specify one of the fixed Character Pitches where you are working in one of the LX fonts or some other PS (proportionally spaced) font. You should always set Character Pitch PS where you want to print using a PS font.

Poor word spacing is typically a consequence of LocoScript having to use the wrong Point Size or the wrong font. The effect is particularly obvious in justified text. LocoScript does what it can to adjust for the different size of characters but the spacing between the words may be either very wide or very narrow.

Note: Spaces in the LX fonts are narrower than in Locomotive's other fonts, in line with other professional fonts.

The text is poorly positioned on the page

Press [PTR] to put LocoScript into its Printer Control State and then use the f6 Left Offset menu to adjust the start position of each line of text. Then use the f7 Document menu to restart printing the document (see Section 4.5).

Converting existing LocoScript files

LocoScript documents and Templates, LocoMail Master documents, LocoMail datafiles and LocoFile datafiles prepared when you were using LocoScript '1' or LocoScript 2 can all be used from LocoScript 3, as can LocoSpell User dictionaries, Phrases files and LocoScript '1' Saved Blocks.

However, they may need to be converted before they can be used fully. In particular, documents that were prepared using LocoScript '1' or LocoScript 2.33 or earlier must be converted to 'LocoScript 3 format' before they can be printed or used in a mailmerge. (Documents prepared using LocoScript 2.50 or later already have this format.)

This conversion is carried out the first time you edit the document in LocoScript 3 and is to a great extent automatic. It simply takes the details in the current document and produces equivalent details for the new LocoScript 3 document. None of the text or the styling is lost – though there may be some extra settings to make, particularly where you are converting from LocoScript '1'. You may also need to re-style documents where you have used more than 30 tabs in a Layout or where you have used Line Pitch, Line Spacing or Character Pitch to produce subtle effects.

This appendix explains the steps you need to take in order to convert each of the different types of file, together with any special information about their conversion.

While it may be easier to convert all your files in one go, there's no actual need to convert any file until you actually want to use it. However, we do recommend converting Templates (TEMPLATE.STD documents) earlier rather than later: while a Template remains unconverted, each document that is created from this Template will itself need to be converted.

Note: (i) Once a document has been converted, it can only be edited or printed using LocoScript 3 or LocoScript 2.50 or later. They can't be edited or printed using earlier versions of LocoScript.

If you need a copy for use with your earlier version of LocoScript, you will need either to make this copy before you work on the document in LocoScript 3 or to recover the old version from Limbo immediately after making the conversion (using the steps given in Section 5.5).

(ii) If you are ever unsure whether a file has been converted or not, either 'inspect' the file (using the f5 Inspect document option: see Section 5.7.1) or just try to use it. If the file hasn't been converted, then depending on the action you've selected, LocoScript 3 will either carry out the conversion at that point or display a message telling you that you haven't picked a suitable file. Simply do whatever is necessary to convert the file, then try again.

Appendix I: Converting to LocoScript 3

I.1 LocoScript '1' documents and templates

In essence, all you do to convert a LocoScript '1' document or template to LocoScript 3 is edit it and save the edited version to disc.

However, the procedure is a little bit more complex than that because it's not possible to be certain in every case precisely what type of paper you had set up the document for. So to start with, the conversion program assumes that if the page length is 70 lines the document was set up for A4 paper, if the page length is 66 lines it was set up for 11" continuous paper, and that anything else represents a special type of continuous stationery. But it then immediately prompts you to check that the various settings it has made are suitable.

The other main change happens to the document's layouts. The Layouts themselves are re-specified as 'Stock Layouts', with Layout 0 (the Base Layout) becoming Stock Layouts 0 and 1; Layout 1 becoming Stock Layout 2; etc. Moreover, if the original layout had more than 15 tabs, the Stock Layout will only have the first 15 of these tabs. However, the effect of the different Layouts set in the document shouldn't have changed – except where there are more than 30 tabs in a layout (LocoScript 3's maximum).

The conversion procedure is as follows:

1. Edit the document in the normal way.

Note: If you want to keep a copy for working with the earlier version of LocoScript, edit a *copy* of the document rather than the original. (The steps used to copy a document are given in Section 5.4.1.)

2. When the message appears advising you to check paper and printer details, press [ENTER].

You are then put into the document's Document Set-up, where these details are set.

3. Press [f5] to display the Page menu, check that Paper type *is highlighted and press* [ENTER].

LocoScript then displays a list of the paper types it knows, together with the 'special' Paper Type *document-name* ? if the conversion program decided this document was set up for a special type of paper. The tick marks the current selection.

4. If the paper actually used is A4, A5 or 11" continuous and this is not ticked:

Place the cursor on the correct paper type and press [⊞] *to tick it. Then press* [ENTER] *to take* Use Paper Type.

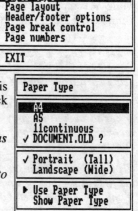

If some other type of paper was used:

Move the cursor to Show Paper Type, *press* [ENTER], *then set the details in the menu so that they describe your paper. (The various settings are explained in Section 12.6.1.) We also recommend setting a suitable name for the paper at the top of the menu.*

When the details are set, press [ENTER], *check that* Use Paper Type *is highlighted, then press* [ENTER] *again.*

5. Back in the Page menu, select Page layout **and press** [ENTER]. **When the Page Layout menu appears, check and if necessary change the Header and Footer Zones (see Section 12.4).**

6. When you have finished setting the Paper and the Page layout, press [EXIT] **followed by** [ENTER] **to leave the Page menu.**

7. Press [EXIT] **followed by** [ENTER] **to leave Document Set-up.**

8. Press [EXIT] **and take the** Save and Print **option to save the LocoScript 3 version of this document to disc and then print it out.**

9. Check the printed version in case there are any adjustments you need to make to the converted document in order to achieve the print-out you require.

In particular, you may need to make changes where you have used Line Pitch and Line Spacing to produce special effects because these settings can give a slightly different result in LocoScript 3.

I.2 LocoScript 2 documents and templates

Converting a LocoScript 2 document or template to LocoScript 3 is simply a matter of editing the document and then saving the edited version on disc.

In general, converting a LocoScript 2 document to LocoScript 3 doesn't alter how it appears when it is printed but there are two cases in which you may have to change some of the styling in the converted document in order to get the same result.

- *If you have used Line Pitch and Line Spacing to produce special effects.*

These settings can give a slightly different result in LocoScript 3.

- *If you have used Character Pitch settings to select different fonts on a laser printer or a DeskJet printer.*

LocoScript 3 gives you direct control over the font that is used. As a result, to get the same print-out from your documents in LocoScript 3 that you did in LocoScript 2, you will have to add the appropriate Font and Point Size settings to each of your Character Pitch settings (as described in Sections 6.1 and 7.1).

Note: If you want to keep a copy for working with the earlier version of LocoScript, edit a *copy* of the document rather than the original. (The steps used to copy a document are given in Section 5.4.1.)

2308

I.3 LocoMail Master documents and datafiles

LocoMail Master documents and datafiles must be converted to LocoScript 3 format before they can either filled or merged in LocoScript 3.

Both the Master documents and the datafiles are simply LocoScript documents and so they need to be converted in the same way – by editing and then saving the edited version to disc. (For more information about the conversion, see either Section I.1 or Section I.2 as appropriate.)

Note: The instructions contained in the LocoMail Masters don't need to be changed in any way as these give the same results in the LocoScript 3 version of LocoMail. However, you may wish to alter them yourself in order to take advantage of the new features this version of LocoMail provides (see the 'Changes in operation' section of your Installation book).

I.4 LocoFile datafiles, LocoSpell User dictionaries and Phrases files

These all have the same format in LocoScript 3 as they did in the earlier versions of LocoScript so they don't need to be converted.

We would, however, like to draw your attention to some of the features offered by the LocoScript 3 versions of LocoFile and LocoSpell. In particular, LocoFile '3' lets you use an existing datafile as a template for a new datafile, while LocoSpell '3' allows you to add unknown words to your User dictionary automatically and to clear out duplicate words between different User dictionaries and between a User dictionary and the System dictionary you now use (first introduced in v2.28).

For further information, see the 'Changes in operation' section of your Installation book.

I.5 LocoScript '1' Saved Blocks

Blocks of text that you saved using LocoScript '1' cannot be inserted directly into LocoScript 3 documents.

However, this doesn't mean that you can no longer use this text. All you need to do to make this text available in LocoScript 3 is to use LocoScript '1' to insert them into a LocoScript '1' document and then convert this document to LocoScript 3.

You will then be able to insert the converted document into LocoScript 3 documents.

Appendix II

The LX fonts

LocoScript 3's LX fonts are professionally-designed fonts which can be used to print good quality text at a range of sizes from 72pt (ie. capital letters about ¾" high) down to 8pt or even as small as 6pt (with extra files).

Moreover, they can be used on almost any printer from the PCW matrix printer and the PcW9512+ inkjet printer to a wide variety of dot-matrix, inkjet and laser printers – whether or not these printers can normally print text at different typesizes. (The printers on which these fonts can't be used are marked ⊗ in the 'Alternative Printers' booklet supplied in your LocoScript 3 pack. These are almost entirely daisy-wheel printers or typewriters, but there are a few other exceptions.)

Two LX fonts – 'LX Roman' and 'LX Sanserif' – are supplied in five standard sizes (8, 10, 12, 14 and 18pt) either in the LocoScript 3 pack or, for external printers, in the LocoScript 3 Printer Support Pack. We give samples of these fonts later in this appendix. Other fonts are available in additional LocoFont LX packs (see Appendix VI). These include a set of 'Decorative' fonts, a set of 'Business' fonts – and one of 'Fixed Pitch' fonts for use where you need to print equally-spaced characters at different sizes. (Samples of these fonts are given in the LocoScript 3 Family brochure.)

The characters of the LX fonts are provided in a series of 'Character Shape' files which the Installation program probably placed on your Start-of-day disc for you when you installed LocoScript 3. This appendix explains how the LX fonts work and which Character Shape files are needed in order to give you the results you require. It also gives some detailed examples of the fonts and point sizes you might use in a document to give particular effects.

Note: A document that uses LocoScript 3's LX fonts can be printed on any printer that supports these fonts: you don't need to print it on the printer for which it has been set up. However, we recommend always printing such a document on the Intended paper if at all possible. If you opt to print on shorter sheets than the Intended stationery, you may find that you get the top part of a line of the text at the bottom of one sheet of paper and the rest of the characters at the top of the next page!

We also strongly recommend setting the Character Pitch to PS and the Line Pitch to Auto wherever you use the LX fonts. In particular, if the Line Pitch you set is too small to accommodate the full height of the characters you are using, you may find that the upper parts of the characters are cut off on the top line of the page. Setting the Line Pitch to Auto will cure this.

Appendix II: LX Fonts

II.1 How the LX fonts work

The different characters offered by the LX fonts are formed from patterns of dots. When you print a document, the patterns of dots for each letter you've used are built up into a 'picture' of your text which LocoScript then sends to the printer to print in Graphics mode.

The patterns of dots required to form each character are held in 'Character Shape' files, which all have a filetype extension of the form .@*xx*. These files are equivalent to the 'Bit Map' font files that are available for some printers.

Each Character Shape file contains the patterns for:

- *A particular set of characters (known as the 'Symbol Set')*
- *In a particular Typeface (or 'Font') – eg. LX Roman or LX Sanserif*
- *At a particular 'Point Size' (character size); and*
- *In a particular Typestyle – 'Regular', 'Bold', 'Italic' or 'Bold+Italic'*

These terms are explained in the Glossary opposite

(To avoid taking up space on disc with patterns for characters you never use, the 500+ characters LocoScript supports have been divided into five 'Symbol Sets' so that you only need to store files that contain characters you actually need. The five Symbol Sets are called Basic, Extended, Greek, Cyrillic and Symbol. Details of the characters in each Symbol Set are given in Appendix III.)

Which Font, Point Size, Symbol Set and Typestyle a Character Shape file offers is revealed by its filename. The first part of this name records the type of printer on which the file is to be used, the Font, the Point Size, the Typestyle and the Symbol Set as shown below. (Different sets of Character Shape files are needed for different types of printer because the size and spacing of the dots they print differs. For example, a LaserJet printer prints at 300 dots per inch but a Bubblejet prints at 360 dots per inch.)

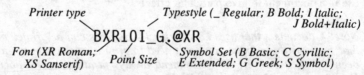

Printer type   *Typestyle (_ Regular; B Bold; I Italic;*
                                                       J Bold+Italic)

BXR10I_G.@XR

Font (XR Roman;   *Point Size*   *Symbol Set (B Basic; C Cyrillic;*
XS Sanserif)   *E Extended; G Greek; S Symbol)*

When you print using the LX fonts, you will need one of these Character Shape files in group 0 (or the 'SYSTEM' group) on Drive M – to cover each combination of Font, Point Size, Typestyle and Symbol Set that you use in your documents.

The five files supplied for each of the LX Roman and LX Sanserif fonts give you just *'Regular'* versions (ie. neither Bold nor Italic) of the characters in the *Basic Symbol Set* in five sizes – *8pt, 10pt, 12pt, 14pt and 18pt* – but these may well be all you need. For a start, the Basic Symbol Set is made up of the 148 characters and accents that cover 99% of people's needs, while the five sizes offered allow you to print everything from 'small print' (using 8pt) to headings (using 14 or 18pt) – as you can see from the samples given in Section II.3.

However, while you will need to buy further files to print a wider range of characters, you won't necessarily need further files to print a wider range of Point Sizes because LocoScript can generate larger-size characters in these fonts by doubling, trebling or even quadrupling the character patterns provided for a smaller size – giving you four sizes from one file. In all, this gives you the following extensive range of sizes to work with:

8pt, 10pt, 12pt, 14pt, 16pt (=2x8pt), 18pt, 20pt (=2x10pt), 24pt (=2x12pt), 28pt (2x14pt), 30pt (=3x10pt), 32pt (=4x8pt), 36pt (=2x18pt), 40pt (=4x10pt), 42pt (=3x14pt), 48pt (=4x12pt), 54pt (=3x18pt), 56pt (=4x14pt) and 72pt (=4x18pt).

We should, however, point out that the characters produced by doubling etc. are not as well formed as those printed at their intended size, particularly at the higher magnifications. You will get better results by adding the Character Shape file specifically for your chosen character size (see Appendix VI).

LocoScript is also able to generate bold and italic characters from a set of 'regular' shapes, so it is not essential to have bold or italic versions of these files – though, again, you will get better-shaped characters if you do.

Section II.2 looks in more detail at which Character Shape files you need.

Glossary of Font terms

Font	The word 'Font' has two possible meanings but, in LocoScript, it is always used to mean the 'Typeface' (or design) of a particular set of characters eg. the ones in a particular Character Shape file. The two LX fonts supplied with LocoScript 3 are called 'LX Roman' and 'LX Sanserif'.
Point Size	The character height expressed in 'Points' – the unit of measure (= ½") used by commercial printers. This height is approximately the distance between the top of a capital letter and the lowest point of a letter like p or g. (LX fonts are available between 6pt* and 72pt.)
Symbol Set	The range of characters supported by a particular file. The characters supported by the different Character Shape files make up one of five Symbol Sets – Basic, Extended*, Symbol*, Greek* and Cyrillic* – which together cover the entire range of characters that LocoScript supports. (The different characters in each of these Symbol Sets are listed in Appendix III.)
Typestyle	The general appearance of the characters supported by a particular file. The LX fonts can be offered in the following typestyles: Regular (ie. upright and not bold), Bold*, Italic* and (in some cases) Bold+Italic*.

* *Available as an optional extra.*

II.2 Which .@*xx* files will you need

To get the best results when using the LX fonts, you need a separate .@*xx* file for each combination of LX font, typestyle (bold, italic, 'regular' etc.), Point Size and Symbol Set you use in your documents. In practice, however, it's generally possible to work with a more restricted range of files – provided you are prepared to accept a few compromises in the quality of the result you achieve. The files you need are therefore as follows:

To print the different Point Sizes you've specified:

To print in a particular font in each Point Size you've specified you need either a file specifically for that Point Size or one for characters a half, a third or a quarter that size because LocoScript can generate larger Point Sizes by doubling, trebling or quadrupling the patterns for a smaller Point Size. So, for example, if you have specified 24pt LX Sanserif, you could use either the 24pt *x*XS24__B.@XS file or, say, the 12pt *x*XS12__B.@XS file. The characters are produced by doubling etc. are not as smooth as ones printed at their intended size but are otherwise quite satisfactory.

(If the specified Point Size isn't provided, LocoScript will simply use the nearest Point Size that is available in this font. How good this looks will depend on how close a match could be found. If the Point Size used was much smaller or much larger than the one you specified, you may find that your lines of text are rather short or, at the other extreme, so long that some of the text is lost off the right-hand edge of the page.)

To print Bold, Italic and Bold+Italic styles:

You don't necessarily need extra files to print text in Bold, Italic etc. because, in the absence of specific Bold etc. files, LocoScript generates the typestyle you want, for example, by skewing regular characters to produce italic or by thickening them to produce bold. The characters so produced aren't as well formed as the ones you would get from the proper Character Shape file and you won't get any of the subtle changes of shape between the different styles, but in general the results will be quite adequate.

To print all the different characters you have used:

The standard set of .@*xx* files all offer the 148 characters and accents that make up the 'Basic' Symbol Set (see Appendix III). This set includes A...Z, a...z, 0...9 and the common punctuation marks that most people need.

If you have only used these standard characters, you won't need any further .@*xx* files. But if you have used any more exotic characters, you will need additional .@*xx* files, specifically to support these extra characters in the fonts and the Point Sizes that you have specified. For example, if your text is printed in 12pt LX Roman and you have included any Greek letters in your text, you will need the *x*XR12__G.@XR file (though the *x*XR10__G.@XR file would do instead as LocoScript is prepared to switch to a different Point Size to print these characters).

If you don't provide a suitable .@*xx* file, LocoScript will simply leave a space so that there's room for you to fill in the character by hand.

IMPORTANT: When working out which .@*xx* files you need, you also need to think whether the text includes any superscripts and subscripts because you'll need Character Shape files for these too. The official size of superscripts and subscripts is 60% that of the main text (rounded down to the next valid point size) so if, for example, your main text is in 12pt, any superscripts and subscripts would technically be 7pt (60% of 12 is 7.2). However, as we don't provide a 7pt file but we do provide an 8pt file, the text is actually laid out for the 8pt characters that in practice you would use instead.

The table below lists the 'true' Super-/Sub-script size for each of the different text sizes you might set with the provided Character Shape files, together with the Point Sizes that would actually be used – again, given the range of files we provide.

Superscript/Subscript Point Size		
Text Point Size	**True Super-/Subscript size**	**Size used in practice**
8	6	8
10	6	8
12	7	8
14	8	8
16 (2x8)	9	8
18	10	10
20 (2x10)	12	12
24 (2x12)	14	14
28 (2x14)	16	16 (2x8)
30 (3x10)	18	18
32 (4x8)	19	18
36 (2x18)	21	20 (2x10)
40 (4x10)	24	24 (2x12)
42 (3x14)	25	24 (2x12)
48 (4x12)	28	28 (2x14)
54 (3x18)	32	32 (4x8)
56 (4x14)	33	32 (4x8)
72 (4x18)	43	42 (3x14)

Appendix II: LX Fonts

II.3 The fonts provided

The Character Shape files provided on the LocoScript 3 disc or in the Printer Support Pack offer two LX fonts – LX Roman and LX Sanserif – each at five different sizes. These produce text as follows:

On a bubblejet such as that provided with some 9512+s:

This is a sample of LX Roman 18pt
This is a sample of LX Roman 14pt
This is a sample of LX Roman 12pt

This is a sample of LX Roman 10pt

This is a sample of LX Roman 8pt

This is a sample of LX Sanserif 18pt
This is a sample of LX Sanserif 14pt
This is a sample of LX Sanserif 12pt

This is a sample of LX Sanserif 10pt

This is a sample of LX Sanserif 8pt

On the PCW matrix printer:

This is a sample of LX Roman 18pt
This is a sample of LX Roman 14pt
This is a sample of LX Roman 12pt

This is a sample of LX Roman 10pt

This is a sample of LX Roman 8pt

This is a sample of LX Sanserif 18pt
This is a sample of LX Sanserif 14pt
This is a sample of LX Sanserif 12pt

This is a sample of LX Sanserif 10pt

This is a sample of LX Sanserif 8pt

II.4 Examples of their use

The following pages show examples of the sort of styling effects that can be achieved using the supplied LX fonts. The examples themselves are on your LocoScript 3 Master disc as BUSINESS, CHAPTER, MINUTES and NEWSLTR. So you can find exact details of the codes used by editing these documents.

Newbell & Company

Chartered Surveyors and Land Agents
25 High Street, Draperston
Tel: (0125) 776432 Fax: (0125) 774611

36pt LX Sanserif bold (18pt doubled)
14pt LX Sanserif
10pt LX Roman
8pt LX Roman

Mr J T Williams
48 West Street
Tillsbury

10th May 1993

Dear Mr Williams

5 Threspan Close

Thank you for your enquiry regarding a full structural survey and valuation of the above property.

Newbell & Co will be happy to carry out this work for you. Moreover, should you instruct us within the next seven days, we will be able to give you the finished report before the end of the month.

Our charges are as follows:

Valuation survey	£99.00
Home purchaser's report	£270.00
Full structural survey	£450.00

In addition, we would recommend taking out our Fallback Insurance (at a cost of £50.00). This will provide you will a second survey on another property free of charge should the purchase of the above property fall through.

All charges are exclusive of VAT which will be charged at the appropriate rate.

We thank you for giving us the opportunity to present our services and look forward to receiving your instruction to proceed.

Yours sincerely

Newbell & Co

E.J. Newbell, P.J. Wellesley, H. James

12pt LX Roman

8pt LX Roman

Uses:

xXR08__B.@XR
xXR10__B.@XR
xXR12__B.@XR
xXS14__B.@XS
xXS18__B.@XS

(Total size on Drive M: Bubblejet 44k; PCW matrix 28k)

9402

The Write Way

_____ *For writers everywhere*

LocoScript 3 breaks new ground

When the Amstrad PCW came out in 1985, it quickly became established as essential equipment for writers everywhere. Locomotive Software's LocoScript word-processing program provided precisely the tools needed to prepare everything from simple letters to major novels.

However, while LocoScript 2 would let you print different documents in different fonts (or typefaces), you could only ever use one font in any document - though you could always vary the type*style* in any way you liked, putting text you wanted to emphasise into Bold or Italic or even Bold+Italic. Also, all the characters would be the same height, though changing the Character Pitch on a dot-matrix printer would vary their width.

LocoScript 3 changes all that. With LocoScript 3, you can use up to four different fonts within one document. And with LocoScript 3's special 'LX' fonts, you can print characters at almost any size between 6pt - that's $^1/_{12}$" - and 72pt (1") in height. True, the LX fonts cannot be used on every type of printer but as they can be used on the PCW8256/8512/9256's built-in matrix printer, the PcW9512+'s Bubblejet printer and a wide range of dot-matrix, Bubblejet, LaserJet and DeskJet printers beside, it's highly likely that you will have a suitable printer.

Writer's Tips: Science Fiction

Story line — Science fiction stories may cover galactic adventures, military conflict or the paranormal. But what they all need is conflict, action, tension and a strong current of suspense. In addition, they need to maintain interest and to finish on a positive note.

The story should also take the reader into the world of Science Fiction and convince them that it's real.

Characters — The characters can be male, female or alien but must be realistic. When facing impossible situations, they must have the strength of character to overcome the enemy.

The Write Way   *March issue*

Annotations (right margin):

— *42pt LX Sanserif bold (14pt trebled)*
— *14pt LX Sanserif italic*
— *18pt LX Sanserif bold*
— *12pt LX Roman*
— *14pt LX Sanserif bold*
— *12pt LX Roman regular & italic*
— *14pt LX Sanserif italic*

Uses: *x*XR12__B.@XR
               *x*XS14__B.@XS
               *x*XS18__B.@XS

(Total size on Drive M: Bubblejet 30k; PCW matrix 18k)

Chapter 4

Backing up your data

This chapter is possibly the most important chapter in the whole book. It describes how to make 'Back-up' copies to use if either a disc or a file is damaged or lost.

Now, don't run away with the wrong idea: data stored on computer discs is pretty reliable. You can leave a disc on a high shelf for years on end and still be able to read the data on it. Discs that you use every day, however, can get lost, be eaten by the dog, have coffee poured over them or simply wear out. Discs can also be damaged if you have a problem with a disc drive. You can also lose files simply through carelessness - formatting the wrong disc, for example! It's in case of accidents such as these that you need Back-ups.

There are two possible approaches to backing up data: you can either make copies of individual files or you can make copies of the whole disc. We can't tell you which is best because it depends how much data you have. Suppose, for example, you are the Secretary of a club with 200 members, whose names you keep in a LocoFile datafile on the same disc as the dozen or so LocoMail Master documents that you use to produce lists of members, subscription reminders etc. etc. The best approach in such a case is probably to start by making a copy of the whole disc in order to back up the LocoMail Masters but thereafter to copy the membership file because the LocoMail Masters won't change.[1]

Your next decision is how often to back up. Again, we can't tell you the answer: it's really a matter of balancing the time and effort spent in making back-ups against that you would have to spend re-doing the changes you have made since the last time you backed up. If you are a one-finger typist, you might begrudge re-typing even one line of text but if you are an expert typist, it may only be worth backing up a file after you have done two or three pages. But beware: if you don't back up at the end of every session and the dog eats your disc, all your hard work will have to be done again!

---

[1] If your membership file contains 2000 names and addresses rather than 200 and almost fills the disc, it may be quicker and easier to copy the whole disc rather than simply this one file.

The Layman's Guide   *page 43*

Callouts:
— *18pt LX Sanserif italic*
— *36pt LX Sanserif bold (18pt doubled)*
— *12pt LX Roman*
— *8pt LX Roman*
— *14pt LX Sanserif bold & italic*

Uses: *x*XR08__B.@XR
            *x*XR12__B.@XR
            *x*XS14__B.@XS
            *x*XS18__B.@XS

(Total size on Drive M: Bubblejet 36k; PCW matrix 22k)

DRAPERSTON CHORAL SOCIETY — *18pt LX Roman bold*

Minutes of the Committee Meeting — *14pt LX Sanserif*
held on Wednesday, 4th August 1993
at 5 Threspan Close, Draperston

Present: William Wykeham-Smythe   (Chairman) — *12pt LX Roman*
Anthea Williams   (Secretary)
Belinda Davison   (Treasurer)
Anthony Robinson   (Librarian)
George Pratt   (Conductor)

1   **Apologies for absence** — *12pt LX Roman bold*
Apologies had been received from Mary Bell (Ladies' Rep.) and Colin Davison (Men's Rep.).

2   **Minutes of the last meeting**
The minutes of the last meeting were read and signed by the Chairman as an accurate record.

3   **Matters arising**
There were no matters arising.

4   **Financial position**
There had been no major expenses to meet over the summer but the Treasurer had been warned that the Festival fees had gone up to £5 per singer. Once again, the importance of the raffles to the choir's funds would need to be emphasised to the members.

5   **New members**   CD
The choir is still very short of male singers. It was agreed that the usual poster should be prepared but this year the poster coverage should be extended to cover Coopernaught in the hope of attracting new members. Mr Davison would organise its distribution.

6   **Music for the Festival**   AR
The Festival organisers had announced the set pieces but hadn't said how many hire copies we would have so it was not known how many extra copies we would have to buy.

7   **Any other business**   AW
Rex Johnston (Hon Life member): The Secretary reported that Mr Johnston had died in July. It was agreed that the choir would make a donation to charity in his memory.

8   The Secretary was thanked for her (and her husband's) kind hospitality in their new home and the meeting closed at 9pm.

———————
Chairman

———————
Date

— *12pt LX Roman italic*

Uses: xXR12__B.@XR
                   xXR18__B.@XR
                   xXS14__B.@XS

(Total size on Drive M: Bubblejet 30k; PCW matrix 18k)

Character Set & Keyboard Layout

LocoScript 3 supports a very wide range of characters and symbols, making it possible to type not only in English but also mathematical equations and text in almost every European language. All of these characters can be displayed on the screen, but the range of characters you can print depends on the printer you use.

To let you type all these characters, they are organised into a number of keyboard layouts, each of which associates either one or two characters with each character key on your PCW's keyboard. There are six layouts in all:

'Normal' – which corresponds to the characters engraved on your PCW's keyboard
'Extra' – which covers all the accents
'Alt' – which covers special language characters like ß ø ð ŋ
'Greek' – which lays out Greek characters in a similar way to keyboards used in Greece
'Cyrillic' – which lays out Cyrillic characters in the way recommended by the AATSEEL Ad Hoc Committee on the Standardisation of Computer Keyboards for Cyrillic
'Symbol' – which covers most of the special symbols LocoScript supports

The keyboard layout that is selected when you press a character key depends on (i) which Supershift is selected (see Section 2.3) and (ii) whether the key is pressed on its own (or with [SHIFT]), with [EXIT] held down, or with [ALT] held down – as follows:

	Keys pressed:		
Supershift	On own	With Extra	With Alt
Normal ([ALT]+[f1])	Normal	Extra	Alt
Greek ([ALT]+[f3])	Greek	Extra	Normal
Cyrillic ([ALT]+[f3])	Cyrillic	Extra	Normal
Symbol ([ALT]+[f3])	Symbol	Extra	Normal

The keyboard layouts are shown on the following pages, together with lists of the characters included on each layout and which LX Font Symbol Sets these characters are included in.

Note: Although you can type all of these characters, you won't necessarily be able to print them. To print them all, you need to be using:
- *the PCW matrix printer and either the Standard or the Sans Serif font (or one of the 'LocoFont' fonts)*
- *the PcW9512+ inkjet printer and a font from the LocoFont BJ set*
- *a suitable 24-pin printer and a font from the LocoFont 24 set*
- *a printer that supports the LX fonts and the full range of LX Symbol Sets*

It also isn't possible to use all these characters in the names you use for documents, Paper Types and the like. The limitations here are explained on page 252.

Normal layout

Selected immediately after loading and returned to by pressing [ALT] + [F1]. Also available from other Supershifts by holding down [ALT] when pressing the given keys.

Description	Keystroke		Description	Keystroke
a...z Lower case letters	*letter*	(	Open parenthesis	[SHIFT] 9
A...Z Upper case letters	[SHIFT] + *letter*	)	Close parenthesis	[SHIFT] 0
0...9 Numerals	*number*	[	Open square bracket	[
- Hyphen (or minus)	-	]	Close square bracket	]
, Comma	, or [SHIFT] ,	{	Open curly brace	[SHIFT] [
. Full stop	. or [SHIFT] .	}	Close curly brace	[SHIFT]]
; Semicolon	;	@	At	[SHIFT] ½
: Colon	[SHIFT] ;	§	Section	§
! Exclamation mark	[SHIFT] 1	£	Pound	[SHIFT] 3
? Question mark	[SHIFT] /	$	Dollar	[SHIFT] 4
& Ampersand	[SHIFT] 7	+	Plus	[SHIFT] =
' Apostrophe	[SHIFT] 6	=	Equals	=
" Double quote	[SHIFT] 2	½	Half	½
_ Underline	[SHIFT] -	<	Less than	[SHIFT] §
* Asterisk	[SHIFT] 8	>	Greater than	[SHIFT] #
# Hash	#	%	Percent	[SHIFT] 5
/ Slash	/			

LX Fonts:

All these characters are included in the Basic Symbol Set.

Note: The Normal and Extra layouts shown on these pages are the ones used on a PCW8256/8512, PcW9256 or PcW10. The layouts used on a PCW9512 or PcW9512+ have the following differences:

Normal layout: § is replaced by |; { by ¼; } by ¾
Extra layout: | is replaced by §; ¼ by {; ¾ by }

Extra layout

Available from all Supershifts and selected by pressing [EXTRA] with the letter keys.

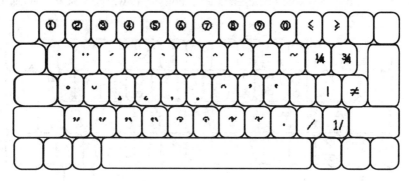

	Description	Keystroke		Description	Keystroke
´	Acute	[EXTRA] E	˘	Breve	[EXTRA] S
`	Grave	[EXTRA] T	˝	Double acute	[EXTRA] R
^	Circumflex	[EXTRA] U	¯	Macron	[EXTRA] O
¨	Umlaut or diaeresis	[EXTRA] W	˵	Double grave	[EXTRA] Y
¸	Cedilla	[EXTRA] D	̨	Ogonek	[EXTRA] F
~	Tilde	[EXTRA] P	,	Latvian tail	[EXTRA] G
°	Ring	[EXTRA] A	.	Dot below	[EXTRA] H
ˇ	Caron or hacek	[EXTRA] I	/	Stroke	[EXTRA] /
˙	Dot	[EXTRA] Q			
ʽ	Rough breathing	[EXTRA] L	¼	One quarter	[EXTRA] [
ʽ/	- with acute	[EXTRA] X	¾	Three quarters	[EXTRA]]
ʽ\	- with grave	[EXTRA] V	|	Vertical bar	[EXTRA] §
ʽ^	- with circumflex	[EXTRA] N	·	Decimal point	[EXTRA] .
ʽ~	- with tilde	[EXTRA] ,	1/	One upon	[EXTRA] ½
ʼ	Smooth breathing	[EXTRA] K	≤	Less than or equal	[EXTRA] -
ʼ/	- with acute	[EXTRA] Z	≠	Not equals	[EXTRA] #
ʼ\	- with grave	[EXTRA] C	≥	Greater than or equal	[EXTRA] =
ʼ^	- with circumflex	[EXTRA] B	⓪...⑨	Circled digits	[EXTRA] 0...9
ʼ~	- with tilde	[EXTRA] M			
^	Greek circumflex	[EXTRA] J			

LX Fonts:

Some of these characters are in the 'Basic' Symbol Set. The rest are in the 'Extended' and 'Greek' Symbol Sets (available as optional extras: see Appendix VI).

Basic	´ ` ^ ¨ ~ ° ¼ ¾ | ·
Extended	˘ ˙ ˝ ¯ ˵ ̨ / 1/ ≤ ≠ ≥ ⓪...⑨
Greek	ʽ ʽ/ ʽ\ ʽ^ ʽ~ ʼ ʼ/ ʼ\ ʼ^ ʼ~ ^

8

Alt layout

Available from the Normal Supershift by holding down $\boxed{\text{ALT}}$ as you press the character keys.

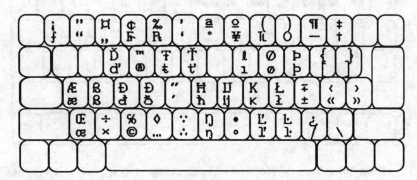

	Description	Keystroke		Description	Keystroke
0	Zero (no slash)	$\boxed{\text{ALT}}$ 0	к K	k (Greenland)	$\boxed{\text{ALT}}$ K
æ Æ	ae diphthong	$\boxed{\text{ALT}}$ A	ŀ Ŀ	L dot	$\boxed{\text{ALT}}$.
œ Œ	oe diphthong	$\boxed{\text{ALT}}$ Z	l' Ľ	L apostrophe	$\boxed{\text{ALT}}$,
ß	Scharfes S	$\boxed{\text{ALT}}$ S	ł Ł	L stroke	$\boxed{\text{ALT}}$ L
		or $\boxed{\text{SHIFT}}\boxed{\text{ALT}}$ S	ℓ	Curly l	$\boxed{\text{SHIFT}}\boxed{\text{ALT}}$ I
ø Ø	O stroke	$\boxed{\text{ALT}}$ O	ŋ Ŋ	Eng	$\boxed{\text{ALT}}$ N
ı	Dotless i (Turkish)	$\boxed{\text{ALT}}$ I	þ Þ	Thorn	$\boxed{\text{ALT}}$ P
đ Đ	D stroke	$\boxed{\text{ALT}}$ D	ŧ Ŧ	T stroke	$\boxed{\text{ALT}}$ T
ð Ð	Eth	$\boxed{\text{ALT}}$ F	ď Ď	(Alternative) d hacek	$\boxed{\text{ALT}}$ E
ħ Ħ	H stroke	$\boxed{\text{ALT}}$ H	ť Ť	(Alternative) t hacek	$\boxed{\text{ALT}}$ Y
ij IJ	IJ	$\boxed{\text{ALT}}$ J			

	Description	Keystroke		Description	Keystroke
'	Open single quote	$\boxed{\text{ALT}}$ 6	¿	Open query	$\boxed{\text{SHIFT}}\boxed{\text{ALT}}$ /
'	Close single quote	$\boxed{\text{SHIFT}}\boxed{\text{ALT}}$ 6	¡	Open shriek	$\boxed{\text{SHIFT}}\boxed{\text{ALT}}$ 1
"	Open double quote	$\boxed{\text{ALT}}$ 2	ª	Feminine ordinal	$\boxed{\text{SHIFT}}\boxed{\text{ALT}}$ 7
"	Close double quote	$\boxed{\text{SHIFT}}\boxed{\text{ALT}}$ 2	º	Masculine ordinal	$\boxed{\text{SHIFT}}\boxed{\text{ALT}}$ 8
‹	Single guillemet	$\boxed{\text{SHIFT}}\boxed{\text{ALT}}$ §			
›		$\boxed{\text{SHIFT}}\boxed{\text{ALT}}$ #	...	Ellipsis	$\boxed{\text{ALT}}$ V
«	Double guillemet	$\boxed{\text{ALT}}$ §	–	Dash	$\boxed{\text{ALT}}$ -
»		$\boxed{\text{ALT}}$ #	©	Copyright	$\boxed{\text{ALT}}$ C
„	German open double quote		®	Registered	$\boxed{\text{ALT}}$ R
		$\boxed{\text{ALT}}$ 3	™	Trade mark	$\boxed{\text{SHIFT}}\boxed{\text{ALT}}$ R

9.

	Description	Keystroke		Description	Keystroke
°	Open circle	[ALT] M	\	Backslash	[ALT] ½
•	Bullet	[SHIFT][ALT] M	°	Degrees	[ALT] 7
¶	Paragraph (Pilcrow)	[SHIFT][ALT] -	´	Minutes	[ALT] G
†	Dagger	[ALT] =	˝	Seconds	[SHIFT][ALT] G
‡	Double dagger	[SHIFT][ALT] =	‰	Per thousand	[SHIFT][ALT] 5
∴	Therefore	[ALT] B	±	Plus or minus	[ALT] ;
∵	Because of	[SHIFT][ALT] B	∓	Minus or plus	[SHIFT][ALT] ;
℅	Care of	[SHIFT][ALT] C	×	Times	[ALT] X
◊	Diamond	[SHIFT][ALT] V	÷	Divide	[SHIFT][ALT] X
¢	Cent	[SHIFT][ALT] 4	/	Slash (large)	[ALT] /
¤	Internatl. currency symbol		(	Bracket (large)	[SHIFT][ALT] 9
		[SHIFT][ALT] 3	)		[SHIFT][ALT] 0
₣	Franc	[ALT] 4	[	Square bracket (large) [ALT] [
ƒ	Florin	[ALT] 1	]		[ALT]]
¥	Yen	[ALT] 8	{	Curly brackets (large) [SHIFT][ALT] [
₧	Peseta	[ALT] 5	}		[SHIFT][ALT]]
₺	Turkish pound	[ALT] 9			

LX Fonts:

Some of these characters are in the 'Basic' Symbol Set. The rest are in the 'Extended' and 'Symbol' Symbol Sets (available as optional extras: see Appendix VI).

Basic 0 æ Æ œ Œ ß ø Ø ı

' ' " " ‹ › « » „ ¿ ¡ ª º

... – © ® ™ ∘ • ¶ † \ °

¢ ¤ ₣ ƒ ¥ ₧

Extended đ Đ ð ħ Ħ ij IJ ĸ ŀ Ŀ ľ Ľ ł Ł ℓ ŋ Ŋ þ Þ ŧ Ŧ ď ť

‡ ∴ ∵ ℅ ◊ ₺ ´ ˝ ‰ ± Ď Ť

Symbol ∓ × ÷ / ( ) [ ] { }

Greek layout

Selected by pressing ALT + f3 to go into the Greek Supershift.

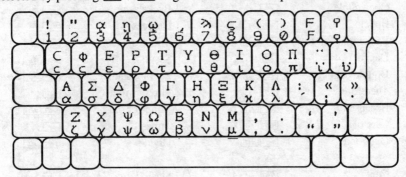

	Description	Keystroke		Description	Keystroke
α A	Alpha	A	ϊ	Iota diaeresis	[
β B	Beta	B	ϋ	Upsilon diaeresis	]
γ Γ	Gamma	G	Ϝ F	Digamma	-
δ Δ	Delta	D	ϙ Ϙ	Qoppa (koppa)	=
ε E	Epsilon	E	c C	Lunate sigma	Q
ζ Z	Zeta	Z	,	Thousands mark	SHIFT 6
η H	Eta	H	ϡ	Sampi	SHIFT 7
θ Θ	Theta	U	ϛ	Stigma	SHIFT 8
ι I	Iota	I	ᾳ	Alpha + iota subscript	SHIFT 3
κ K	Kappa	K	ῃ	Eta + iota subscript	SHIFT 4
λ Λ	Lambda	L	ῳ	Omega + iota subscript	SHIFT 5
μ M	Mu	M			
ν N	Nu	N	0...9	Numerals	*number*
ξ Ξ	Xi	J	,	Comma	, or SHIFT ,
o O	Omicron	O	.	Full stop	. or SHIFT .
π Π	Pi	P	;	Semicolon	§
ρ P	Rho	R	:	Colon	SHIFT ;
σ Σ	Sigma	S	!	Exclamation mark	SHIFT 1
ς		W	"	Double quote	SHIFT 2
τ T	Tau	T	'	Open single quote	SHIFT /
υ Y	Upsilon	Y	'	Close single quote	SHIFT ½
φ Φ	Phi	F	"	Open double quote	/
φ		SHIFT W	"	Close double quote	½
χ X	Chi	X	(	Open parenthesis	SHIFT 9
ψ Ψ	Psi	C	)	Close parenthesis	SHIFT 0
ω Ω	Omega	V			
			´	Acute	;
·	Greek semicolon	#	`	Grave	SHIFT]
			¨	Umlaut or diaeresis	SHIFT [

LX Fonts:

Some of these characters are in the 'Basic' Symbol Set but the majority are in the 'Greek' Symbol Set (available as an optional extra: see Appendix VI).

Cyrillic layout

Selected by pressing ⌐ALT⌐ + ⌐f5⌐ to go into the Cyrillic Supershift.

	Description	Keystroke		Description	Keystroke
a A	A	A	ц Ц	Ts	C
б Б	B	B	ч Ч	Ch	H
в В	V	V	ш Ш	Sh	W
г Г	G; H (BR, U)	G	щ Щ	Shch; Sht (Blg)	]
г Г	G (BR, U)	-	ъ Ъ	hard sign; A (Blg)	=
д Д	D	D	ы Ы	Y (postcon. BR,R)	Y
e E	E; Ye (BR, R)	E	ь Ь	soft sign	;
є Є	Ye (U)	½	э Э	E (BR, R)	#
ж Ж	Zh	§	ю Ю	Yu	[
з З	Z	Z	я Я	Ya	Q
и И	I (Blg, R); Y (U)	I			
й Й	Y (postvocalic)	J	№	Number	⌐SHIFT⌐ 3
i I	I (BR, U)	/			
к К	K	K	0...9	Numerals	*number*
л Л	L	L	,	Comma	,
м М	M	M	.	Full stop	.
н Н	N	N	;	Semicolon	⌐SHIFT⌐ ,
о О	O	O	:	Colon	⌐SHIFT⌐ .
п П	P	P	!	Exclamation mark	⌐SHIFT⌐ 1
p Р	R	R	?	Question mark	⌐SHIFT⌐ 4
с С	S	S	"	Double quote	⌐SHIFT⌐ 2
т Т	T	T	'	Close single quote	⌐SHIFT⌐ 6
y У	U	U	(	Open parenthesis	⌐SHIFT⌐ 9
ф Ф	F	F	)	Close parenthesis	⌐SHIFT⌐ 0
x Х	Kh	X	%	Percent	⌐SHIFT⌐ 5

Note: Blg = Bulgarian; BR = Byelorussian; R = Russian; U = Ukrainian.

LX Fonts:

Some of these characters are in the 'Basic' Symbol Set but the majority are in the 'Cyrillic' Symbol Set (available as an optional extra: see Appendix VI). To print й Й, you will also need the 'Extended' Symbol Set.

Symbol layout

Selected by pressing [ALT] + [f7] to go into the Symbol Supershift.

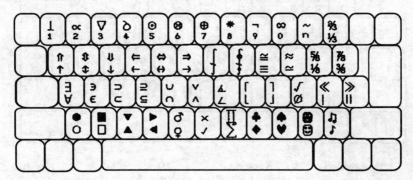

	Description	Keystroke		Description	Keystroke
⅛*	One eighth	[	∃	Exists	[SHIFT] A
⅓*	One third	=	∍	Such that	[SHIFT] S
⅜*	Three eighths	]	∀	Universal	A
⅝*	Five eighths	[SHIFT] [	∨	Logical Or	[SHIFT] H
⅔*	Two thirds	[SHIFT] =	∧	Logical And	H
⅞*	Seven eighths	[SHIFT]]	¬	Logical Not	[SHIFT] 9
$^{0...9}$	Superscript 0...9	0...9	Ø	Empty set	;
^{n}	Superscript n	-	∩	Intersection	G
≃*	Approx. equal to	P	∪	Union	[SHIFT] G
≈*	Nearly equal to	[SHIFT] P	⊂	Proper subset	D
≪	Much less than	[SHIFT] §	⊃	Proper superset	[SHIFT] D
~	Asymptotically equal to	[SHIFT] -	⊆	Reflex subset	F
≫	Much greater than	[SHIFT] #	⊇	Reflex superset	[SHIFT] F
≡	Equivalent	O	∈	Element	S
≅	Congruent	[SHIFT] O	⌊	Floor	K
∝	Proportional to	[SHIFT] 2	⌋		L
|	Modulus	§	⌈	Ceiling	[SHIFT] K
‖	Parallel	#	⌉		[SHIFT] L
⊥	Perpendicular	[SHIFT] 1	⊙	Circle dot (arrow out)	[SHIFT] 5
∞	Infinity	[SHIFT] 0	⊗	Circle times	[SHIFT] 6
√	Root	[SHIFT] ;	⊕	Circle plus	[SHIFT] 7
∠	Angle	J			
∠		[SHIFT] J			

Description		Keystroke	Description		Keystroke
Σ	Sum	M	∫	Integral	U
Π	Product	⌜SHIFT⌝ M	∮	Contour integral	I
∂	Partial differential	⌜SHIFT⌝ 4	∫	Integral (large)	⌜SHIFT⌝ U
∇	Gradient	⌜SHIFT⌝ 3	∮	Contour integral (large)	⌜SHIFT⌝ I

Description		Keystroke	Description		Keystroke
↑	Up arrow	Q	○	Large open circle	Z
↕	Up and down arrow	W	●	Large bullet	⌜SHIFT⌝ Z
↓	Down arrow	E	□	Box	X
←	Left arrow	R	■	Filled Box	⌜SHIFT⌝ X
↔	Left and right arrow	T	✓	Tick	N
→	Right arrow	Y	×	Cross	⌜SHIFT⌝ N
⇑	Wide up arrow	⌜SHIFT⌝ Q	✮	Star	⌜SHIFT⌝ 8
⇕	Wide up and down arrow ⌜SHIFT⌝ W		☺	Smiling face	/
⇓	Wide down arrow	⌜SHIFT⌝ E	☻	Black smiling face	⌜SHIFT⌝ /
⇐	Wide left arrow	⌜SHIFT⌝ R	♂	Mars	⌜SHIFT⌝ B
⇔	Wide left and right arrow ⌜SHIFT⌝ T		♀	Venus	B
⇒	Wide right arrow	⌜SHIFT⌝ Y	♣	Clubs	⌜SHIFT⌝ ,
▲	Up triangle	C	♦	Diamonds	,
▼	Down triangle	⌜SHIFT⌝ C	♥	Hearts	.
◄	Left triangle	V	♠	Spades	⌜SHIFT⌝ .
►	Right triangle	⌜SHIFT⌝ V	♪	Note	½
			♫	Two-note	⌜SHIFT⌝ ½

LX Fonts:

The characters marked * are in the 'Extended' Symbol Set. The others are included in the 'Symbol' Symbol Set. Both these Symbol Sets are optional extras (see Appendix VI).

Characters for names within LocoScript

A number of items within LocoScript have names: Documents; Groups; Discs; Layouts; Paper Types; Printers; Character Sets (and Styles); Identity text

The names used for your printers and their Character Sets and for the supplied range of Paper Types are set for you. But you get to choose the names for everything else and there are rules about how these names should be constructed – in particular, about the range of characters and the number of characters that can be used. By no means all the characters that you can type using LocoScript 3 can be used in these names.

The items split into two groups, in terms of the range of characters that can be used in their names – as follows:

Documents, Groups and Discs

Documents, Groups and Discs are restricted to the following range of characters:
- the capital letters A...Z
- the digits 0...9
- the characters " # $ % ' @ _ § { } ½ ◊

No other characters may be used: in particular, you cannot include any spaces in these names.

Note: Document and Disc names have a main part which is between one and eight characters long, to which you can add an extension of up to three characters which you separate from the main part by a full stop. The names for Groups are simply between one and eight characters long.

Layouts, Paper Types, Character Styles, Identity

The range of characters you can use for Layouts, Paper Types and Character Styles, and for the Identity text is very much wider – comprising:
- a...z, A...Z, Ø...9 0 , æ, Æ, œ, Œ
- these accented characters only:
  á...ú, à...ù, â...û, ãõ, ç, ÄÖÜ, ä...üÿ, Å, å, Ñ, ñ, ġ
- all the Greek characters
- đ Ð ð ħ Ħ ı ij IJ ĸ KĿ Ŀ łŁ ℓ ŋ Ŋ ø Ø ß þ Þ t Ŧ ďť
- - , . ; : ... ! ? (space) & ' " _ * # / ( ) [ ] { } @ © ® ™ § ∘ • ¶ ◊
- « » ¿ ¡ ª º
- $ + / = | \ ½ . < > %

The principal groups of characters you can't use are:
- the Cyrillic characters
- many of the special mathematical symbols
- symbols like ○ ● □ ■ ✓ × ☺ ☻ ♂ ♀ ♣ ♦ ♥ ♠ ♪ ♫

Note: Each of these names can be up to 12 characters long.

Appendix IV

Glossary

Alert	A type of message that LocoScript displays to draw your attention eg. to an error
ASCII	(American Standard Code for Information Interchange) System used by most computers to represent characters. Defines the codes used for upper and lower case letters, the numbers 0...9 and a range of punctuation symbols
ASCII file	A file containing only simple ASCII text characters
Back-up copy	A copy of a file or a disc, made for use in case of accidents
Bail bar	The bar on a printer that holds the paper against the platen (rubber roller)
Block	An area of memory used to hold sections of text, ready for pasting into a document
Block editing	Changing the text by copying sections into Blocks, then pasting them back into the document in different positions
Bold	A way of styling text that makes characters darker when printed (each character is printed twice with the second printing shifted slightly to the right – cf. Double-strike)
Bottom Gap	The area at the bottom of a page in which the printer never prints
Booting LocoScript 3	Loading the LocoScript 3 program into the PCW's memory
BubbleJet printer	A printer which creates characters by firing ink drops at the paper from thin nozzles – in particular, the inkjet printer provided with some models of the PcW9512+
Byte	Unit of storage space either in memory or on a disc. Each byte can hold one character
Caps Lock	Special key combination ([ALT]+[ENTER]) that tells LocoScript to convert any lower case letters you type to upper case – until you type [ALT]+[ENTER] again
Case (of a character)	Whether the character is a capital letter (upper case) or a small letter (lower case)
Centre tab ↔	Tab that aligns text segments so that the centre of each text segment is at the tab position
Centring (of a line)	Positioning the text on the line centrally between the margins
Centronics port	Connector into which you can plug a printer which has the Centronics type of interface. Also known as a Parallel port

Appendix IV: Glossary

LocoScript 3 User Guide

253

308

Character keys	The keys on the keyboard that produce text characters
Character Pitch	The spacing of the characters along a line
Character Set	The range of characters available (see also Symbol Set). On a daisy-wheel printer, it identifies the 'family' to which a printwheel belongs
Character Set file	Printer file supporting a particular font. Identified by the filetype .#xx
Character Shape file	Printer file, identified by the filetype .@xx, providing patterns for printing one of the LX fonts. Each file contains the patterns for printing the characters of one Symbol Set in one of the LX fonts at one particular Point Size (and multiples thereof)
Character Style	The part of the printer set-up that identifies the printwheel on a daisy-wheel printer (Can be ignored on other types of printer)
Commands menu	A menu offering a choice of actions. An arrow or a diamond marks the action that will be carried out when [ENTER] is pressed
Confirmation menu	Menu used to set up and confirm the details of a task to be carried out
Continuous stationery	Paper on a continuous roll or 'fanfolded' with pages divided by a line of perforations
Carriage Return (↵)	The special character that tells LocoScript to start a new line, typed by pressing [RETURN]
CR Extra Spacing	Additional line spacing following a Carriage Return
Cursor	Blob or band of highlighting used either to mark where you are working or to pick out items on the screen
Cursor keys	The four 'Arrow' keys – used to move Cursors
Daisy-wheel printer	A printer that produces characters by hitting the 'petals' of a printwheel with a hammer
Data discs	Discs used to store documents and datafiles (cf. Start-of-day and Start-up discs)
Decimal tab	Tab that aligns numbers in such a way that their decimal points are at the tab position
Disc Manager Screen	The display showing the documents, etc. on the discs currently in your disc drives
Document	The text of a letter, chapter of a book, report etc. as stored in memory or on disc
Document Set-up	The area of a document in which general information about the document is recorded eg. which type of paper the document has been prepared for

---

Dot-matrix printer	A printer that produces characters by making patterns of dots on the paper
Double-spaced text	Text that has a blank line between each line of text
Double-strike	Making text darker by printing each character twice in the same position (cf. Bold)
Download mode	Several printers, including the PcW9512+ inkjet printer, can – with suitable additional software – print characters downloaded from LocoScript: such printers are described as having a Download mode
Draft quality	The quality of text produced quickly by using a low density of dots (dot-matrix and inkjet printers only)
Drive M	The area of the PCW's memory used to store documents and data files (temporarily)
Editing	Changing the text of a document
End-of-page line	Special line used on the screen to mark the end of each page of the document
End-page-here (↓)	Special character which tells LocoScript to start a new page, typed by holding down ⎯ALT⎯ and pressing ⎯RETURN⎯. Also known as a Form Feed
Exchange Text	Text that LocoScript will substitute for examples of the Find Text in the document (see Find Text)
External printer	Printer that is used instead of the PCW's built-in printer
Fanfold paper	Continuous stationery with the pages divided by lines of perforations and folded
File	Collection of related data or the text of a document, as stored in memory or on a disc
File cursor	Band of highlighting on the Disc Manager Screen used to pick out the document or file you want to work with
Find Text	Text that you supply which LocoScript tries to match against the text in the document
Fixed Pitch text	Text in which the characters all take up the same amount of space along the line
Font	The word 'Font' has two possible meanings but, in LocoScript, it is always used to mean the 'Typeface' (or design) of a particular set of characters eg. the ones supported by a particular Character Set (.#xx) file.
Footer	Optional text printed at the bottom of one or more pages of your document
Footer Zone	Section of the page reserved for the Footer
Form Feed (↓)	Special character which tells LocoScript to start a new page, typed by holding down ⎯ALT⎯ and pressing ⎯RETURN⎯. Also known as the End-page-here character

Formatting	The process of marking out a new blank disc ready to store data and documents
Function keys	Keys on the keyboard marked f1, f2 etc. used in particular to bring menus onto the screen
Group	Group of documents and datafiles on a disc. You can have up to eight different groups on each disc
Group cursor	Band of highlighting in the upper part of the Disc Manager Screen used to pick out the group you want to work with
Hard hyphen	Special type of hyphen that tells LocoScript not to break the line at this hyphen (typed by pressing ⊞ and then typing a hyphen)
Hard Space	Special type of space that tells LocoScript not to break the line at this space (typed by pressing ⊞ and then typing a space)
Header	Optional text printed at the top of one or more pages of your document
Header Zone	Section of the page reserved for the Header
Hidden files	Files on the Start-of-day disc which are vital to the running of LocoScript and so have been hidden to protect them against accidental erasure
High Quality	The quality of text produced using a high density of dots. Also known as NLQ or 'Near Letter Quality'
Indent tab (↦)	Special character (typed by holding down ALT and pressing TAB) that tells LocoScript to use the next tab position as the left margin for the text until the next Carriage Return
Information lines	The three lines at the top of the screen, displaying details of the current task and of the facilities that are available
Inkjet printer	A printer which creates characters by squirting jets of ink at the paper (cf. Bubble Jet printer)
Italic	A way of styling text in which the characters are slanted
Justification	Increasing the spaces between words so that the right-hand edge of the text is straight as well as the left
K	A Kilobyte or 1024 bytes. Used to express the size of files, the amount of storage space on a disc etc.
Landscape	Orientation of a sheet of paper widthways instead of lengthways (cf. Portrait)
Layout	The specification of the margins, tabs etc. used to lay out text in the part of the document that uses this layout
Layout Editor	The part of LocoScript that helps you set up or change the Layout for the current text

Left Offset	The distance the print start position is moved to the right of its normal start position (normally zero)
Limbo files	Files that have been 'erased' but remain on disc until the storage space they occupy is needed to store another file
Line Break	The point in continuous text at which LocoScript decides to move onto the next line
Line Pitch	The standard spacing of the lines down the page – usually set either to 6 lines per inch or to 'Auto' (which makes the spacing 20% more than the Point Size)
Line Spacing	The number of standard lines the printer advances between printing one line and printing the next (but see CR Extra Spacing)
Loading LocoScript 3	The process of loading the LocoScript 3 program into the PCW's memory so that you can start using the program
LocoFile	Integrated pop-up database for use with LocoScript 3
LocoFont/LocoFont 24/LocoFont BJ/LocoFont LX	Sets of additional fonts for use with LocoScript 3. For example, LocoFont LX provides additional LX fonts for printing at multiple sizes (see below). For further information, see the LocoScript 3 Family brochure
LocoMail	The program that works alongside LocoScript, merging information eg. from datafiles into documents
LocoSpell	The program that works alongside LocoScript, checking words against dictionaries of standard spellings
Lower case characters	Small letters (cf. Upper case characters)
LX font	Special LocoScript Graphics font which can be printed at a range of different sizes. Available for printing on a wide range of different printers (except daisy-wheels)
Menu cursor	Band of highlighting used to pick out options in menus
Memory disc	Section of the PCW's memory used as a temporary store for files and documents (referred to as Drive M)
NLQ (Near Letter Quality)	The quality of text produced using a high density of dots. Also known as High Quality
Num Lock	Special key combination ($\boxed{\text{ALT}}$+$\boxed{\text{RELAY}}$) that sets/clears the use of the Textual Movement Keys as a numeric keypad
Page Break	Point in the text at which LocoScript decides to move onto the next page (shown on the screen by an End-of-page line)
Page printer	A printer which only handles single sheet stationery, feeding each sheet out automatically as it is completed
Pagination text	Text for use at the top and bottom of one or more pages of the document (also referred to as Headers and Footers)
Paper Type	Record of Height, Width, etc. of a particular type of paper

Paragraph	Block of text separated from other text by one or more lines of 'white'
Parallel Port	A connector into which you can plug a printer which has a 'Parallel' interface. Often described as a Centronics port
Phrases	Short pieces of text, including word-processing codes, stored on disc for easy insertion into documents
PHRASES.STD	File of Phrases made available as part of loading LocoScript 3 (if stored in group 0 of Start-of-day disc)
Pitch	Number of characters per inch on a line
Platen	Rubber roller in the printer against which paper is held
Points	Measure used by commercial printers. 1 Point = ½"
Point Size	The height of characters from the top of a capital letter to the lowest point of a letter like p or g, expressed in Points
Portrait	Orientation of the paper lengthways (cf. Landscape)
Printer Control State	Phase of using LocoScript in which all actions affect how the printer is set up (entered by pressing [PTR])
Printer Support Pack	Set of Printer files needed to support a wide range of external printers
Printwheel	Interchangeable unit on a daisy-wheel printer with characters on each 'petal'
Proportional Spacing (PS)	System of positioning characters so that wide characters take more space on a line than narrow characters
Relaying	Re-adjusting how the text is laid out to take account of changes that have been made
Resetting	Restarting LocoScript 3 by pressing [SHIFT], [EXTRA] and [EXIT]. Equivalent to switching off and switching on again
Reverse	A way of styling text so that words are shown on the screen as dark text against a light background
Right Aligning	Positioning text so that the last character is at the right-hand margin
Right tab	A tab that marks the position of the last character in any segment of text using this tab
RS232 Interface	The standard type of Serial Interface (see Serial Port)
Ruler cursor	Marker on the Ruler Line showing how far across the page you are working
Ruler Line	Line displaying the current set of margins and tabs
Scale Pitch	Character Pitch used to mark out the Ruler Line
Scrolling	Moving the screen display up, down, left or right to see other parts of the document or other lines of files
Serial Port	Socket into which you can plug a printer that has a serial (RS232) interface

Selection menu	A menu of options that can be either 'Set' or 'Cleared'. Ticks mark the options that are set
Settings file	File of information about the facilities of your system (stored as SETTINGS.STD on the Start-of-day disc) – in particular, it records the types of paper you use and the printer and paper LocoScript is initially set up to print on
Sheet feeder	A device for automatically feeding separate sheets of paper into a printer
Simple tab	A tab that marks the position of the first character in any segment of text using this tab
Single sheet stationery	Separate sheets of paper
Single-spaced text	Text that has no extra space between the lines
Soft Hyphen	Special type of hyphen that can be inserted into a long word, giving LocoScript the option of breaking the line at this hyphen. The hyphen only appears when the line is broken at this point (typed by pressing ⬒ and then typing a hyphen)
Soft Space	Special type of space that can be inserted into a long word, giving LocoScript the option of breaking the line at this space (typed by pressing ⬒ and then typing a space)
Start-of-day disc	The disc inserted in Drive A when LocoScript is loaded – or the first such disc if you have more than one. Contains the programs that need to be loaded (cf. Start-up disc; Data disc)
Start-up disc	A disc used alongside your Start-of-day disc when you load LocoScript. Contains additional Support files for copying to Drive M
Stock Layout	Pattern for a Layout stored as part of the Document Set-up
Subscript	Character written below the normal line of the text
Superscript	Character written above the normal line of the text
Supershift	Special key combination that puts the keyboard into a particular character mode, eg. Greek or Symbol (typed by holding down ⟨ALT⟩ and pressing one of the Function keys)
Support files	Printer files, dictionaries, Templates etc. that support different areas of LocoScript. Normally stored on a Start-up disc and copied to Drive M as part of loading LocoScript
Symbol Set	Range of characters printed by a particular Character Shape file. Each Character Shape file prints one of five Symbol Sets – Basic, Extended*, Symbol*, Greek* and Cyrillic* – which together cover the entire range of characters LocoScript supports.

Available as an optional extra – see Appendix VI

Appendix IV: Glossary

System files	Special files that LocoScript uses, usually stored on Drive M. Details of these files are never displayed
Template	Document called TEMPLATE.STD used as the pattern for new documents, especially those in the same group
Text cursor	Marker showing the point in the document at which you are currently working
Textual Movement Keys	Keys on the keyboard marked Para, EOL etc. used to move the Text cursor through the document
Toggle	Using the same action to switch from 'Set' to 'Clear' or from 'Clear' to 'Set'
Top Gap	The area at the top of a page in which the printer never prints
Top of Form	First line on a sheet of paper on which your printer is able to print
Tractor Feed	The part of the printer designed for handling continuous stationery
Typeface	*See Font*
Typestyle	General appearance of characters eg. Bold, Italic, Regular (ie. upright and not bold)
Underline	Underlining both words and spaces (cf. Word Underline)
Upper case characters	Capital letters (cf. Lower case characters)
Widows and Orphans	Single lines of paragraphs separated from the rest of the paragraph by a page break
Wild card character	Special character used in Find Text to match any character including space
Word processor codes	Special codes embedded in text to tell LocoScript how the text should be laid out and styled
Word Underline	Underlining of the words but not the spaces between the words (cf. Underline)
Word Wrap	Automatic movement of a word onto the next line when there isn't room for the whole word on the current line

Appendix V

Printer Settings

Each printer used with LocoScript is initially set up to be used in a standard way. In particular, every printer is set up expecting you to use A4 paper, while the PCW9512 daisy-wheel printer is set up expecting you to work with multi-strike ribbons and the Prestige Pica 10 wheel supplied with this printer.

The way in which a printer is set up is part of the information about this printer recorded in your Settings file, and this appendix describes:

- *How to set the type of paper used as standard on your printer*
- *How to record further printwheels and how to set the printwheel used as standard*
- *How to set the type of ribbon used on the 9512 daisy-wheel printer*
- *How to adjust the print strength used on the 9512 daisy-wheel printer*

It also gives the DIP switch and Control Panel settings that are required when printing LocoScript documents on the Inkjet printer supplied with some models of the PcW9512+.

Note: The additional settings associated with an 'External' printer (ie. one used as an alternative to your PCW's built-in printer) are described in the External Printers Guide supplied in the LocoScript 3 Printer Support Pack (which you need in order to use any External printer from LocoScript 3).

V.1 Setting the standard type of paper

Every printer is initially set up expecting you to use A4 single sheet paper. If you usually use some other type of paper in your printer, you should record this as the 'default' paper used on this printer as follows:

1. Finish whatever you are currently working on and display the Disc Manager Screen.
You cannot change your Settings while you are still working on a document.

2. Press [f6] to display the Settings menu, move the cursor to Printer defaults *and press [ENTER] to display the Printer defaults menu.*

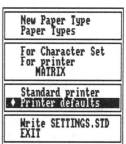

Appendix V: Printer Settings

LocoScript 3 User Guide 261

3. If you have more than one printer on your system, check the correct printer is named at the top of the menu.

If the wrong printer is shown, place the cursor on Defaults for printer, press [ENTER], tick the printer you want in the menu that is shown and then press [ENTER] to return to the Printer Defaults menu.

4. Move the cursor to Default Paper Type and press [ENTER]. When the list of paper types is displayed, tick the type of paper you normally use in the printer; if this is single sheet stationery, tick whether this is used Portrait or Landscape; then press [ENTER] to return to the Printer Defaults menu.

```
┌──────────────────────────────┐
│  Printer defaults            │
├──────────────────────────────┤
│ ♦ Defaults for printer       │
│       BJ130E                 │
├──────────────────────────────┤
│   Default Paper Type         │
│        A4                    │
├──────────────────────────────┤
│   Default Set                │
│       Courier                │
├──────────────────────────────┤
│   Printer options            │
├──────────────────────────────┤
│   EXIT                       │
└──────────────────────────────┘
```

If the type of paper you want isn't listed, you need to press [CAN] twice to return to the main Settings menu and then set up a standard Paper Type for this paper as described in Section 12.6 before returning to this point.

5. Press [EXIT] followed by [ENTER] to return to the main Settings menu, then press [EXIT] followed by [ENTER] again to leave the Settings menu. When the message appears, offering to write the updated Settings file to your Start-of-day disc, insert your Start-of-day disc in Drive A and then press [ENTER] to take this option.

Your Start-of-day disc is the first disc that you insert in Drive A when you load LocoScript.

6. Re-load LocoScript to put the setting you have made into action.

V.2 Adding further printwheels

Each printwheel for a daisy-wheel printer needs to be recorded as a separate Character *Style* in LocoScript's Settings file as follows:

1. Display the Disc Manager Screen. Then press [f6] to display the Settings menu.

2. If you have more than one printer on your system, check the correct printer is named under the For printer line of the menu.

If the wrong printer is shown, place the cursor on For printer, press [ENTER], tick your daisy-wheel printer in the menu that is shown and then press [ENTER] to return to the main Settings menu.

3. Select For character set and press [ENTER].

You then see a list of the Character Sets associated with this printer. *Note:* If the Character Set for this printwheel is not in this list, you need extra Character Set files – such as those provided by the PCW9512 Printwheels Pack (see Appendix VI).

4. Tick the Character Set which represents the 'family' the new wheel belongs to and press [ENTER].

LocoScript returns you to the Settings menu, which now shows the names of the printer and the Character Set you have just picked out.

5. You are now ready to start defining the Character Style. Select New Character Style *and press* [ENTER]*: a menu like this will then appear:*

Type in the name of your new printwheel, then move the cursor to the next line of the menu, type its pitch and press [ENTER]*.*

These details are on the wheel itself, which will have something like Elite 12 written on it. Here, the name of the wheel is Elite and its pitch is 12.

```
Character Style
───────────────────────
Name  : Thesis
Pitch : PS
───────────────────────
For Character Set
       England
For printer
       PCW9512
───────────────────────
▶ Create new Style
```

Often you can just copy the name on the printwheel but you will have to shorten any names that are more than 12 characters. The name doesn't have to be exactly what is marked on the wheel, just near enough to remind you. The pitch, however, does need to be correct.

7 Press [ENTER] *to select the* Create new Style *command at the bottom of the menu.*

When you press [ENTER], LocoScript returns you to the Settings menu. If you have another new wheel to install on your system, you could do this now by repeating Steps 6 – 7 (if the wheel uses the same Character Set) or 4 – 7 (if it uses a different Character Set).

8 Press [EXIT]*, and then press* [ENTER]*. LocoScript now offers to update the SETTINGS.STD on your Start-of-day disc. Make sure that you have your Start-of-day disc in Drive A and then press* [ENTER]*.*

V.3 Setting the printwheel used as standard

The printwheel used as standard on a daisy-wheel printer is defined by a Default Set and a Default Style. The Default Set records the 'family' to which the printwheel belongs, while the Default Style identifies the printwheel from among others belonging to this family. Set this printwheel as follows:

1. Finish whatever you are currently working on and display the Disc Manager Screen.
You cannot change your Settings while you are still working on a document.

2. Press [f6] *to display the Settings menu, move the cursor to* Printer defaults *and press* [ENTER] *to display the Printer defaults menu.*

3. If you have more than one printer on your system, check that the correct printer is named at the top of this menu.
If the wrong printer is shown, place the cursor on

```
Printer defaults
───────────────────────
◆ Defaults for printer
       PCW9512
───────────────────────
Default Paper Type
       A4
───────────────────────
Default Style
       PrestigePica 10
Default Set
       England
───────────────────────
Printer options
───────────────────────
EXIT
```

Defaults for printer, press [ENTER], tick the printer you want in the menu that is shown and then press [ENTER] to return to the Printer Defaults menu.

9308

4. *Move the cursor to* Default Set *and press* [ENTER]. *When the list of Character Sets is displayed, tick the appropriate Character Set for your standard printwheel, then press* [ENTER] *to return to the Printer Defaults menu.*

5. *Now move the cursor to* Default Style *and press* [ENTER]. *When the list of Character Styles associated with the Default Character Set is displayed, tick the one for your standard printwheel, then press* [ENTER] *to return to the Printer Defaults menu.*

6. *Press* [EXIT] *followed by* [ENTER] *to return to the main Settings menu, then press* [EXIT] *followed by* [ENTER] *again to leave the Settings menu. When the message appears,*

Printer defaults
Defaults for printer PCW9512
Default Paper Type A4
Default Style PrestigePica 10
◆ Default Set England
Printer options
EXIT

offering to write the updated Settings file to your Start-of-day disc, insert your Start-of-day disc in Drive A and then press [ENTER] *to take this option.*

Your Start-of-day disc is the first disc that you insert in Drive A when you load LocoScript.

6. *Re-load LocoScript to put the setting you have made into action.*

V.4 Setting the type of ribbon used on the 9512 daisy-wheel printer

The standard type of ribbon to use on the PCW9512 daisy-wheel printer are multi-strike ribbons, and so this is what this printer is set up for by default. If you use either cloth ribbons or single-strike ribbons on this printer, you should record this as follows:

1. *Finish whatever you are currently working on and display the Disc Manager Screen.*

You cannot change your Settings while you are still working on a document.

2. *Press* [f6] *to display the Settings menu, move the cursor to* Printer defaults *and press* [ENTER] *to display the Printer defaults menu.*

3. *If you have more than one printer on your system, check that the PCW9512 printer is named at the top of this menu.*

If the wrong printer is shown, place the cursor on Defaults for printer, press [ENTER], tick PCW9512 in the menu that is shown and then press [ENTER] to return to the Printer Defaults menu.

4. *Move the cursor to* Printer options *and press* [ENTER].

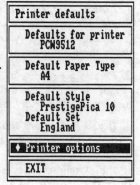

Printer defaults
Defaults for printer PCW9512
Default Paper Type A4
Default Style PrestigePica 10 Default Set England
◆ Printer options
EXIT

LocoScript 3 User Guide

5. *Tick the type of ribbon you use in the printer, then press* [ENTER] *to return to the Printer Defaults menu.*

6. *Press* [EXIT] *followed by* [ENTER] *to return to the main Settings menu, then press* [EXIT] *followed by* [ENTER] *again to leave the Settings menu. When the message appears, offering to write the updated Settings file to your Start-of-day disc, insert your Start-of-day disc in Drive A and then press* [ENTER] *to take this option.*

Your Start-of-day disc is the first disc that you insert in Drive A when you load LocoScript.

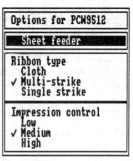

7. *Re-load LocoScript to put the setting you have made into action.*

V.5 Adjusting the print strength on the 9512 daisy-wheel printer

The 9512 daisy-wheel printer is normally set to give you medium strength printing, but if you find that the documents printed are always a bit too light or a bit too dark, you can adjust its print strength as follows:

1. *Finish whatever you are currently working on and display the Disc Manager Screen.*
You cannot change your Settings while you are still working on a document.

2. *Press* [f6] *to display the Settings menu, move the cursor to* Printer defaults *and press* [ENTER] *to display the Printer defaults menu.*

3. *If you have more than one printer on your system, check that the PCW9512 printer is named at the top of this menu.*
If the wrong printer is shown, place the cursor on Defaults for printer, press [ENTER], tick PCW9512 in the menu that is shown and then press [ENTER] to return to the Printer Defaults menu.

4. *Move the cursor to* Printer options *and press* [ENTER]. *When the menu appears, tick the print strength you would prefer, then press* [ENTER] *to return to the Printer Defaults menu.*
If you think that the standard print strength has made the documents a bit dark, tick Low; if you think that it has made the documents a bit light, tick High.

5. *Press* [EXIT] *followed by* [ENTER] *to return to the main Settings menu, then press* [EXIT] *followed by* [ENTER] *again to leave the Settings menu. When the message appears, offering to write the updated Settings file to your Start-of-day disc, insert your Start-of-day disc in Drive A and then press* [ENTER] *to take this option.*
Your Start-of-day disc is the first disc that you insert in Drive A when you load LocoScript.

6. *Re-load LocoScript to put the setting you have made into action.*

9308

V.6 PcW9512+ Inkjet printer settings

The following summarises the DIP switch and Control Panel settings that are required when printing LocoScript documents on the inkjet printer supplied with some models of the PcW9512+.

Note: These are settings required on the printer itself – NOT in your Settings file!

DIP Switches

Switch 1-1   Auto Sheetfeeder   Should be set to reflect reality.

LocoScript works equally well with or without a sheetfeeder. There is no need to change anything in LocoScript when adding this sheetfeeder.

Switch 1-2   Graphics density   Don't care; Not relevant to LocoScript

Switch 1-3   Automatic LineFeed   Don't care; Overridden by LocoScript

Switch 1-4   Page Length   Don't care; Overridden by LocoScript

However, the printer cannot be fooled into thinking that paper is shorter than it really is. If you have mail-merges which use this trick eg. to print labels you should alter the mail-merge accordingly. This effect also affects Direct Printing, which will use a new sheet of paper for each direct print invocation (though not for every line).

Switch 1-5   Character Set   Don't care; LocoScript sends suitable
                                         sequences.

Switch 1-6   Automatic CR   Don't care; Overridden by LocoScript

Switch 1-7   Alternative Graphics   Don't care

Switch 1-8   Download Enable   Needs to be set to ON when the printer is
                                         used with the LocoFont BJ software. When
                                         the printer is driven in its standard mode,
                                         the setting doesn't matter though setting
                                         the switch to OFF gives the printer a
                                         bigger buffer to work with.

Switch 1-9   Code Page Selection   Don't care

LocoScript automatically switches between code pages to print all the characters that the printer is capable of. This is not the entire LocoScript character set: for that, you need either the LX Symbol pack (see Appendix VI) or the LocoFont BJ software.

Switch 1-10 Mode   Don't care

LocoScript will drive the printer in either mode. There are, however, some

---

differences between the two modes, as noted on the following page. These are nothing to do with LocoScript, but are merely characteristics of the Inkjet printer.

Note: In mode 1, 12 pitch characters are printed in a Prestige style. In mode 2 and in all other pitches in both modes the characters are in a Courier style. In mode 1 the vertical bar characters are solid (l). In mode 2 they are broken (¦).

In both modes printing in "draft" is taken to be printing using the Economy (low ink consumption) mode. In mode 1 it is not possible to print in PS and Economy at the same time – so LocoScript uses the HQ (darker) mode instead. In mode 2 all pitches can be printed in both Economy and HQ modes.

Control Panel

The printer must be ON-LINE before LocoScript will print.

The Print Mode, Pitch and HQ/Economy selections will be overridden whenever LocoScript starts to print a document. It is not recommended that these functions be used whilst LocoScript is printing because unpredictable results may occur.

General restrictions

The INKJET.PRI driver used with this printer in its Standard mode assumes that the inkjet printer is attached to the "built-in" Centronics port. In particular it will not work with a Centronics interface on a CPS8256 interface or with the Centronics interface on the Locomotive Power Pack.

The printer can only print in italics or at 15 pitch when you are using either the LX fonts or the LocoFont BJ software.

9308

Related products

Locomotive Software have a number of additional products to enhance your use of LocoScript 3. These products are in two principal areas:

- *Extra Character Shape files – providing further typefaces, point sizes and/or characters*
- *Additional space on Drive M*

The following sections introduce the different products and explain what they offer. For further information and prices, refer to the 'LocoScript 3 Family' brochure supplied in your most recent LocoScript 3 product pack.

VI.1 Additional Character Shape files

Note: When ordering any additional Character Shape files, remember to say which type of printer you will be using these on.

Extra point sizes (LX Size pack)

Wherever you want to print text in a particular Point Size, you will always get the best results if you have the Character Shape file specifically for that size. Where you specify a size for which you don't have a Character Shape file, LocoScript simply substitutes characters of the nearest Point Size that is available – if necessary doubling, trebling or even quadrupling the patterns from another file in order to get as close as possible to the Point Size you specified. If the exact Point Size isn't available, the resulting text may look either too cramped or too widely spaced. In addition, the characters themselves can look a little 'lumpy' where LocoScript has doubled, trebled or quadrupled shapes provided for a smaller Point Size.

The standard range of files contain character shapes for 8pt, 10pt, 12pt, 14pt and 18pt text in both the LX Roman and LX Sanserif fonts. The 'LX Size' pack for your printer extends the range of sizes at which you can print these fonts by adding Character Shape files for a range of further sizes from 6pt to 36pt.

Additional characters (LX Symbol pack)

There are approximately 450 different characters and accents that you can insert into your LocoScript documents. However, to save cluttering up Drive M with characters you don't use, we divided these characters into five 'Symbol Sets' and provide files containing the 'Basic' Symbol Set as standard. This Symbol Set includes the 148 characters and accents that cover 99% of people's needs.

If you want to print characters outside the Basic Symbol Set, you need to add further Character Shape files to provide these additional characters in the typeface and at the Point Size you require. In particular, if you want to print any Greek characters, you will need files containing the Greek Symbol Set while if you want to print any Cyrillic characters, you will need files containing the Cyrillic Symbol Set. The 'LX Symbol' pack for your printer provides the four extra Symbol Sets in both LX Roman and LX Sanserif and in the standard range of sizes.

The characters in the different Symbol Sets are listed in Appendix III.

True Bold & Italic (LX Style pack)

The standard set of Character Shape files just define the shapes of normal weight, upright ('Regular') characters. So where you ask for Bold or Italic styling, LocoScript generates bold/italic versions of these characters itself.

Specific Character Shape files for the different typestyles are provided in the 'LX Style' pack. The files in this pack give you Italic and Bold versions of the Basic Symbol Set in both LX Roman and LX Sanserif and in each of the five standard sizes.

Not only will you get better formed characters from these Character Shape files but the characters also have their true forms. (Italic characters in particular often have a significantly different shape from their upright counterpart or are slanted at a particular angle.)

Extra LX fonts (LocoFont LX)

Further LX fonts are provided in our various 'LocoFont LX' packs.

We have, for example, a set of 11 'Decorative' fonts that you might use in invitations, adverts or menus – including Dom Casual, Park Avenue, Old English and Broadway fonts. (These fonts have been prepared by Agfa, a leading company in the world of computer typesetting.)

We also have a similar set of eight 'Business' fonts – including Futura, Century Schoolbook, Garamond and Antique Olive – and a set of three 'Fixed' fonts for use anywhere that it is important to have evenly spaced characters, for example tables of numbers.

All the fonts are provided in a range of sizes. The Business and Fixed Fonts are each provided in 8, 10, 12, 14 and 18pt. The Decorative fonts are provided either in 10, 12, 14 and 18pt or in 14, 18 and 24pt depending on the font.

There are samples of each of the fonts in the LocoScript 3 Family brochure.

Note: It is possible that other manufacturers will make their fonts available in LX format. For the latest information, contact Locomotive Software's Sales Department.

VI.2 Memory and other products

Locomotive LPP512 Power Pack

This is a single unit to attach to the Expansion port on the back of your PCW, which adds both 512k to the memory of your machine (eg. increasing 256k to 768k or 512k to 1M) and a 'Parallel' printer port to your PCW. This port may then be used to attach an 'external' printer which uses a Parallel or 'Centronics' interface to your PCW (as most printers do). The pack also includes a cable with which to attach your printer to the LPP512. It could also be used to attach the printer to a PCW9512/PcW9512+'s built-in Parallel port.

The LPP512 fits any type of PCW.

Note: The LPP512 can also be used from LocoScript 2 v2.32c/33c or later and from CP/M provided you are using v1.14/2.14 or later.

New LocoSpell dictionary – *to recover 64k of Drive M*

If the System dictionary you currently use to check the spelling of your documents occupies around 160k of your Drive M, we would recommend upgrading to the new version of this 78,000-word dictionary. This includes all the same words as your current dictionary but occupies about 64k less space on disc (approx. 96k instead of approx. 160k). Checking spelling against this dictionary is also about three times faster than with the old version.

The only thing to note about the new dictionary is that it *has* to be used from Drive M: it cannot be used directly from floppy disc. The spelling checking facilities offered by the program haven't changed.

Printer Support Pack

If you want to take advantage of the quality, speed, range of typefaces etc. offered by the various printers on the market today, you need a copy of the Printer Support Pack. This provides the files needed to support a vast range of printers from simple daisy-wheel printers and typewriters with computer interfaces to relatively sophisticated laser printers. It also includes the files needed to use LocoScript 3's LX fonts on such printers. (A list of the printers currently supported is given in the 'Alternative Printers' booklet supplied in the LocoScript 3 pack – and in other LocoScript product packs.)

PCW9512 Printwheels Pack

A vast array of different national printwheels are available for the PCW9512/9512+ daisy-wheel printer. You automatically get the files needed to work with the standard printwheels for your PCW ('England' and 'Swiss-French' in the UK), but further files are needed to use printwheels from any other national family. The Printwheels Pack provides the software needed to support the full range of printwheels available for this printer.

INDEX

LocoScript 3 User Guide

LocoScript 3 User Guide